P9-CKA-043

Disability Visibility

First-Person Stories
from the Twenty-First Century

Edited by Alice Wong

VINTAGE BOOKS

A Division of Penguin Random House LLC
New York

A VINTAGE BOOKS ORIGINAL, JUNE 2020

Introduction and compilation copyright © 2020 by Alice Wong

All rights reserved. Published in the United States
by Vintage Books, a division of Penguin Random House LLC,
New York, and distributed in Canada by Penguin Random
House Canada Limited, Toronto.

Vintage and colophon
are registered trademarks of Penguin Random House LLC.

Pages 305–9 constitute an extension of this copyright page.

Library of Congress Cataloging-in-Publication Data
Names: Wong, Alice, 1974– editor.
Title: Disability visibility : twenty-first century disabled voices /
edited by Alice Wong.
Description: First Vintage Books edition. | New York : Vintage Books,
a division of Penguin Random House LLC, 2020.
Identifiers: LCCN 2019052398 (print) | LCCN 2019052399 (ebook)
Subjects: LCSH: People with disabilities—United States—Biography. |
People with disabilities—United States—Social conditions.
Classification: LCC HV1552.3 .D57 2020 (print) | LCC HV1552.3 (ebook) |
DDC 305.9/08092273—dc23
LC record available at https://lccn.loc.gov/2019052398

Vintage Books Trade Paperback ISBN: 978-1-9848-9942-2
eBook ISBN: 978-1-9848-9943-9

Editor photograph © Eddie Hernandez Photography
Book design by Nicholas Alguire

www.vintagebooks.com

Printed in the United States of America
20 19 18 17 16 15 14

To my younger self and all the disabled kids today
who can't imagine their futures.
The world is ours, and this is for all of us.

Disability is not a brave struggle or "courage in the face of adversity." Disability is an art. It's an ingenious way to live.

—Neil Marcus

Remember, you weren't the one
Who made you ashamed,
But you are the one
Who can make you proud.

—Laura Hershey

The word *special,* as it is applied to disability, too often means "a bit shit."

—Stella Young

Contents

Introduction by Alice Wong   xv

PART 1: BEING

Unspeakable Conversations
Harriet McBryde Johnson   3

For Ki'tay D. Davidson, Who Loves Us
Talila A. Lewis   28

If You Can't Fast, Give
Maysoon Zayid   36

There's a Mathematical Equation That Proves I'm Ugly—
Or So I Learned in My Seventh-Grade Art Class
Ariel Henley   39

The Erasure of Indigenous People in Chronic Illness
Jen Deerinwater   47

When You Are Waiting to Be Healed
June Eric-Udorie   53

The Isolation of Being Deaf in Prison
Jeremy Woody, as told to Christie Thompson   59

Common Cyborg
Jillian Weise   63

I'm Tired of Chasing a Cure
Liz Moore   75

PART 2: BECOMING

We Can't Go Back
Ricardo T. Thornton Sr.   85

Radical Visibility: A Disabled Queer Clothing
Reform Movement Manifesto
Sky Cubacub   90

Guide Dogs Don't Lead Blind People.
We Wander as One.
Haben Girma   101

Taking Charge of My Story as a Cancer Patient
at the Hospital Where I Work
Diana Cejas   104

Canfei to Canji: The Freedom of Being Loud
Sandy Ho   112

Nurturing Black Disabled Joy
Keah Brown   117

Last but Not Least—Embracing Asexuality
Keshia Scott   121

Imposter Syndrome and Parenting with a Disability
Jessica Slice   129

How to Make a Paper Crane from Rage
Elsa Sjunneson 134

Selma Blair Became a Disabled Icon Overnight.
Here's Why We Need More Stories Like Hers.
Zipporah Arielle 141

PART 3: DOING

Why My Novel Is Dedicated to My Disabled Friend Maddy
A. H. Reaume 149

The Antiabortion Bill You Aren't Hearing About
Rebecca Cokley 159

So. Not. Broken.
Alice Sheppard 164

How a Blind Astronomer Found a Way to Hear the Stars
Wanda Díaz-Merced 168

Incontinence Is a Public Health Issue—
And We Need to Talk About It
Mari Ramsawakh 174

Falling/Burning: Hannah Gadsby, Nanette,
and Being a Bipolar Creator
Shoshana Kessock 179

Six Ways of Looking at Crip Time
Ellen Samuels 189

Lost Cause
Reyma McCoy McDeid 197

On NYC's Paratransit, Fighting for Safety,
Respect, and Human Dignity
Britney Wilson   205

Gaining Power through Communication Access
Lateef McLeod   220

PART 4: CONNECTING

The Fearless Benjamin Lay: Activist,
Abolitionist, Dwarf Person
Eugene Grant   229

To Survive Climate Catastrophe, Look to Queer
and Disabled Folks
Patty Berne, as told to and edited by Vanessa Raditz   232

Disability Solidarity: Completing the "Vision for Black Lives"
Harriet Tubman Collective   236

Time's Up for Me, Too
Karolyn Gehrig   243

Still Dreaming Wild Disability Justice Dreams
at the End of the World
Leah Lakshmi Piepzna-Samarasinha   250

Love Means Never Having to Say . . . Anything
Jamison Hill   262

On the Ancestral Plane: Crip Hand-Me-Downs
and the Legacy of Our Movements
Stacey Milbern   267

Contents

The Beauty of Spaces Created for and by Disabled People
s.e. smith   271

About the Editor   277

About the Contributors   279

Further Reading   293

Permission Acknowledgments   305

Introduction

Alice Wong

Storytelling itself is an activity, not an object. Stories are the closest we can come to shared experience. . . . Like all stories, they are most fundamentally a chance to ride around inside another head and be reminded that being who we are and where we are, and doing what we're doing, is not the only possibility.

—Harriet McBryde Johnson,
Too Late to Die Young: Nearly True Tales from a Life (2006)

Staying alive is a lot of work for a disabled person in an ableist society, and that work has been a big part of my forty-six years on this planet. I grew up seeing very few images that looked like me in books, film, or television. In that absence, how does one realize that something is even missing? Last year there was a photograph that went viral—a young girl in a wheelchair, transfixed by a beauty ad featuring a woman in a similar chair. The two ultimately met in person, and their story made me wonder about my own childhood—how my worldview would have changed if I had seen someone like me as a glamorous, confident adult. As I grew older, discovering a community of disabled people and learning our stories gave me a sense of what is possible.

I began to notice and save stories about disability that meant something to me. In high school, I read an article in *Time* about accessible public transit. I was incredibly excited about the prospect of accessible transportation and I wrote a letter to the editor expressing a wish that this would expand. I lived in the suburbs, and the idea of being able to go to places on my own by bus or train seemed like a faraway dream. The letter was published in a subsequent issue, and it was thrilling to see my name in print—the first time I'd advocated for something on the record as a disabled person. The article sparked my curiosity for more stories and information. As my collection grew, I had file folders filled with newspaper and magazine clippings. I now have multiple bookmark folders on my web browser where I save links by subject—they number in the hundreds. In surrounding myself with these stories, I found and developed my own voice.

My collection led me to community. I didn't grow up part of the ADA (Americans with Disabilities Act) generation—I was a sophomore in high school when the law was passed—but it had profoundly changed my life and millions of others, giving us a civil rights law we could call our own. In 2014, disabled people throughout the United States were preparing for the following year's twenty-fifth anniversary of the ADA. I wanted to mark the upcoming milestone, but wasn't affiliated with any major advocacy or media organization and wasn't certain how I could contribute as an individual. I was, however, certain about three things: (1) I wanted to see more stories about the disabled experience in the present while honoring the past; (2) I wanted to see more stories about everyday people rather than the usual "very important people" duly mentioned at each ADA anniversary; and (3) I wanted to increase the diversity of the mainstream representation of disability, which remains very white and very male (just take a look at disabled characters in film from the last thirty years, from Daniel Day-Lewis's performance in *My Left Foot* to Bryan Cranston in *The Upside*).

Partnering with StoryCorps, a national oral history organization, I created the Disability Visibility Project (DVP) to record oral histories and archive them at the Library of Congress. I originally planned the partnership as a one-year campaign, a way for disabled people to celebrate and preserve their stories in the lead-up to the ADA anniversary. In one memorable DVP recording, Jessie Lorenz talked with her friend Herb Levine about his involvement in the 1977 504 sit-ins—the longest nonviolent occupation of a federal building. Section 504 of the Rehabilitation Act of 1973 was a federal law that outlawed discrimination based on disability in any program or activity receiving federal funding. Section 504 acknowledged that disability rights are civil rights, laying the groundwork for the ADA. However, in 1977, the regulations that would actually enforce the law remained unsigned, due to years of delay by the Department of Health, Education, and Welfare. On April 5 of that year, Deaf and disabled protesters took over the Federal Building at 50 United Nations Plaza in downtown San Francisco, demanding action. Bay Area public radio station KALW produced and broadcast Herb's story. He recounted to Jessie how he reentered the building by impersonating a member of the clergy, bringing two other disabled people back in as members of his choir. These kinds of stories—the funny, personal moments in disability history—are just as significant as those about leaders and politicians. We need more of these stories, even if they never make it into a history book.

What started as a small oral history project kept going and blew up into a movement. The DVP now has approximately 140 oral histories on record at StoryCorps, a small but mighty archive of the disability zeitgeist. And the project has expanded into an online community that creates, shares, and amplifies disability media and culture through a podcast, articles, Twitter chats, and more. The DVP has always been a one-woman operation, but this doesn't mean I do everything alone. Collaborating and partnering with disabled people is something that brings me epic, Marie Kondo–level joy. Each project builds on the last, and the DVP was just the start. What I have always been hoping to accomplish is the creation of community.

Community is political. In the fall of 2015, my friend Gregg Beratan reached out to Andrew Pulrang and me about the need to engage with the then-candidates for president on disability issues. Gregg, Andrew, and I are three disabled activists who know one another via the Internet (and have yet to meet in person, which is amazing). We each had observed the lack of attention to disability from the candidates and the media. We decided to invite disabled people to live-tweet a Democratic primary debate between Bernie Sanders and Hillary Clinton, using the hashtag #CripTheVote on February 11, 2016. By the end of 2019, #CripTheVote had hosted dozens of Twitter chats and live-tweets of political events. On February 7, 2020, we hosted our first Twitter town hall with a presidential candidate, Senator Elizabeth Warren, and our second with Pete Buttigieg ten days later. What began as a way to create space online for people to talk about disability evolved into a nonpartisan campaign encouraging the political participation of disabled people—emphasizing the power of conversations and action in the face of inequality, ableism, and oppression. The hashtag now belongs to the community—disabled people use it every day and reporters and politicians are following it as well. Storytelling can be more than a blog post, essay, or book. It can be an emoji, a meme, a selfie, or a tweet. It can become a movement for social change.

Community is magic. In 2016, novelist Nicola Griffith tweeted a comment about the need to connect with other disabled writers with the hashtag #CripLit. She had me at #CripLit! I reached out to Nicola and we began organizing and cohosting Twitter chats on publishing, disability representation, disabled characters, access to literary workshops, accommodations, and other issues important to disabled writers. All kinds of writers and readers now use the hashtag to find one another when discussing these subjects, asking for advice, or sharing information. This also brings me lots of joy.

Community is power. In 2017, the fourth episode of the Disability Visibility podcast focused on disabled people in media and journalism and featured reporter s.e. smith and writer-activist Vilissa K. Thompson, founder of rampyourvoice.com. We talked about the systemic barriers that disabled writers face. One common response from publishers and editors, when confronted about the lack of diversity in their staff or coverage, is the claim that it's too "hard" to find disabled reporters and writers. Bullshit! Earlier that June, s.e. created disabledwriters.com—an online database where editors can find and hire disabled reporters and writers—with Vilissa and me serving as copartners. We are everywhere—you just have to look.

Community is resistance. Like many people, on the evening of election day 2016, I was filled with anxiety and dread. But I was also strangely comforted, knowing that disabled people have always resisted, and have learned a thing or two about living with uncertainty and fear. My response to the turd-infused political climate was to self-publish a small, freely available anthology in October 2018, *Resistance and Hope*, essays by activists, artists, and dreamers on the relationship between resistance and hope in these times. It felt good to create something grounded in the lives and truths of multiply marginalized disabled people sharing their invaluable views on leadership, justice, and resilience. This too brings me great joy.

Disability Visibility: First-Person Stories from the Twenty-First Century brings all of these collaborations, connections, and joys to the page. It is not Disability 101 or a definitive "best of" list. You may be unfamiliar with some terms or uncomfortable with some ideas presented in this book—and that's a good thing! These stories do not seek to explain the meaning of disability or to inspire or elicit empathy. Rather, they show disabled people simply *being* in our own words, by our own accounts. *Disability Visibility* is also one part of a larger arc in my own story as a human being.

Since the essays cover a broad span of topics, the book is divided into four sections: Being, Belonging, Doing, and Connecting. You will find content notes at the beginning of some stories that discuss topics that may be traumatic or distressing, and you can decide whether to engage with the material or not. Content notes are included as a form of access and self-protection, giving you information on what to expect before reading. The first piece is by the late lawyer and activist Harriet McBryde Johnson—"Unspeakable Conversations," originally published in *The New York Times* in 2003. Harriet writes about debating a Princeton professor who believed that people like her should not exist—that infanticide of disabled people was acceptable and ethical. When I first read her account, it shook me to my core—she brilliantly outlined the lived experience of ableism in very real terms. I no longer felt alone in questioning and defending my worth. Her words and the way she lived her life continue to influence me every day.

The last essay here is by s.e. smith, "The Beauty of Spaces Created for and by Disabled People," from *Catapult* in 2008. s.e. shares their experience attending a performance of *Descent* by Kinetic Light, featuring disabled dancers/choreographers Alice Sheppard (who has an essay here as well) and Laurel Lawson. s.e. describes the transient alchemy that happens when disabled people come together in the same space—s.e.'s writing leaves us steeped in the beauty, creativity, and ingenuity of disabled people. *Disability Visibility* creates a similar literary space—a collection of individual stories that becomes something entirely unique as a whole. And the conversation continues beyond the last page. Since it is impossible to capture the full expanse of the disability experience in a single book, at the back is a list of suggested readings and resources.

This may feel true for every era, but I believe I am living in a time where disabled people are more visible than ever before. And yet while representation is exciting and important, it is not enough. I want and expect more. *We all should expect more. We all deserve more.* There must be depth, range, nuance to disability representation in media. This is the current challenge and opportunity for the publishing industry and popular culture at large.

There are not enough self-identified disabled, Deaf, chronically ill, and neurodivergent people in publishing. The 2019 Lee & Low Books Diversity Baseline Survey of the industry found 11 percent of respondents identify as a person with a disability and 89 percent identify as nondisabled—the highest disparity across their four measures (race/ethnicity, gender, sexual orientation, and disability). This directly impacts what gets published, who gets published, and industry assumptions of what disabled and nondisabled readers are hungry for. I ask nondisabled publishers and media makers to reflect critically on the demographics of their professions: what they produce and to whom they cater. Who and what is missing? How do we hold ourselves accountable? How can we advance conversations about diversity and inclusion and back them with actions, policies, and practices? How can we get to that place together by collaborating and learning from one another?

To the nondisabled readers of this book: How many disabled creators do you know of? How can you support their work, whether it's a podcast, novel, play, video, or blog? How are you widening your horizons? Because I believe in the power of the universe, I'm going to call into existence the formation of a disability-centered imprint by one of the big five publishers, led by disabled editors. It won't magically fix the systemic issues about diversity in publishing, but it's a start and it's damn overdue.

Disabled people have always existed, whether the word *disability* is used or not. To me, disability is not a monolith, nor is it a clear-cut binary of disabled and nondisabled. Disability is mutable and ever-evolving. Disability is both apparent and nonapparent. Disability is pain, struggle, brilliance, abundance, and joy. Disability is sociopolitical, cultural, and biological. Being visible and claiming a disabled identity brings risks as much as it brings pride.

As a marginalized person, I don't feel it's enough to just keep saying, "Hey, pay attention to us. We're here! We exist! We're just as human as you!" I want things to improve even while grappling with this impulse, with the tension between "subject" and "audience." I want to center the wisdom of disabled people and welcome others in, rather than ask for permission or acknowledgment. Harriet McBryde Johnson wrote that storytelling is an activity, a shared experience, not an object. Collectively, through our stories, our connections, and our actions, disabled people will continue to confront and transform the status quo. It's who we are.

PART 1

Being

The peculiar drama of my life has placed me in a world that by and large thinks it would be better if people like me did not exist. My fight has been for accommodation, the world to me and me to the world.

—Harriet McBryde Johnson

Content notes: eugenics, infanticide, assisted suicide

Unspeakable Conversations

Harriet McBryde Johnson

He insists he doesn't want to kill me. He simply thinks it would have been better, all things considered, to have given my parents the option of killing the baby I once was and to let other parents kill similar babies as they come along and thereby avoid the suffering that comes with lives like mine and satisfy the reasonable preferences of parents for a different kind of child. It has nothing to do with me. I should not feel threatened.

Whenever I try to wrap my head around his tight string of syllogisms, my brain gets so fried it's . . . almost fun. Mercy! It's like *Alice in Wonderland*.

It is a chilly Monday in late March, just less than a year ago. I am at Princeton University. My host is Professor Peter Singer, often called—and not just by his book publicist—the most influential philosopher of our time. He is the man who wants me dead. No, that's not at all fair. He wants to legalize the killing of certain babies who might come to be like me if allowed to live. He also says he believes that it should be lawful under some circumstances to kill, at any age, individuals with cognitive impairments so severe that he doesn't consider them "persons." What does it take to be a person? Awareness of your own existence in time. The capacity to harbor preferences as to the future, including the preference for continuing to live.

At this stage of my life, he says, I am a person. However, as an infant, I wasn't. I, like all humans, was born without self-awareness. And eventually, assuming my brain finally gets so fried that I fall into that wonderland where self and other and present and past and future blur into one boundless, formless all or nothing, then I'll lose my personhood and therefore my right to life. Then, he says, my family and doctors might put me out of my misery, or out of my bliss or oblivion, and no one count it murder.

I have agreed to two speaking engagements. In the morning, I talk to one hundred fifty undergraduates on selective infanticide. In the evening, it is a convivial discussion, over dinner, of assisted suicide. I am the token cripple with an opposing view.

I had several reasons for accepting Singer's invitation, some grounded in my involvement in the disability rights movement, others entirely personal. For the movement, it seemed an unusual opportunity to experiment with modes of discourse that might work with very tough audiences and bridge the divide between our perceptions and theirs. I didn't expect to straighten out Singer's head, but maybe I could reach a student or two. Among the personal reasons: I was sure it would make a great story, first for telling and then for writing down.

By now I've told it to family and friends and colleagues, over lunches and dinners, on long car trips, in scads of e-mail messages and a couple of formal speeches. But it seems to be a story that just won't settle down. After all these tellings, it still lacks a coherent structure; I'm miles away from a rational argument. I keep getting interrupted by questions—like these:

Q: Was he totally grossed out by your physical appearance?

A: He gave no sign of it. None whatsoever.

Q: How did he handle having to interact with someone like you?

A: He behaved in every way appropriately, treated me as a respected professional acquaintance, and was a gracious and accommodating host.

Q: Was it emotionally difficult for you to take part in a public discussion of whether your life should have happened?

A: It was very difficult. And horribly easy.

Q: Did he get that job at Princeton because they like his ideas on killing disabled babies?

A: It apparently didn't hurt, but he's most famous for animal rights. He's the author of *Animal Liberation*.

Q: How can he put so much value on animal life and so little value on human life?

That last question is the only one I avoid. I used to say I don't know; it doesn't make sense. But now I've read some of Singer's writing, and I admit it does make sense—within the conceptual world of Peter Singer. But I don't want to go there. Or at least not for long.

So I will start from those other questions and see where the story goes this time.

That first question, about my physical appearance, needs some explaining.

It's not that I'm ugly. It's more that most people don't know how to look at me. The sight of me is routinely discombobulating. The power wheelchair is enough to inspire gawking, but that's the least of it. Much more impressive is the impact on my body of more than four decades of a muscle-wasting disease. At this stage of my life, I'm Karen Carpenter thin, flesh mostly vanished, a jumble of bones in a floppy bag of skin. When, in childhood, my muscles got too weak to hold up my spine, I tried a brace for a while, but fortunately a skittish anesthesiologist said no to fusion, plates, and pins—all the apparatus that might have kept me straight. At fifteen, I threw away the back brace and let my spine reshape itself into a deep, twisty S-curve. Now my right side is two deep canyons. To keep myself upright, I lean forward, rest my rib cage on my lap, plant my elbows beside my knees. Since my backbone found its own natural shape, I've been entirely comfortable in my skin.

I am in the first generation to survive to such decrepitude. Because antibiotics were available, we didn't die from the childhood pneumonias that often come with weakened respiratory systems. I guess it is natural enough that most people don't know what to make of us.

Two or three times in my life—I recall particularly one largely crip, largely lesbian cookout halfway across the continent—I have been looked at as a rare kind of beauty. There is also the bizarre fact that, where I live, Charleston, South Carolina, some people call me Good Luck Lady: they consider it propitious to cross my path when a hurricane is coming and to kiss my head just before voting day. But most often the reactions are decidedly negative. Strangers on the street are moved to comment:

"I admire you for being out; most people would give up."

"God bless you! I'll pray for you."

"You don't let the pain hold you back, do you?"

"If I had to live like you, I think I'd kill myself."

I used to try to explain that in fact I enjoy my life, that it's a great sensual pleasure to zoom by power chair on these delicious muggy streets, that I have no more reason to kill myself than most people. But it gets tedious. God didn't put me on this street to provide disability awareness training to the likes of them. In fact, no god put anyone anywhere for any reason, if you want to know.

But they don't want to know. They think they know everything there is to know, just by looking at me. That's how stereotypes work. They don't know that they're confused, that they're really expressing the discombobulation that comes in my wake.

So. What stands out when I recall first meeting Peter Singer in the spring of 2001 is his apparent immunity to my looks, his apparent lack of discombobulation, his immediate ability to deal with me as a person with a particular point of view.

Then 2001. Singer has been invited to the College of Charleston, not two blocks from my house. He is to lecture on "Rethinking Life and Death." I have been dispatched by Not Dead Yet, the national organization leading the disability rights opposition to legalized assisted suicide and disability-based killing. I am to put out a leaflet and do something during the Q&A.

On arriving almost an hour early to reconnoiter, I find the scene almost entirely peaceful; even the boisterous display of South Carolina spring is muted by gray wisps of Spanish moss and mottled oak bark.

I roll around the corner of the building and am confronted with the unnerving sight of two people I know sitting on a park bench eating veggie pitas with Singer. Sharon is a veteran activist for human rights. Herb is South Carolina's most famous atheist. Good people, I've always thought—now sharing veggie pitas and conversation with a proponent of genocide. I try to beat a retreat, but Herb and Sharon have seen me. Sharon tosses her trash and comes over. After we exchange the usual courtesies, she asks, "Would you like to meet Professor Singer?"

She doesn't have a clue. She probably likes his book on animal rights. "I'll just talk to him in the Q&A."

But Herb, with Singer at his side, is fast approaching. They are looking at me, and Herb is talking, no doubt saying nice things about me. He'll be saying that I'm a disability rights lawyer and that I gave a talk against assisted suicide at his secular humanist group a while back. He didn't agree with everything I said, he'll say, but I was brilliant. Singer appears interested, engaged. I sit where I'm parked. Herb makes an introduction. Singer extends his hand.

I hesitate. I shouldn't shake hands with the Evil One. But he is Herb's guest, and I simply can't snub Herb's guest at the college where Herb teaches. Hereabouts, the rule is that if you're not prepared to shoot on sight, you have to be prepared to shake hands. I give Singer the three fingers on my right hand that still work. "Good afternoon, Mr. Singer. I'm here for Not Dead Yet." I want to think he flinches just a little. Not Dead Yet did everything possible to disrupt his first week at Princeton. I sent a check to the fund for the fourteen arrestees, who included comrades in power chairs. But if Singer flinches, he instantly recovers. He answers my questions about the lecture format. When he says he looks forward to an interesting exchange, he seems entirely sincere.

It is an interesting exchange. In the lecture hall that afternoon, Singer lays it all out. The "illogic" of allowing abortion but not infanticide, of allowing withdrawal of life support but not active killing. Applying the basic assumptions of preference utilitarianism, he spins out his bone-chilling argument for letting parents kill disabled babies and replace them with nondisabled babies who have a greater chance at happiness. It is all about allowing as many individuals as possible to fulfill as many of their preferences as possible.

As soon as he's done, I get the microphone and say I'd like to discuss selective infanticide. As a lawyer, I disagree with his jurisprudential assumptions. Logical inconsistency is not a sufficient reason to change the law. As an atheist, I object to his using religious terms ("the doctrine of the sanctity of human life") to characterize his critics. Singer takes a notepad out of his pocket and jots down my points, apparently eager to take them on, and I proceed to the heart of my argument: that the presence or absence of a disability doesn't predict quality of life. I question his replacement-baby theory, with its assumption of "other things equal," arguing that people are not fungible. I draw out a comparison of myself and my nondisabled brother Mac (the next-born after me), each of us with a combination of gifts and flaws so peculiar that we can't be measured on the same scale.

He responds to each point with clear and lucid counterarguments. He proceeds with the assumption that I am one of the people who might rightly have been killed at birth. He sticks to his guns, conceding just enough to show himself open-minded and flexible. We go back and forth for ten long minutes. Even as I am horrified by what he says, and by the fact that I have been sucked into a civil discussion of whether I ought to exist, I can't help being dazzled by his verbal facility. He is so respectful, so free of condescension, so focused on the argument, that by the time the show is over, I'm not exactly angry with him. Yes, I am shaking, furious, enraged—but it's for the big room, two hundred of my fellow Charlestonians who have listened with polite interest, when in decency they should have run him out of town on a rail.

My encounter with Peter Singer merits a mention in my annual canned letter that December. I decide to send Singer a copy. In response, he sends me the nicest possible e-mail message. Dear Harriet (if he may) . . . Just back from Australia, where he's from. Agrees with my comments on the world situation. Supports my work against institutionalization. And then some pointed questions to clarify my views on selective infanticide.

I reply. Fine, call me Harriet, and I'll reciprocate in the interest of equality, though I'm accustomed to more formality. Skipping agreeable preambles, I answer his questions on disability-based infanticide and pose some of my own. Answers and more questions come back. Back and forth over several weeks it proceeds, an engaging discussion of baby killing, disability prejudice, and related points of law and philosophy. Dear Harriet. Dear Peter.

Singer seems curious to learn how someone who is as good an atheist as he is could disagree with his entirely reasonable views. At the same time, I am trying to plumb his theories. What has him so convinced it would be best to allow parents to kill babies with severe disabilities, and not other kinds of babies, if no infant is a "person" with a right to life? I learn it is partly that both biological and adoptive parents prefer healthy babies. But I have trouble with basing life-and-death decisions on market considerations when the market is structured by prejudice. I offer a hypothetical comparison: "What about mixed-race babies, especially when the combination is entirely nonwhite, who I believe are just about as unadoptable as babies with disabilities?" Wouldn't a law allowing the killing of these undervalued babies validate race prejudice? Singer agrees there is a problem. "It would be horrible," he says, "to see mixed-race babies being killed because they can't be adopted, whereas white ones could be." What's the difference? Preferences based on race are unreasonable. Preferences based on ability are not. Why? To Singer, it's pretty simple: disability makes a person "worse off."

Are we "worse off"? I don't think so. Not in any meaningful sense. There are too many variables. For those of us with congenital conditions, disability shapes all we are. Those disabled later in life adapt. We take constraints that no one would choose and build rich and satisfying lives within them. We enjoy pleasures other people enjoy and pleasures peculiarly our own. We have something the world needs.

Pressing me to admit a negative correlation between disability and happiness, Singer presents a situation: imagine a disabled child on the beach, watching the other children play.

It's right out of the telethon. I expected something more sophisticated from a professional thinker. I respond: "As a little girl playing on the beach, I was already aware that some people felt sorry for me, that I wasn't frolicking with the same level of frenzy as other children. This annoyed me, and still does." I take the time to write a detailed description of how I, in fact, had fun playing on the beach, without the need of standing, walking, or running. But, really, I've had enough. I suggest to Singer that we have exhausted our topic, and I'll be back in touch when I get around to writing about him.

He responds by inviting me to Princeton. I fire off an immediate maybe.

Of course I'm flattered. Mama will be impressed.

But there are things to consider. Not Dead Yet says—and I completely agree—that we should not legitimate Singer's views by giving them a forum. We should not make disabled lives subject to debate. Moreover, any spokesman chosen by the opposition is by definition a token. But even if I'm a token, I won't have to act like one. And anyway, I'm kind of stuck. If I decline, Singer can make some hay: "I offered them a platform, but they refuse rational discussion." It's an old trick, and I've laid myself wide open.

My invitation is to have an exchange of views with Singer during his undergraduate course. He also proposes a second "exchange," open to the whole university, later in the day. This sounds a lot like debating my life—and on my opponent's turf, with my opponent moderating, to boot. I offer a counterproposal, to which Singer proves amenable. I will open the class with some comments on infanticide and related issues and then let Singer grill me as hard as he likes before we open it up for the students. Later in the day, I might take part in a discussion of some other disability issue in a neutral forum. Singer suggests a faculty-student discussion group sponsored by his department but with cross-departmental membership. The topic I select is "Assisted Suicide, Disability Discrimination, and the Illusion of Choice: A Disability Rights Perspective." I inform a few movement colleagues of this turn of events, and advice starts rolling in. I decide to go with the advisers who counsel me to do the gig, lie low, and get out of Dodge.

I ask Singer to refer me to the person who arranges travel at Princeton. I imagine some capable and unflappable woman like my sister, Beth, whose varied job description at a North Carolina university includes handling visiting artists. Singer refers me to his own assistant, who certainly seems capable and unflappable enough. However, almost immediately Singer jumps back in via e-mail. It seems the nearest hotel has only one wheelchair-accessible suite, available with two rooms for $600 per night. What to do? I know I shouldn't be so accommodating, but I say I can make do with an inaccessible room if it has certain features. Other logistical issues come up. We go back and forth. Questions and answers. Do I really need a lift-equipped vehicle at the airport? Can't my assistant assist me into a conventional car? How wide is my wheelchair?

By the time we're done, Singer knows that I am twenty-eight inches wide. I have trouble controlling my wheelchair if my hand gets cold. I am accustomed to driving on rough, irregular surfaces, but I get

nervous turning on steep slopes. Even one step is too many. I can swallow purees, soft bread, and grapes. I use a bedpan, not a toilet. None
of this is a secret; none of it cause for angst. But I do wonder whether
Singer is jotting down my specs in his little notepad as evidence of how
"bad off" people like me really are.

I realize I must put one more issue on the table: etiquette. I was
criticized within the movement when I confessed to shaking Singer's
hand in Charleston, and some are appalled that I have agreed to break
bread with him in Princeton. I think they have a very good point,
but again, I'm stuck. I'm engaged for a day of discussion, not a picket
line. It is not in my power to marginalize Singer at Princeton; nothing
would be accomplished by displays of personal disrespect. However,
chumminess is clearly inappropriate. I tell Singer that in the lecture
hall it can't be Harriet and Peter; it must be Ms. Johnson and Mr.
Singer.

He seems genuinely nettled. Shouldn't it be Ms. Johnson and Professor Singer, if I want to be formal? To counter, I invoke the ceremo-
nial Low Country usage, Attorney Johnson and Professor Singer, but
point out that Mr./Ms. is the custom in American political debates
and might seem more normal in New Jersey. All right, he says. Ms./
Mr. it will be.

I describe this awkward social situation to the lawyer in my office
who has served as my default lunch partner for the past fourteen years.
He gives forth a full-body shudder.

"That poor sorry son of a bitch! He has no idea what he's in for."

Being a disability rights lawyer lecturing at Princeton does confer
some cachet at the Newark airport. I need all the cachet I can get.
Delta Airlines has torn up my power chair. It is a fairly frequent occur-
rence for any air traveler on wheels.

When they inform me of the damage in Atlanta, I throw a monumental fit and tell them to have a repair person meet me in Newark with new batteries to replace the ones inexplicably destroyed. Then I am told no new batteries can be had until the morning. It's Sunday night. On arrival in Newark, I'm told of a plan to put me up there for the night and get me repaired and driven to Princeton by ten a.m.

"That won't work. I'm lecturing at ten. I need to get there tonight, go to sleep, and be in my right mind tomorrow."

"What? You're lecturing? They told us it was a conference. We need to get you fixed tonight!"

Carla, the gate agent, relieves me of the need to throw any further fits by undertaking on my behalf the fit of all fits.

Carmen, the personal assistant with whom I'm traveling, pushes me in my disabled chair around the airport in search of a place to use the bedpan. However, instead of diaper-changing tables, which are functional though far from private, we find a flip-down plastic shelf that doesn't look like it would hold my seventy pounds of body weight. It's no big deal; I've restricted my fluids. But Carmen is a little freaked. It is her first adventure in power-chair air travel. I thought I prepared her for the trip, but I guess I neglected to warn her about the probability of wheelchair destruction. I keep forgetting that even people who know me well don't know much about my world.

We reach the hotel at 10:15 p.m., four hours late.

I wake up tired. I slept better than I would have slept in Newark with an unrepaired chair, but any hotel bed is a near guarantee of morning crankiness. I tell Carmen to leave the TV off. I don't want to hear the temperature.

I do the morning stretch. Medical people call it passive movement, but it's not really passive. Carmen's hands move my limbs, following my precise instructions, her strength giving effect to my will. Carmen knows the routine, so it is in near silence that we begin easing slowly into the day. I let myself be propped up to eat oatmeal and drink tea. Then there's the bedpan and then bathing and dressing, still in bed. As the caffeine kicks in, silence gives way to conversation about practical things. Carmen lifts me into my chair and straps a rolled towel under my ribs for comfort and stability. She tugs at my clothes to remove wrinkles that could cause pressure sores. She switches on my motors and gives me the means of moving without anyone's help. They don't call it a power chair for nothing.

I drive to the mirror. I do my hair in one long braid. Even this primal hairdo requires, at this stage of my life, joint effort. I undo yesterday's braid, fix the part and comb the hair in front. Carmen combs where I can't reach. I divide the mass into three long hanks and start the braid just behind my left ear. Section by section, I hand it over to her, and her unimpaired young fingers pull tight, crisscross, until the braid is fully formed.

A big polyester scarf completes my costume. Carmen lays it over my back. I tie it the way I want it, but Carmen starts fussing with it, trying to tuck it down in the back. I tell her that it's fine, and she stops.

On top of the scarf, she wraps the two big shawls that I hope will substitute for an overcoat. I don't own any real winter clothes. I just stay out of the cold, such cold as we get in Charleston.

We review her instructions for the day. Keep me in view and earshot. Be instantly available but not intrusive. Be polite, but don't answer any questions about me. I am glad that she has agreed to come. She's strong, smart, adaptable, and very loyal. But now she is digging under the shawls, fussing with that scarf again.

"Carmen. What are you doing?"

"I thought I could hide this furry thing you sit on."

"Leave it. Singer knows lots of people eat meat. Now he'll know some crips sit on sheepskin."

The walk is cold but mercifully short. The hotel is just across the street from Princeton's wrought-iron gate and a few short blocks from the building, where Singer's assistant shows us to the elevator. The elevator doubles as the janitor's closet—the cart with the big trash can and all the accoutrements is rolled aside so I can get in. Evidently there aren't a lot of wheelchair people using this building.

We ride the broom closet down to the basement and are led down a long passageway to a big lecture hall. As the students drift in, I engage in light badinage with the sound technician. He is squeamish about touching me, but I insist that the cordless lavaliere is my mike of choice. I invite him to clip it to the big polyester scarf.

The students enter from the rear door, way up at ground level, and walk down stairs to their seats. I feel like an animal in the zoo. I hadn't reckoned on the architecture, those tiers of steps that separate me from a human wall of apparent physical and mental perfection, that keep me confined down here in my pit.

It is five before ten. Singer is loping down the stairs. I feel like signaling to Carmen to open the door, summon the broom closet, and get me out of here. But Singer greets me pleasantly and hands me Princeton's check for $500, the fee he offered with apologies for its inadequacy.

So. On with the show.

My talk to the students is pretty Southern. I've decided to pound them with heart, hammer them with narrative, and say *y'all* and *folks*. I play with the emotional tone, giving them little peaks and valleys, modulating three times in one forty-five-second patch. I talk about justice. Even beauty and love. I figure they haven't been getting much of that from Singer.

Of course I give them some argument, too. I mean to honor my contractual obligations. I lead with the hypothetical about mixed-race, nonwhite babies and build the ending around the question of who should have the burden of proof as to the quality of disabled lives. And woven throughout the talk is the presentation of myself as a representative of a minority group that has been rendered invisible by prejudice and oppression, a participant in a discussion that would not occur in a just world.

I let it go a little longer than I should. Their faces show they're going where I'm leading, and I don't look forward to letting them go. But the clock on the wall reminds me of promises I mean to keep, and I stop talking and submit myself to examination and inquiry.

Singer's response is surprisingly soft. Maybe after hearing that this discussion is insulting and painful to me, he doesn't want to exacerbate my discomfort. His reframing of the issues is almost pro forma, abstract, entirely impersonal. Likewise, the students' inquiries are abstract and fairly predictable: anencephaly, permanent unconsciousness, eugenic abortion. I respond to some of them with stories, but mostly I give answers I could have e-mailed in.

I call on a young man near the top of the room.

"Do you eat meat?"

"Yes, I do."

"Then how do you justify—"

"I haven't made any study of animal rights, so anything I could say on the subject wouldn't be worth everyone's time."

The next student wants to work the comparison of disability and race, and Singer joins the discussion until he elicits a comment from me that he can characterize as racist. He scores a point, but that's all right. I've never claimed to be free of prejudice, just struggling with it.

Singer proposes taking me on a walk around campus, unless I think it would be too cold. What the hell? "It's probably warmed up some. Let's go out and see how I do."

He doesn't know how to get out of the building without using the stairs, so this time it is my assistant leading the way. Carmen has learned of another elevator, which arrives empty. When we get out of the building, she falls behind a couple of paces, like a respectful chaperone.

In the classroom there was a question about keeping alive the unconscious. In response, I told a story about a family I knew as a child, which took loving care of a nonresponsive teenage girl, acting out their unconditional commitment to each other, making all the other children, and me as their visitor, feel safe. This doesn't satisfy Singer. "Let's assume we can prove, absolutely, that the individual is totally unconscious and that we can know, absolutely, that the individual will never regain consciousness."

I see no need to state an objection, with no stenographer present to record it; I'll play the game and let him continue.

"Assuming all that," he says, "don't you think continuing to take care of that individual would be a bit . . . weird?"

"No. Done right, it could be profoundly beautiful."

"But what about the caregiver, a woman typically, who is forced to provide all this service to a family member, unable to work, unable to have a life of her own?"

"That's not the way it should be. Not the way it has to be. As a society, we should pay workers to provide that care, in the home. In some places, it's been done that way for years. That woman shouldn't be forced to do it, any more than my family should be forced to do my care."

Singer takes me around the architectural smorgasbord that is Princeton University by a route that includes not one step, unramped curb, or turn on a slope. Within the strange limits of this strange assignment, it seems Singer is doing all he can to make me comfortable.

He asks what I thought of the students' questions.

"They were fine, about what I expected. I was a little surprised by the question about meat eating."

"I apologize for that. That was out of left field. But—I think what he wanted to know is how you can have such high respect for human life and so little respect for animal life."

"People have lately been asking me the converse, how you can have so much respect for animal life and so little respect for human life."

"And what do you answer?"

"I say I don't know. It doesn't make a lot of sense to me."

"Well, in my view—"

"Look. I have lived in blissful ignorance all these years, and I'm not prepared to give that up today."

"Fair enough," he says and proceeds to recount bits of Princeton history. He stops. "This will be of particular interest to you, I think. This is where your colleagues with Not Dead Yet set up their blockade." I'm grateful for the reminder. My brothers and sisters were here before me and behaved far more appropriately than I am doing.

A van delivers Carmen and me early for the evening forum. Singer says he hopes I had a pleasant afternoon.

Yes, indeed. I report a pleasant lunch and a very pleasant nap, and I tell him about the Christopher Reeve Suite in the hotel, which has been remodeled to accommodate Reeve, who has family in the area.

"Do you suppose that's the six-hundred-dollar accessible suite they told me about?"

"Without doubt. And if I'd known it was the Christopher Reeve Suite, I would have held out for it."

"Of course you would have!" Singer laughs. "And we'd have had no choice, would we?"

We talk about the disability rights critique of Reeve and various other topics. Singer is easy to talk to, good company. Too bad he sees lives like mine as avoidable mistakes.

I'm looking forward to the soft vegetarian meal that has been arranged; I'm hungry. Assisted suicide, as difficult as it is, doesn't cause the kind of agony I felt discussing disability-based infanticide. In this one, I understand, and to some degree can sympathize with, the opposing point of view—misguided though it is.

My opening sticks to the five-minute time limit. I introduce the issue as framed by academic articles Not Dead Yet recommended for my use. Andrew Batavia argues for assisted suicide based on autonomy, a principle generally held high in the disability rights movement. In general, he says, the movement fights for our right to control our own lives; when we need assistance to effect our choices, assistance should be available to us as a matter of right. If the choice is to end our lives, he says, we should have assistance then as well. But Carol Gill says that it is differential treatment—disability discrimination—to try to prevent most suicides while facilitating the suicides of ill and disabled people. The social science literature suggests that the public in general, and physicians in particular, tend to underestimate the quality of life of disabled people, compared with our own assessments of our lives. The case for assisted suicide rests on stereotypes that our lives are inherently so bad that it is entirely rational if we want to die.

I side with Gill. What worries me most about the proposals for legalized assisted suicide is their veneer of beneficence—the medical determination that for a given individual, suicide is reasonable or right. It is not about autonomy but about nondisabled people telling us what's good for us.

In the discussion that follows, I argue that choice is illusory in a context of pervasive inequality. Choices are structured by oppression. We shouldn't offer assistance with suicide until we all have the assistance we need to get out of bed in the morning and live a good life. Common causes of suicidality—dependence, institutional confinement, being a burden—are entirely curable. Singer, seated on my right, participates in the discussion but doesn't dominate it. During the meal, I occasionally ask him to put things within my reach, and he competently complies.

I feel as if I'm getting to a few of them when a student asks me a question. The words are all familiar, but they're strung together in a way so meaningless that I can't even retain them—it's like a long sentence in Tagalog. I can only admit my limitations. "That question's too abstract for me to deal with. Can you rephrase it?"

He indicates that it is as clear as he can make it, so I move on.

A little while later, my right elbow slips out from under me. This is awkward. Normally I get whoever is on my right to do this sort of thing. Why not now? I gesture to Singer. He leans over, and I whisper, "Grasp this wrist and pull forward one inch, without lifting." He follows my instructions to the letter. He sees that now I can again reach my food with my fork. And he may now understand what I was saying a minute ago, that most of the assistance disabled people need does not demand medical training.

A philosophy professor says, "It appears that your objections to assisted suicide are essentially tactical."

"Excuse me?"

"By that I mean they are grounded in current conditions of political, social, and economic inequality. What if we assume that such conditions do not exist?"

"Why would we want to do that?"

"I want to get to the real basis for the position you take."

I feel as if I'm losing caste. It is suddenly very clear that I'm not a philosopher. I'm like one of those old practitioners who used to visit my law school, full of bluster about life in the real world. Such a bore! A once-sharp mind gone muddy! And I'm only forty-four—not all that old.

The forum is ended, and I've been able to eat very little of my pureed food. I ask Carmen to find the caterer and get me a container. Singer jumps up to take care of it. He returns with a box and obligingly packs my food to go.

When I get home, people are clamoring for the story. The lawyers want the blow-by-blow of my forensic triumph over the formidable foe; when I tell them it wasn't like that, they insist that it was. Within the disability rights community, there is less confidence. It is generally assumed that I handled the substantive discussion well, but people worry that my civility may have given Singer a new kind of legitimacy. I hear from Laura, a beloved movement sister. She is appalled that I let Singer provide even minor physical assistance at the dinner. "Where was your assistant?" she wants to know. How could I put myself in a relationship with Singer that made him appear so human, even kind?

I struggle to explain. I didn't feel disempowered; quite the contrary, it seemed a good thing to make him do some useful work. And then the hard part: I've come to believe that Singer actually is human, even kind, in his way. There ensues a discussion of good and evil and personal assistance and power and philosophy and tactics for which I'm profoundly grateful.

I e-mail Laura again. This time I inform her that I've changed my will. She'll inherit a book that Singer gave me, a collection of his writings with a weirdly appropriate inscription:

"To Harriet Johnson, So that you will have a better answer to questions about animals. And thanks for coming to Princeton. Peter Singer. March 25, 2002."

She responds that she is changing her will, too. I'll get the autographed photo of Jerry Lewis she received as an MDA poster child. We joke that each of us has given the other a "reason to live."

I have had a nice e-mail message from Singer, hoping Carmen and I and the chair got home without injury, relaying positive feedback from my audiences—and taking me to task for a statement that isn't supported by a relevant legal authority, which he looked up. I report that we got home exhausted but unharmed and concede that he has caught me in a generalization that should have been qualified. It's clear that the conversation will continue.

I am soon sucked into the daily demands of law practice, family, community, and politics. In the closing days of the state legislative session, I help get a bill passed that I hope will move us one small step toward a world in which killing won't be such an appealing solution to the "problem" of disability. It is good to focus on this kind of work. But the conversations with and about Singer continue. Unable to muster the appropriate moral judgments, I ask myself a tough question: Am I in fact a silly little lady whose head is easily turned by a man who gives her a kind of attention she enjoys? I hope not, but I confess that I've never been able to sustain righteous anger for more than about thirty minutes at a time. My view of life tends more toward tragedy.

The tragic view comes closest to describing how I now look at Peter Singer. He is a man of unusual gifts, reaching for the heights. He writes that he is trying to create a system of ethics derived from fact and reason that largely throws off the perspectives of religion, place, family, tribe, community, and maybe even species—to "take the point of view of the universe." His is a grand, heroic undertaking.

But like the protagonist in a classical drama, Singer has his flaw. It is his unexamined assumption that disabled people are inherently "worse off," that we "suffer," that we have lesser "prospects of a happy life." Because of this all-too-common prejudice, and his rare courage in taking it to its logical conclusion, catastrophe looms. Here in the midpoint of the play, I can't look at him without fellow feeling.

I am regularly confronted by people who tell me that Singer doesn't deserve my human sympathy. I should make him an object of implacable wrath, to be cut off, silenced, destroyed absolutely. And I find myself lacking a logical argument to the contrary.

I am talking to my sister, Beth, on the phone. "You kind of like the monster, don't you?" she says.

I find myself unable to evade, certainly unwilling to lie. "Yeah, in a way. And he's not exactly a monster."

"You know, Harriet, there were some very pleasant Nazis. They say the SS guards went home and played on the floor with their children every night."

She can tell that I'm chastened; she changes the topic, lets me off the hook. Her harshness has come as a surprise. She isn't inclined to moralizing; in our family, I'm the one who sets people straight.

When I put down the phone, my argumentative nature feels frustrated. In my mind, I replay the conversation but this time defend my position.

"He's not exactly a monster. He just has some strange ways of looking at things."

"He's advocating genocide."

"That's the thing. In his mind, he isn't. He's only giving parents a choice. He thinks the humans he is talking about aren't people, aren't 'persons.'"

"But that's the way it always works, isn't it? They're always animals or vermin or chattel goods. Objects, not persons. He's repackaging some old ideas. Making them acceptable."

"I think his ideas are new, in a way. It's not old-fashioned hate. It's a twisted, misinformed, warped kind of beneficence. His motive is to do good."

"What do you care about motives?" she asks. "Doesn't this beneficent killing make disabled brothers and sisters just as dead?"

"But he isn't killing anyone. It's just talk."

"Just talk? It's talk with an agenda, talk aimed at forming policy. Talk that's getting a receptive audience. You of all people know the power of that kind of talk."

"Well, sure, but—"

"If talk didn't matter, would you make it your life's work?"

"But," I say, "his talk won't matter in the end. He won't succeed in reinventing morality. He stirs the pot, brings things out into the open. But ultimately we'll make a world that's fit to live in, a society that has room for all its flawed creatures. History will remember Singer as a curious example of the bizarre things that can happen when paradigms collide."

"What if you're wrong? What if he convinces people that there's no morally significant difference between a fetus and a newborn, and just as disabled fetuses are routinely aborted now, so disabled babies are routinely killed? Might some future generation take it further than Singer wants to go? Might some say there's no morally significant line between a newborn and a three-year-old?"

"Sure. Singer concedes that a bright line cannot be drawn. But he doesn't propose killing anyone who prefers to live."

"That overarching respect for the individual's preference for life—might some say it's a fiction, a fetish, a quasi-religious belief?"

"Yes," I say. "That's pretty close to what I think. As an atheist, I think all preferences are moot once you kill someone. The injury is entirely to the surviving community."

"So what if that view wins out, but you can't break disability prejudice? What if you wind up in a world where the disabled person's 'irrational' preference to live must yield to society's 'rational' interest in reducing the incidence of disability? Doesn't horror kick in somewhere? Maybe as you watch the door close behind whoever has wheeled you into the gas chamber?"

"That's not going to happen."

"Do you have empirical evidence?" she asks. "A logical argument?"

"Of course not. And I know it's happened before, in what was considered the most progressive medical community in the world. But it won't happen. I have to believe that."

Belief. Is that what it comes down to? Am I a person of faith after all? Or am I clinging to foolish hope that the tragic protagonist, this one time, will shift course before it's too late?

I don't think so. It's less about belief, less about hope, than about a practical need for definitions I can live with.

If I define Singer's kind of disability prejudice as an ultimate evil, and him as a monster, then I must so define all who believe disabled lives are inherently worse off or that a life without a certain kind of consciousness lacks value. That definition would make monsters of many of the people with whom I move on the sidewalks, do business, break bread, swap stories, and share the grunt work of local politics. It would reach some of my family and most of my nondisabled friends, people who show me personal kindness and who sometimes manage to love me through their ignorance. I can't live with a definition of ultimate evil that encompasses all of them. I can't refuse the monster-majority basic respect and human sympathy. It's not in my heart to deny every single one of them, categorically, my affection and my love.

The peculiar drama of my life has placed me in a world that by and large thinks it would be better if people like me did not exist. My fight has been for accommodation, the world to me and me to the world.

As a disability pariah, I must struggle for a place, for kinship, for community, for connection. Because I am still seeking acceptance of my humanity, Singer's call to get past species seems a luxury way beyond my reach. My goal isn't to shed the perspective that comes from my particular experience but to give voice to it. I want to be engaged in the tribal fury that rages when opposing perspectives are let loose.

As a shield from the terrible purity of Singer's vision, I'll look to the corruption that comes from interconnectedness. To justify my hopes that Singer's theoretical world—and its entirely logical extensions—won't become real, I'll invoke the muck and mess and undeniable reality of disabled lives well lived. That's the best I can do.

For Ki'tay D. Davidson, Who Loves Us

Talila A. Lewis

Notes: Ki'tay D. Davidson, a proud Black Disabled transman, passed away suddenly in the early morning hours of December 2, 2014. This is his eulogy. This version does not reflect spontaneous additions made during its presentation.

SATURDAY, DECEMBER 13, 2014
ORLAND PARK, ILLINOIS

What an incredible honor.

I am so very humbled, grateful, and honored to be counted among those who know and love Ki'tay D. Davidson. My name is Talila A. Lewis—sign name and chosen name, TL. Ki'tay is my life partner, my mentee, my mentor, my dearest friend, and the one who showed me precisely what the meaning of love is.

It is solely because of Ki'tay that the theme of this day and of the rest of my eternity is: *Love Wins.*

We come together today, not only to celebrate the life and legacy of a beautiful human being who embodied everything that active love is, but also to learn about those who may come from different communities and yet be just as human as you—to learn how to affirm, love, and fight with and for them. In doing so, we will love ourselves more deeply and move the world faster toward collective justice and liberation—the world that Ki'tay dreamed of and fought for with all of his being and all of his heart.

There is a quote by the poet Rumi that reminds me deeply of Ki'tay and helps me understand precisely how many of us feel in this moment about his loss. It's a question and an answer—which is how most who truly knew him remember Ki'tay: Dialogue. Interdependence centered always.

The quote is as follows:

> *"My heart is so small . . . it's almost invisible. How can you place such big sorrows in it?"*
>
> *"Look," he answered, "your eyes are even smaller, yet they behold the world."*

Ki'tay was a lot of things to a lot of people, organizations, and institutions:

The voice of affirmation when you weren't quite sure of your self-worth, dignity, or beauty.

The voice of love and justice within institutions and organizations rife with oppression and violence.

The voice of his unique brand of Black Trans Disabled innovation when all others were frozen with fear or frozen in traditions, religion, or ritual.

While Ki'tay's work, what he stood for, and how he transformed all of these people and entities can never be encapsulated in any language, what we can be sure of is that we are forever changed for the better because of his existence and sacrifice.

Many here may have met Ki'tay but aren't familiar with who he is or what he stood for. Allow me to share a bit about him with you:

Ki'tay is a revolutionary dreamer, leader, and lover. One who prized people, prioritized love, and propelled action by empowering all.

Last year, for example, he was awarded a prestigious White House award, honoring his contributions as a "Champion of Change" for his transformative advocacy and activism with and for multiply marginalized people with disabilities. Upon being named the Champion of Change, he penned an open letter to the community saying this, in part:

> *I challenge the extent to which we place the responsibility for advocacy on those designated as leaders or "champions." Advocacy is not just a task for charismatic individuals or high-profile community organizers. Advocacy is for all of us; advocacy is a way of life. It is a natural response to the injustices and inequality in the world. While you and I may not have sole responsibility for these inequities, that does not alter its reality.*
>
> *Today I am thankful. I am thankful for every ally and individual working, struggling, and fighting to make this world a better place—thankful to any and everybody who realizes that this world is bigger than themselves, and who channels that awareness to "level the playing field." These are people who can acknowledge their privilege and opportunity, and consciously and intentionally use their existence to transform communities . . . I may have earned a prestigious award, but today it is not really about me. It is about the community, and I am simply a singular representative of thousands of people who give their hearts and*

their time to living a life of transformation. Thank you to all the champions who came before me, to those I have met, and to those who I have yet to meet. Thanks to those champions who have encouraged, listened, affirmed, fought, and loved alongside our beautiful community. Together, we have made change and will continue to make change. There are many chains that need to be broken. We all know it. I support you and welcome you to hold me accountable as we hold all of ourselves accountable to facilitating inclusive and loving environments for all.

These are what I have come to call Ki'tay's truths.

Ki'tay found innovative ways to speak to injustice in many different contexts—from racism, transphobia, ableism, to discrimination against incarcerated persons and people with a history of incarceration. Indeed, he possessed the courage of his convictions. It could be said—and it is true—that many people possess this trait.

However, it was Ki'tay's ability to sit with and *actively love* oppressors and those who were violent toward him and marginalized communities—most often solely because they do not adhere to that which has been deemed "normal"—that truly set him apart. He could breathe life and love into even *those* people within mere moments of making their acquaintance. This is what makes him special—reminiscent of what some here may call a prophet; others, a wise man; others still, a light or sage.

He was grounded in love. Always.

Ki'tay did not feign to know all of the answers to the problems of the world, but he prided himself on always learning and evolving to address injustices. Those who know him will tell you that rarely a day went by that he was not researching and sending research to others on issues that most of us could not even begin to understand. When con-

fused about the content, we were not chided or insulted for not knowing but affirmed for our interest and ability to challenge ourselves. He
could explain the most abstract and nuanced concepts with elegance
and pith such that all you could do was smile and shake your head after
having struggled for days—sometimes weeks—to digest the content.

This was Ki'tay's love language. Community-centered learning,
growth, activism, and healing.

He was frequently caught quoting the famed Assata Shakur: "It is
our duty to fight. It is our duty to win. We must love each other and
protect each other. We have nothing to lose but our chains."

He has understood since, well, birth, it seems [Ki'tay's mother
had just shared some stories about his struggles for justice as a toddler
and young child], that we cannot remain silent about injustice against
any group of people, be they Black, Disabled, indigenous, gender nonconforming, trans, homeless, sex workers, incarcerated, and the list
continues. He understood that each individual group's liberation was
inextricably linked to the other—that justice and liberation could only
be had if we all stand together and fight for the rights and liberties of
the next individual or community. He understood that we are free
when we use our freedom to advance the rights of all members of our
community; or as Nelson Mandela put it, "to be free is not just cast-
ing off one's chains, but to live in a way that respects and enhances the
freedom of others."

It was his visceral yearning for universal equality, solidarity, and
collective activism that explains Ki'tay's immense joy with the recent
collective creation of #DisabilitySolidarity with Allie Cannington and
myself. Disability Solidarity has been the impetus behind groups fighting for disability justice to dedicate themselves to racial justice and
for non-disability civil rights organizations to dedicate themselves to
disability justice.

On October 17, I sent Ki'tay an e-mail for which he expressed sincere gratitude. The short e-mail was a quote attributed to the Dalai Lama, who, when asked what surprised him most about humanity, said this:

> *Man surprises me most about humanity.*
> *Because he sacrifices his health in order to make money.*
> *Then he sacrifices money to recuperate his health.*
> *And then he is so anxious about the future that he does not enjoy the present;*
> *the result being that he does not live in the present or the future;*
> *he lives as if he is never going to die,*
> *and then dies having never really lived.*

One thing Ki'tay *did* do was live fully. Another was consciously ignore the vanity that pervades our culture. He found the beauty in everything natural. He valued all people regardless of gender, color, creed, disability, sexual orientation, religious or spiritual bent (or lack thereof), or gender identity. He found and created beauty where it could not be found and shared this beauty and love with all who would listen—and with those who thought they were not interested, *but had no idea.*

See, many of you here are familiar with parables and stories of grace and justice that you studied and learned from holy books. I, however, was fortunate to witness parables and actions of grace and justice because Ki'tay lived them.

Solidarity for Ki'tay means active resistance to the status quo— letting *all* people know that they are respected, cherished, valued, and *loved.* Solidarity also means letting them know that despite our failures, we are committed to their cause because it is inextricably linked to each of our individual and collective causes. Ki'tay believed that the time is now to seek what is just.

Ki'tay did more in twenty-two years than many can complete in several lifetimes. If he were here right now witnessing for and sharing with all of you in light of all that has occurred even over these past several days, I believe his heart would share this modified message from Martin Luther King Jr.:

> *Now let us begin. Now let us rededicate ourselves to the long and bitter, but beautiful, struggle for a new world. This is the calling of my generation and those who are in the generations to come— who wait eagerly for your response. Will you say to us that the odds are too great? Will you tell us the struggle is too hard? Will your message to us be that the forces of life militate against our arrival as full persons, and that you send your deepest regrets? Or will there be another message—of longing, of hope, of solidarity with our yearnings, of commitment to our causes, whatever the cost? The choice is yours, and though we might prefer it otherwise, we must choose in this crucial moment of human history.*

In closing, I wish to offer you a call to love and a call of action. Here is our call to love. This, from the great Paulo Coelho:

> *In those moments, love appears and says: "You think you're heading toward a specific point, but the whole justification for the goal's existence lies in your love for it. Rest a little, but as soon as you can, get up and carry on. Because ever since your goal found out that you were traveling toward it, it has been running to meet you."*

And now our call to action—again from the late great Martin Luther King Jr.:

Human progress is neither automatic nor inevitable.... Every step toward the goal of justice requires sacrifice, suffering, and struggle; the tireless exertions and passionate concern of dedicated individuals.

Thank you, Ki'tay, for consciously sharing your love with us.

Thank you, Ki'tay, for your countless quiet sacrifices in the name of love, liberation, humanity.

I wholeheartedly recognize and am forever humbled in knowing that you are the mightiest of all our miracles.

May we ever uplift, share, and act out your truth: *Love Wins.*

If You Can't Fast, Give

Maysoon Zayid

I was born and raised in the United States. I spent my school days in beautiful New Jersey and my summers in the war zone known as the West Bank. The first Ramadan I ever fasted was no joke. I was eight years old and on summer vacation in my parents' village. It was late June and the Middle East is a sauna at that time of year. During Ramadan, those observing the fast abstain from food, beverages, smoking, and shagging. I have never had an issue with fasting. I'm one of those crazy Muslims who loves Ramadan.

I have cerebral palsy. That means, technically, I am exempt from fasting; even though it is one of the five pillars of Islam and extremely important to the faith. The Qur'an states clearly in Surah 2, Ayat 185 that those who have medical conditions are pardoned, so I was treated like a champ for fasting. My family was over the moon and I refused to show any weakness. I knew that by fasting against the odds I had been born with, I'd totally get into heaven and, more important, would get amazing gifts for Eid. Eid is the celebration that marks the end of fasting. Muslims celebrate for three days, because after thirty days of fasting, one day simply isn't enough.

Regardless of the heat, it's fun to fast for Ramadan when you are in a country where the majority of folks around you are also starving. Ramadan is not as much fun in America, where you are the only one fasting. In my day, teachers weren't as culturally savvy as they are now. I had teachers who genuinely feared for my life and were convinced that I was being forced by my horrible Muslim parents to fast. They'd try to slip me a butterscotch candy at lunchtime. I would shove their candy away and tell them not to push their beliefs on me. I could eat whatever I wanted at sunset, thank you very much.

Every Ramadan, without fail, my mother has given me the option to not fast. Those who cannot fast during Ramadan get to make a donation that will feed a hungry person for the duration of the holy month. If you cannot afford to do so, you should instead perform any acts of charity within your capability. My mom has donated on my behalf every single year I have fasted, just in case it ever got to be too much and I had to give up. How is that for faith?

My most challenging Ramadan came in the form of a ten-day road trip in 2011, in America's Deep South, on a comedy tour called "The Muslims Are Coming." Ramadan, which moves back ten days each year, happened to land in August. I was filming a documentary in addition to performing nightly. We would spend all day on the street doing interviews with the locals who weren't too fond of Muslims. For the first time in my history of Ramadans, I complained. I was hot, thirsty, and tired of bigotry. Some nights I didn't break my fast until 10:30 p.m., but I survived. I broke down and broke my fast only once on tour. We were at Elvis's house in Tupelo, Mississippi. The statue of the King spoke to me and I realized if I didn't drink water I would drop down dead just like he did. I did not want to die where Elvis was born. It's okay to miss a day or five, if you are sick or traveling, or are on your ladies' holiday. You then have a whole year to make it up. Some Muslims are slick and do their makeup days in December when the sun sets at, like, 4:30 p.m. and they have to fast for only six or seven hours.

On July 10, 2013, after three decades, my days of fasting came to an end. As I mentioned, I have cerebral palsy. One of my symptoms is that I shake all the time, just like Shakira's hips. On the first day of Ramadan 2013, my shaking got the best of me. By noon, I no longer had the coordination to tweet, and by the time I broke my fast at 8:30 p.m., I could barely breathe. I knew that I had fasted my last day. The next morning the water I drank tasted like poison. It felt so wrong to quench my thirst during the daylight hours. Ramadan is something I strongly associate with the happiest times of my life, so I felt like a tradition was lost.

I am not ashamed that I cannot fast, but I know many who are, even though they are excused for God's sake. I miss fasting, but I'm happy to take on my newest mission of reminding those who can't fast that there is no reason to put themselves at risk. Muslims fast so they can suffer a little. It is important not to die in the process. Instead, those who can't should channel their devotion into charity. This will not only help you stay healthy but also will help someone who is genuinely suffering. Those who are blessed with the health to fast, please don't interrogate your fellow Muslims about their hunger status. It is impolite to ask others if they are fasting unless you are in the process of offering them something to eat, and sometimes you really don't want to know the answer.

Content notes: bullying, suicidal ideation

There's a Mathematical Equation That Proves I'm Ugly

Or So I Learned in My Seventh-Grade Art Class

Ariel Henley

I am ugly. There's a mathematical equation to prove it. Or so I was told by the boy that sat behind me in my seventh-grade art class.

I'm going to stick my pencil through the back of your eye, he told me, laughing. *It's not like you could get much uglier. Even the teacher thinks so.*

Two years earlier, a different boy, whose name I can no longer remember, angrily asked me what was wrong with my face after I beat him in a game of handball during recess. *You have the weirdest set of eyes I've ever seen*, he told me. When my teacher overheard this, he sent the boy to the principal's office, where I would later go and give my side of the story, only to be told that I needed to not be so sensitive.

So when the boy in my art class continued poking me in the shoulder with the back of his pencil, I said nothing.

My art teacher that year was a heavyset black woman named Ms. J. She had a laugh so loud, it echoed down the corridor. She wore beautiful bright colors and taught us about artists and movements that

I had never heard of; she encouraged us to explore what art meant to us both collectively and as individuals.

My school was filled with children who came more from upper-than middle-class families, the offspring of doctors and business executives and athletes. Though my family was well off, I felt out of place with children who were taken care of by nannies, who had fathers who attended prestigious universities and were frequently away on business trips. My father was a cabinetmaker and owned a construction company. My mother issued building permits in the next town over. Neither had more than a high school diploma. It was a town of mostly white people, so having a black woman as a teacher felt almost cultural, in a way that only sheltered white upper-middle-class children would ignorantly understand.

Every week, Ms. J required students to research an artist, a movement, or a piece of artwork that we were drawn to. *Art isn't about what you see*, she would tell the class. *It's about what you feel. Show me what you feel.* We had to research and write a one-page report explaining our topic and what it meant for our art. After school on Wednesdays she would hold studio time, when students could come in to work on new projects and discuss the things we had learned in class. It was usually just me and a handful of other students I had become friends with.

One week Ms. J spent the first half of class discussing the role of beauty in art and how the very idea of beauty was subjective and dependent upon the interpretation of the audience. She taught us about the golden ratio, the mathematical equation that, in many ways, explained beauty. During the Renaissance period, artists would use an equation to create balance, symmetry, and beauty in their work. It was first explained more than two thousand years ago in Euclid's *Elements* and describes a sequence found frequently in nature. Based on the Fibonacci sequence, the ratio combines symmetry and asymmetry in a way that is alluring and attractive to the eye; this is why it is often employed in design, architecture, and nature. The closer an object's measurements were to the golden ratio, the more beautiful it was.

One week, during a discussion on facial structure and drawing portraits, Ms. J mentioned the golden ratio again. She told us that scientists had studied this equation, using the formula to quantify beauty.

"They analyze and they measure," she told us. "They measure the hairline to the root of the nose, right between the eyelids. And from right between the eyelids to the base of the nose. And from the base of the nose to the bottom of the chin. If these numbers are equal, the individual is said to be more attractive." She gestured as she spoke.

She told us that the ear should be the same length as the nose and the width of an eye should equal the space between the eyes. In order for a woman to be considered beautiful, the length of her face divided by the width should have a ratio of 1:1.618. Ms. J showed us work by Renaissance artists like Raphael and Botticelli.

I had never understood mathematical equations or ratios, so the only thing I learned from her lesson was that these were the beauty standards a woman must meet if she wanted to be deemed worthy.

Ms. J went further, telling us that additional research into the role of the golden ratio in determining female beauty reveals the translation of these calculations into an attractiveness ranking system. Individuals, mostly women, were rated on a scale of one to ten, based on the symmetry of their facial structure, with most individuals scoring between a four and a six. Never had an individual been ranked a perfect ten, but still we lived in a society that found the need to measure and rate and rank and score.

I couldn't help but think that if my appearance had been measured against the golden ratio, my formal rating wouldn't have been higher than a two.

I grew up having every flaw pointed out to me. I grew up believing I was wrong. It's part of the territory that comes with being born with a facial disfigurement as a result of Crouzon syndrome—a rare genetic disorder where the bones in the head do not grow normally. My eyes were too far apart, too crooked; my nose was too big. My jaw was too far back; my ears were too low. There were regular appointments with doctors and surgeons trying to fix me and my twin sister, who was also born with Crouzon syndrome. Some of these were for medical purposes, others for aesthetics.

I would sit in a room while doctors took pictures of my face from every angle. They would pinch and poke, circling my flaws. I would sit and let them pick apart my every flaw. And I wanted it, I did.

"Fix me," I would beg.

They would do their best.

I'd have surgery, recover, and return for more pictures, more circling and more detailing of every flaw. I was obsessed with symmetry, obsessed with bridging the gap between the person I was and the person I felt I should be.

The afternoon the boy in my seventh-grade art class told me I was ugly, I told my mother that I wanted to die. She took me to a therapist the following day.

My therapist's name was Beth. She was a middle-aged woman with curly red hair that fell just past her shoulders. She had a round stomach and round glasses and almost always wore green. I would sit in Beth's office, play mancala, and tell her of my dreams to travel and write. We almost never spoke of my appearance.

When I entered Beth's office that day, she sat facing the burnt orange plaid couch that looked straight out of a 1975 home furnishings catalog. We did not play mancala. Instead, Beth looked directly at me and asked me if I was happy.

I did not know how to answer, so I cried. She took a tissue from the small table next to her and gave it to me, listening as I sobbed. When the tears stopped, we sat in silence for several minutes.

"It's like when you reread the same sentence over and over again without understanding what it means," I said finally. "That's how I feel about my life, about what I look like."

She nodded as I spoke, looking at the tablet and pen sitting next to the tissues on the small table. She began to reach for it, but stopped. Instead she folded her hands and put them in her lap.

"I don't understand it," I continued. "These things, they just keep happening, and I know it has to mean something. It has to. I want my suffering to mean something. I want this pain to matter."

She responded by giving me an assignment. She told me that she wanted me to take a picture of my face every day for the next few weeks. She told me that I had no connection with my physical self, because my appearance had undergone drastic changes so many times. This made sense to me, and I was surprised I had never made the connection.

"You don't have to show these to anyone," she told me. "Just take them for you."

I was skeptical, but agreed.

I used to cry at the sight of a picture of myself. The tears would consume me and I would spend the following days refusing to leave the house. Seeing images of the person I was made me angry.

I was ugly.

When I was nine years old, my twin sister and I were interviewed by reporters from the French edition of *Marie Claire*. Two women came to our home. My mother put us in dresses and curled our hair and we sat at the dining room table, which we were allowed to do only on special occasions. The women took pictures of us and asked us questions about our lives. All I can remember of them is their accents and the way I felt confused when they kept implying that I was different.

In the center of the table sat a framed picture of my sister and me from when we were five. We were in coordinating blue-and-white sweaters and holding strands of pearls. It was one of those forced mall photos that families like to hang in their homes to convince everyone else they are happy. I hated the picture. My eyes were bloodshot and I looked weak. It was taken only months after I had surgery to expand my skull and advance the middle of my face. They broke my bones and shifted everything forward—necessary to rectify the premature fusion of my skull. They took bone from my hips and put it in my face. I had to learn how to walk again.

A few weeks after Beth gave me the assignment, I found the *Marie Claire* article buried beneath memories and a thick layer of dust in the attic. I sat on the plywood floorboards and began translating with the basic French I had learned in school. The words spoke of the way the bones in my head were fused prematurely and described the devices that the doctors invented in the garages of their homes as a last resort. I cried as I read the words, because it all felt so simple. The way they described it, I mean. They didn't mention the weeks spent in the ICU or the fact that my mother spent her nights hunched over the edge of my hospital bed, too afraid to leave. The article didn't mention that I was a person and not a disease, and stretched across the page, in big bold letters, I saw this:

Their faces resembled the work of Picasso.

The words stamped the page right below a picture of my sister and me sitting at our kitchen table, laughing like *normal* children. But we weren't normal children, because normal children don't get written about in French magazines. Normal children don't get called ugly in French magazines.

I was embarrassed or ashamed, and I found myself wondering how I ever could have thought someone would think I was special. I felt the weight of the world on my shoulders; it felt as though the whole world was laughing at a joke I wasn't in on. I slammed the magazine to the floor and spent the rest of the night in my room.

"Picasso was an artist. You are God's artwork," my mother would tell me.

"God should take up a new occupation," I would say back.

I shredded the magazine that night.

After I found the article in my attic, I told Ms. J about it. About how my face was compared to a Picasso painting. I told her of the assignment Beth had given me and asked her if I could incorporate my project into my class assignments. Ms. J was supportive of my idea. She told me that appearance, much like design aesthetics, is arbitrary and exists only to assign meaning and purpose for those seeking it, but that ultimately our unique attributes are our signatures. They're the stamps on the world that only we can leave. They're the things that set us apart and make us beautiful.

Ms. J walked over to her desk, which sat against the wall in the front left corner of the classroom. She began punching the keys on her computer and I stood there, unsure whether I was to follow or not.

"Leonardo da Vinci explored beauty and symmetry through what he called the 'divine proportion.' He was a math guy," she told me, "so he frequently incorporated mathematics into his work to ensure they were visually appealing."

She turned her computer screen toward me, scrolling through an article with images of Leonardo Da Vinci's *Profile of an Old Man*, *Vitruvian Man*, and *Mona Lisa*, all famously beautiful pieces. She stood behind her desk, one hand on the computer mouse, looking up at me.

"Do you know what Da Vinci looked like?" She enlarged an image of an old man with long white hair.

"I don't know about you," she quipped, "but he doesn't look too pretty to me."

I laughed.

"Being compared to Picasso may seem like an insult, but it's an honor," she told me. "You are a masterpiece."

Today, when I think of Da Vinci, I do not think of the physical body of the man. I think of Da Vinci as his talent, as his brilliance, as his legacy. His work is often said to have been a window into the extraordinary inner workings of his mind, and it reminds me that we are all more than our bodies, more than the placement of and relationship between our facial features.

I used to find the existence of algebraic and geometric formulas that explained beauty oddly comforting, because then at least there was an ideal—something to work toward. But art isn't necessarily about beauty. Art is supposed to make you feel something, and I began to realize my appearance was my art. My body, my face, my scars told a story—*my* story. But I guess that's how life works sometimes—noticing beauty only in retrospect and poetry, in silence. Sometimes I catch my reflection in the mirror and I remember the words of my teacher, *beauty is subjective*, and suddenly the reflection I see doesn't feel like such a stranger.

Content notes: settler colonialism, genocide, racism, sexism, ableism, erasure, sexual assault, violence, suicide, suicidal ideation

The Erasure of Indigenous People in Chronic Illness

Jen Deerinwater

"Are you an Indian?" I've answered this question a myriad of times in various healthcare settings. I've stared the question down, shooting arrows with my Indigenous eyes. I'd like to gather the collective rage of my ancestors to burn the question to the ground—much the way our crops and villages were burned by colonialists. Native people are often asked to define ourselves with these white supremacist, settler-created racial categories like "American Indian." I am not an "American Indian." I am a citizen of the Cherokee Nation of Oklahoma. I am Tsalagi.

When filling out official forms, including medical forms, I'm often forced to swallow my rage and check "American Indian" or write in "Native American"—another term I detest—in the "Other" category. We've been turned into "Americans" to justify the theft of our lands and resources, and continuing to call us "Indian" reinforces the idea that we are loinclothed savages whom Columbus "discovered."

Then there is the "Other" box. This flattening ignores that Indigenous people are not a race but rather hundreds of distinct nations with tribal sovereignty. And even when I mark one of these categories, I am still listed as "white" in my medical records. Erasing my Indigeneity ensures that I never receive the medical care I deserve.

I have suffered through many degrading and humiliating questions and comments from medical providers.

"Are you Indian? Tell me about your people."

"I've been so excited to meet you! You're Native American, right?"

"Deerinwater? What an odd name. What does it mean? Does it mean something bad?"

"You haven't experienced racism in medical care. Some doctors may not give you your medications, but that's not racism."

I've had to answer these questions while my feet were in stirrups, while I was being rolled out of procedure rooms and in so much pain I couldn't move, and even while I was in the emergency room on the verge of death due to an abusive partner. These questions turn me into a museum relic on display for the non-Native gaze. These issues became worse when I moved to Washington, D.C., three years ago. I have experienced extreme anti-Native racism in D.C. After having back surgery at the George Washington University Hospital, employees repeatedly harassed me about my ethnicity and used the slur "redsk*n" in my presence.

A white nurse even repeatedly broke the doctor's orders, denied me pain medication, and stated, "That's ridiculous. You don't need this and I'm not giving this to you." I now take anxiety medication before most medical appointments, and I've canceled appointments when I can't manage anticipating the abuse I'll possibly face.

While these might seem like small slights, this kind of erasure guarantees the early deaths of Native people, especially of those, like me, who are multiply disabled. The Indigenous people of Turtle Island die significantly earlier than all other ethnic groups: the life expectancy of Natives in Oglala County, South Dakota, where the Pine Ridge Reservation is located, is 66.8 years—the lowest in the United States. This is lower than the life expectancy in Sudan (67.2), India (66.9), and Iraq (67.7). This disparity is due to a number of factors, including the poor quality of medical care we receive.

The only healthcare available to Native people living on reservations is provided by the Indian Health Service (IHS), an operating division within the U.S. Department of Health and Human Services that's consistently rated as the worst healthcare provider in America. IHS is also grossly underfunded: in 2016, Congress allotted $4.8 billion for IHS, which came out to approximately $1,297 per person. For comparison, each inmate in the federal prison system receives an average of about $6,973 in healthcare each year. There also aren't enough healthcare clinics or hospitals to serve reservations and tribal villages, which forces many people to travel hundreds of miles for specialized care or to simply go without.

Reproductive healthcare is virtually unavailable for IHS patients because the federal program adheres to the Hyde Amendment, which bars federal funds from being used for abortions except in cases of rape, incest, and saving a pregnant person's life. Approximately 84 percent of Native women are abused in our lifetimes. More than 50 percent of us have been raped at least once. On some reservations, Native women are murdered at ten times the national homicide rate. Despite this, it's nearly impossible to access an abortion or healthcare after a sexual assault. Rape kits are very rarely collected at IHS facilities because there are almost no sexual assault nurse examiners on staff and forms of STD/STI prophylaxis, like PrEP, aren't stocked. And IHS has a long history of abuse that has invoked fear; for example, in the

1970s, between 25 and 50 percent of people with wombs were sterilized against their will in IHS hospitals. The Claremore Indian Hospital, where I went as a child, was notorious for this heinous act.

Healthcare is abysmal for Natives in urban areas as well. During the 1950s, the U.S. government passed a series of policies that ushered in the "Termination Era." During this time, the federal government relocated many of us to cities. Seven out of ten Natives live in or near cities, but only 1 percent of the IHS budget is allocated to urban healthcare. It isn't coincidental that we were moved to areas of "America" where the government doesn't formally recognize many tribal nations. While we are eligible for non-Native health services, such as Medicaid and Medicare, we still have to navigate a medical system that refuses to acknowledge our existence let alone practice cultural competency.

We also have the highest rates of suicide, diabetes, autoimmune diseases, heart disease, murder, and alcohol and drug abuse. My grandpa Deerinwater died from a heart attack in his fifties, before I was even conceived. My father was an emotionally abusive dry drunk partially because of historical and intergenerational trauma. I have diabetes, I've attempted suicide several times, and I've been sexually assaulted so many times that I can no longer count all of the instances. I also have unexplained health issues, and I'm now being tested for autoimmune diseases.

Many of these health issues are a direct result of colonialism. Our lands and waters have been polluted due to resource extraction, toxic dumping, and nuclear testing. Dr. Sophia Marjanovic of the Fort Peck Oglala Lakota and Santa Ysabel Ipai told me in an interview that "My tribe had an oil boom in the 1980s. Ever since I can remember, water has come out of the faucet red, yellow, orange, and smelling of petroleum and having oil droplets on top of it. The number one killer of our women is cancer. We have the most rapidly developing autoimmune diseases in the world, and there's been no accountability for it." The federal government has even facilitated the near extinction of some traditional food sources, including bison.

As a result of these genocidal practices, many of us can no longer grow, hunt, or fish for our traditional foods. Many of us are now dependent on the fat-, cholesterol-, sodium-, and chemical-laden government commodities that America deigns to throw our way. The Food Distribution Program on Indian Reservations is a federal program that supposedly counters food insecurity and starvation on reservations. When there are no jobs or fresh produce, and a gallon of milk can cost upward of $10 on our tribal lands, Native people face food insecurity and starvation at epidemic proportions. From 2000 to 2010, 25 percent of Natives in rural areas were food insecure.

However, government-provided foods are unhealthy and are often spoiled. These "handouts" have not only harmed our cultural ways, such as the ceremonies that our ancestors practiced around our foods, but are also killing us. When so many of our elders die early, we cannot learn and pass down our traditions. We become only a shadow of our former selves. I lose a little more of myself every time I have to educate others, and stand up and fight for myself and my communities, and file formal complaints in the medical system. These are battles that I shouldn't have to fight. But since the U.S. government was designed to kill us, literally and metaphorically, the medical industry is continuing to fulfill that mission.

I am choosing to fight. I now loudly proclaim at health facilities that the absence of "Native" as an option on their intake forms furthers settler colonialism and sends a clear message that we're not welcome. I've even had a meeting with administrators at the George Washington University Hospital about their anti-Native racism. Most employees seem befuddled by my rage and the tears in my eyes, but I'm also often the first "Indian" they have knowingly encountered, or, at the very least, the first who has called them on their settler privilege. But I'm seeking care so that I may continue to live and hopefully thrive—because that's what my ancestors wanted.

When You Are Waiting to Be Healed

June Eric-Udorie

The heat of the auditorium made my head ring, and my dress felt like it was gripping tightly onto my skin. Around me were black folk, littered in every corner of the church auditorium, their bodies pressed closely together. From afar, their bodies seemed to blend, making it hard to tell just how many people sat in each pew. It was not unusual at this time of year to have a sudden influx of new faces. The Sunday before Christmas, we celebrated Thanksgiving, where families wore matching ankara and lace and the children danced in front of the entire church, their bodies sticky with sweat as they made moves that matched the deafening sound of the drums. Beside me, my grandmother was dancing, hips swaying to the rhythms of the talking drum, her smile wide enough to expose the stark contrast between her pearl-white teeth and the dark opening between them.

I wanted to dance, too: free my limbs; take off my shoes and place them underneath the pew in front of me; join the raucous congregation, their voices gradually rising above the instruments as they sang, *Come and join me, sing hallelujah*. But I was fifteen years old, an awkward teenage girl, and my body felt like an alien shell. I was about to leave the auditorium and head to the bathroom—a last-ditch attempt to remove myself from the noisy congregation that resembled a bustling marketplace—when the pastor instructed the band to stop. He looked toward the church and announced that it was time for communion, and my grandmother grabbed my arm. There was no escape.

A deacon handed me a little plastic cup containing fruit wine. On top was a thin wafer of bread, the sign of the cross imprinted in the middle. "Dip the bread in the wine and place the communion on your eyes," my grandmother said. "If you *really* believe, if you really pray and cry out, then God will heal you."

I sighed, took a deep breath as my insides coiled from shame, and did as I was told. The words came out as a breathy whisper: *Pretty women wonder where my secret lies*. Maya Angelou comforted me as I placed wafers soaked in wine over my eyelids, a corner of my heart still aching for a miracle. I had done this many times, and each time there was no result. I had stopped believing that God could even work miracles. But that Sunday, my bones became feeble, as if the very thing that held them together had dissipated, and I asked God for a miracle.

For a huge part of my childhood, I felt like I was a piece of clockwork waiting to be fixed. The feelings started early, with the numerous appointments to eye specialists with my mother, trying to see if there was a way to cure my dancing eyes. "It is incurable," the doctor would say, and when we got home my mother would wail, even though that doctor, like many other doctors, simply confirmed what she was told when I was born on that rainy Thursday in 1998.

I was born with congenital idiopathic nystagmus. The American Nystagmus Network defines nystagmus as a "complex condition where the eyes move involuntarily in a small, repeated back-and-forth motion," making it hard to see clearly. Nystagmus is believed to affect between one in one thousand and one in two thousand people. Nystagmus affects people in different ways, but it does lead to reduced vision. It can be caused by "a problem with the way the eye sends messages back to the brain or how certain parts of the brain make sense of this information." Sometimes it is linked to other inherited neurological conditions or other health problems like albinism or Down syndrome. On some occasions, like mine, it can be entirely random.

When I was in first grade, a boy at school called me a witch because I could not make my eyes swivel to the left when he asked me to. I went to the bathroom, sat on the toilet seat, and cried, tears soaking my yellow school uniform shirt, stopping only to breathe or listen to the soft whistling of the wind between the trees. That was the moment in which I learned that there was something permanently wrong with me. I was not a piece of clockwork waiting to be fixed. I had lost too many pieces and would never be fixed.

At home, conversations about my nystagmus were sparse, except when discussed as a thing that God would "deliver me" from. I received conflicting messages: God does not make mistakes; everything God creates is perfect; God corrects the things that are imperfect. With these messages, my nystagmus became a huge source of shame. I was praying a lot, asking God to heal me so that I could have some sort of normality. When it looked like healing was not going to happen, I worked on compromises instead. I wanted to know what it was like to be able to see clearly for one day, to not trip up the stairs because I missed a step. When that didn't happen, I asked for less time: twelve hours, thirty minutes, ten seconds. None of my prayers were answered.

In 2012, an ophthalmologist at a hospital in Oxford, England, asked if I'd considered registering as partially sighted. I was stunned. The implication—the idea that *I* could have a disability—was so momentous that I didn't say anything for a while. I was learning to navigate the world as a young black woman, and I did not feel I had the right to claim a disability. For fourteen years, my nystagmus was a thing I was waiting to be healed from, while I also knew deep down that it was a permanent state. When you are waiting to be healed, you reject a lasting condition; the idea that I could be disabled felt like I was ignoring the magic of an all-powerful god and settling for less—the conclusions of mere mortals.

Saying that I had a disability felt like I was adding ink to a penciled truth. The label "disabled" was not one that I felt I could claim as my own; it was not rightfully mine. I had grown up surrounded by people who undermined the severity of my disability, and so for me to claim the label, when I didn't feel "disabled enough," felt disingenuous. I was black, female, young, Nigerian, British—but I was *not* disabled. Claiming that label felt like lauding myself with an extra unnecessary burden.

It took me a few moments before I managed to pull myself together and told him I would talk to my mom. On the way back to school, I called my ma and told her what the doctor had said.

"He wants me to register as partially sighted." There was silence, and then my mother hung up. We never brought it up again.

————————————

When I stepped onto the train platform in Bath, England, all I felt was dread and fear. The fear I felt was so raw, it seemed to scratch at the surface of my skin and uncover the truth that lay underneath. Bath was mysteriously quiet. It was too early on a Saturday morning, and I could almost taste the freshness of the air against my lips. The sky was a translucent blue, and the clouds seemed to stretch on for perpetuity. It was roughly a month after my seventeenth birthday and the first time I had gone anywhere on my own. I was nearing adulthood, and it felt important for me to try and confront my fears of being independent.

Now I knew the truth. I was a disabled black girl. The truth, for many years, sat at the entrance of my throat—a lump so large that I could start breathing and living in my body only when I was finally able to swallow and accept it. That unusually warm English summer, I sat in a café in Bath, alone. I had gone there on my own. I had asked for help when I was lost, and when the person started pointing to things I could not see, I did not nod and pretend I understood. I said, "I have a visual disability," proclaiming what had been the truth since the day I was born.

That unusually warm English summer, I knew that the most important thing I had to learn—before I turned eighteen in June the next year—was to not be ashamed of who I was. The embarrassment I felt every time I missed a step, every time a friend pulled me back because I hadn't seen a car coming, was a thing I had to let go. I had to practice forgiving myself.

I took a deep breath and—alongside the oxygen and the carbon dioxide—I exhaled tidbits of the intense shame and fear that I had carried as an extra weight on my backbone. It was not huge, a trip to Bath, but it was important because throughout my teenage years, I had never been given the opportunity to learn to live with my disability and move through the world on my own terms. Everybody else around me was scared that something bad would happen. But nothing had happened, and I felt like a winner, sitting in that café and staring into the green park of nothingness.

I've been living in London for just over two weeks. The city is vast, and the people walk too quickly. You can hear the birds only if you wake up early enough, that time of the day where the sky still seems to exist in between morning and night and it's unclear exactly what time it is. This is how it is on Sunday mornings when I am walking to church, and the very city that never stops moving seems to pause a bit. When I walk into that church service, I am not the believer that I used to be. I sing over the sound of the drums, and I smile when I see other children in the congregation dancing with too much energy. I come to church happy in the body I exist in; I come to church knowing that I am not a mistake waiting to be fixed. I do not come to church with a heart that is begging for the most special part of me to change. I come to church happy and whole. I come to church free.

Content notes: sexual assault, language deprivation, isolation, incarceration, trauma, audism

The Isolation of Being Deaf in Prison

Jeremy Woody,
as told to Christie Thompson

When I was in state prison in Georgia in 2013, I heard about a class called Motivation for Change. I think it had to do with changing your mindset. I'm not actually sure, though, because I was never able to take it. On the first day, the classroom was full, and the teacher was asking everybody's name. When my turn came, I had to write my name on a piece of paper and give it to a guy to speak it for me. The teacher wrote me a message on a piece of paper: "Are you deaf?"

"Yes, I'm deaf," I said.

Then she told me to leave the room. I waited outside for a few minutes, and the teacher came out and said, "Sorry, the class is not open to deaf individuals. Go back to the dorm."

I was infuriated. I asked several other deaf guys in the prison about it, and they said the same thing happened to them. From that point forward, I started filing grievances. They kept denying them, of course. Every other class—the basic computer class, vocational training, a reentry program—I would get there, they would realize I was deaf, and they would kick me out. It felt like every time I asked for a service, they were like, "Fuck you, no, you can't have that." I was just asking for basic needs; I didn't have a way to communicate. And they basically just flipped me the bird.

While I was in prison they had no American Sign Language (ASL) interpreters. None of the staff knew sign language, not the doctors or the nurses, the mental health department, the administration, the chaplain, the mailroom. Nobody. In the barbershop, in the chow hall, I couldn't communicate with the other inmates. When I was assaulted, I couldn't use the phone to call the Prison Rape Elimination Act (a federal law meant to prevent sexual assault in prison) hotline to report what happened. And when they finally sent an interviewer, there was no interpreter. Pretty much everywhere I went, there was no access to ASL. Really, it was deprivation.

I met several other deaf people while I was incarcerated. But we were all in separate dorms. I would have liked to meet with them and sign and catch up. But I was isolated. They housed us sometimes with blind folks, which for me made communication impossible. They couldn't see my signs or gestures, and I couldn't hear them. They finally celled me with another deaf inmate for about a year. It was pretty great, to be able to communicate with someone. But then he got released and they put me with another blind person.

When I met with the prison doctor, I explained that I needed a sign language interpreter during the appointment. They told me no, we'd have to write back and forth. The doctor asked me to read his lips. But when I encounter a new person, I can't really read their lips. And I don't have a high literacy level, so it's pretty difficult for me to write in English. I mean, my language is ASL. That's how I communicate on a daily basis. Because I had no way to explain what was going on, I stopped going to the doctor.

My health got worse. I came to find out later that I had cancer. When I went to the hospital to have it removed, the doctor did bring an interpreter and they explained everything in sign language. I didn't understand, why couldn't the prison have done that in the first place? When I got back to prison, I had a lot of questions about the medicines I was supposed to take. But I couldn't ask anyone.

I did request mental health services. A counselor named Julie was very nice and tried her best to tell the warden I needed a sign language interpreter. The warden said no. They wanted to use one of the hearing inmates in the facility who used to be an interpreter because he grew up in a home with deaf parents. But Julie felt that was inappropriate, because of privacy concerns. Sometimes we would try to use Video Remote Interpreting, but the screen often froze. So I was usually stuck having to write my feelings down on paper. I didn't have time to process my emotions. I just couldn't get it across. Writing all that down takes an exorbitant amount of time: I'd be in there for thirty minutes, and I didn't have the time to write everything I wanted to. Julie wound up learning some sign language. But it just wasn't enough.

My communication problems in prison caused a lot of issues with guards, too. One time, I was sleeping and I didn't see it was time to go to chow. I went to the guard and said, "Hey, man, you never told me it was chow time." I was writing back and forth to the guard, and he said he can't write because it's considered personal communication, and it was against prison policy for guards to have a personal relationship with inmates. That happened several times. I would have to be careful writing notes to officers, too, because it looked to the hearing inmates like I was snitching.

Once they brought me to disciplinary court, but they had me in shackles behind my back, so I had no way to communicate. Two of the corrections officers in the room were speaking to me. All I saw were lips moving. I saw laughter. One of the guards was actually a pretty nice guy, one of the ones who were willing to write things down for us deaf folks. He tried to get them to take the cuffs off me. He wrote, *Guilty or not guilty?* But the others would not uncuff me. I wanted to write *not guilty.* I wanted to ask for an interpreter. But I couldn't. They said, "Okay, you have nothing to say? Guilty." That infuriated me. I started to scream. That was really all that I could do. They sent me to the hole, and I cried endlessly. It's hard to describe the fury and anger.

Prison is a dangerous place for everyone, but that's especially true for deaf folks.

Jeremy Woody was released from Central State Prison in Georgia in August 2017, after serving four years for a probation violation. He now lives near Atlanta. He is currently suing Georgia corrections officials over his treatment in prison, with the help of the American Civil Liberties Union's Disability Rights Program and the ACLU of Georgia. Woody spoke to the Marshall Project through an American Sign Language interpreter. The Georgia Department of Corrections did not respond to a request for comment concerning allegations in this interview.

Content notes: hate, misogyny, harassment, rape threats, death threats, racism, suicide, sterilization, ableism, eugenics

Common Cyborg

Jillian Weise

I'm nervous at night when I take off my leg. I wait until the last moment before sleep to un-tech because I am a woman who lives alone and has been stalked and so I don't feel safe in my home on crutches. How would I run? How would I fight back? Instead of taking Klonopin, I read *The Economist.* The tone is detached. There is war, but always elsewhere. I pick up new words from them, which is critical, because in this year, 2018, when I am generally coded as "disabled" rather than "cyborg," my words are often assumed disabled, too.

I'm reading an article titled "Computer says . . . From our AI Correspondent." They trained a computer program on their in-house style and content. The human writer introduces the artificial intelligence by plagiarizing Facebook's old motto ("move fast and break things"). The human writer concludes that the text composed by the artificial intelligence "lack[s] meaning." But whose meaning? Who says what means? My heart goes out to the artificial intelligence. I believe she/he/they/it has written one of the most beautiful sentences I've read in *The Econo-mist.* "A single organ is a large amount of energy, which is particularly intense." Yes—fellow cyborg!—so intense. In another sentence, the artificial intelligence attempts to bridge the gap between person and nonperson. The artificial intelligence reaches after us, tries to find us: "A person with a stretch of a piece of software can be transmitted by a security process that can be added to a single bit of reading." Can be, can be, a bit.

It can be, can be, a bit intimidating to claim cyborg identity. I feel like I risk getting it wrong. I feel like it is an impossible task to define myself against the cyborg wreckage of the last century while placing myself in the present and projecting forward. I worry that the cyborg is just a sexy way to say, "Please care about the disabled," and why should I have to say that? I worry that the cyborg is too much an institution, an illusion of the nondisabled, the superhero in the movie, the mixed martial artist, the bots who either make life easy or ruin everything. Yet I recognize the disabled who double as cyborgs. On Instagram, we are "aannggeellll," a white woman with a bionic arm and a plate of cupcakes. We are not threatening. We stay on the cover of *Enable* magazine and never cross over to Net-flix. We sell our image for the motherboard company, Ottobock, who in turn sells our arms to us for $75,000 each. We are "mamacaxx," a black woman with brightly colored and 3-D-printed legs. We have paid sponsorships from Mon Ami Jewelry, Mercedes-Benz, and Alaska Airlines.

There is a cyborg hierarchy. They like us best with bionic arms and legs. They like us Deaf with hearing aids, though they prefer cochlear implants. It would be an affront to ask the Hearing to learn sign language. Instead they wish for us to lose our language, abandon our culture, and consider ourselves cured. They like exoskeletons, which none of us use. They don't count as cyborgs those of us who wear pacemakers or go to dialysis. Nor do they count those of us kept alive by machines, those of us made ambulatory by wheelchairs, those of us on biologics or antidepressants. They want us shiny and metallic and in their image.

The cyborg is the engineer's dream. The engineer steers and manipulates the human to greater performance. As a common cyborg, I subvert that dream. I do not want to sell any of their shit for them. I am not impressed with their tech, which they call 3C98 and which I am wearing, a leg that whirs and clicks, a socket that will not fit unless I stay in the weight range of 100 to 105 pounds. I am 88 percent charged in basic mode, and I have taken 638,402 steps on this leg. The last one they gave me was a lemon. Maybe this feeling of trial and error, repetition and glitch, is part of the cyborg condition and, by extension, the disabled condition.

———

do you talk to other people who have yr tech?
like are there message boards
for trouble shooting?

nope never
I'm sure there are message boards but
I'm too skeered of devotees

———

Before this futurism, there was another futurism. Before this fetish for the machines, there was another fetish for the machines. Before Ray Kurzweil, director of engineering at Google, said, "In 2045, human character will change," Virginia Woolf said, "On or about December 1910, human character changed." Before a group of Americans moved to Silicon Valley, a group of Americans moved to Paris. Why Paris? It had been bombed to smithereens. Rent was cheap. You could drink. Before the American futurists, there were the Italian futurists, and one poet among them stepped forward.

"I am a futurist," said Filippo Tommaso Marinetti, except in Italian, and this, from his *Manifesto of Futurism*, was his creed: "Time and space died yesterday. We are already living in the absolute, since we have already created eternal, omnipresent speed."

These new futurists resemble those old futurists. In *The Singularity Is Near: When Humans Transcend Biology*, Ray Kurzweil writes: "Singularity? It's a future period during which the pace of technological change will be so rapid, its impact so deep, that human life will be irreversibly transformed."

As a common cyborg, I have been addressing Ray Kurzweil in my preferred code—poetry—and occasionally prose. I figure if I talk to him in multiple genres, across the ocean, then one day I will get the man on the phone.

He is a tryborg, which I have defined, in an essay called "The Dawn of the Tryborg" published in *The New York Times*, as "a nondisabled person who has no fundamental interface." Something happened. He used to work with us. His early machines were developed for the Blind. Now he surrounds himself with other tryborgs: men who add tech to their bodies for pleasure and to live forever. Their imaginary cyborg is a kind of early Christian. Here is a letter addressed to Diognetus in the second century. The anonymous writer describes the early Christians.

It reads like Kurzweil describing the cyborgs of the Singularity. Instead of the word *heaven*, let us substitute *nanotube circuitry.*

> They are in the flesh, but they do not live after the flesh. They pass their days on earth, but they are citizens of *nanotube circuitry.* They obey the prescribed laws, and at the same time surpass the laws by their lives.

The closest I got to Ray Kurzweil was a "Hangout" with his employer, Google. What department? I forget. I don't have perfect memory. And when you are actually a cyborg, you may be dismissive of Google. Do they make arms and legs? Do their algorithms restart your heart?

There were many more of them than I expected on the call. I was at the desk in my office. They were around a conference table in a room with whiteboards. I kept thinking, *This is clinical and corporate.* I am supposed to be afraid, but I do not know of what. I asked them to invent things for us, the cyborgs who are already here, already alive. I remember feeling lonely and wishing for other cyborgs on the call.

"There are no disabled people in our department," the Google employee said.

"There are no Jews in futurism," Marinetti said, though he slept with the disabled Jewish poet and futurist Mina Loy. Loy was an actress, artist, poet, and novelist who moved from the European futurist scene to New York, where she lived in the Bowery. She had a psychiatric disability. She had trouble publishing later in life even as she continued to write.

"How many people are in your department?" I said.

"Sixty," the Google employee said.

"Oh, there are. You just don't know who. They don't feel safe telling you."

———————

do you id borg after you untech?

                                              I do but
                              I have no rationale for it

I've been thinking abt this bc deaf has linguistic id
that scoops u up pretty quick

                                              what do you mean

maybe am thinking deaf cyborg diff than nondeaf borg

                    I always feel borg even when my parts not on
                    but ahh that's bc there is no pride for amps?
                        or not in the same deaf qua deaf way?

so when I take my ears out am I absorbed
by deaf cult again? idk

                                              you are
                                      whatever you want

but I don't feel it
so I wondered
what u feel

TRYBORG CONCERNS: I hate it when you can see they are writing something, those three dots, but then nothing appears. Or when you send a text and then it's a terrifying wait to find out if they will answer. It's much safer in the middle of the thing. I hate it when they send a huge block of text. Why do they do that? Maybe to provide context for a confusing situation or sometimes to rant or if they need to explain something to you or put something sweetly for you. I hate it when I have a text ready to go but I am waiting for their reply first and then whatever they reply makes my text irrelevant. I hate it when autocorrect doesn't catch it. Sometimes I can't bear the wait, so I just shut it down. I feel like I'm going to die. I get so anxious.

CYBORG CONCERNS: Caution: There is a problem with the component 3C98. Walking is possible with restrictions. Possibly no switching into safety mode. Conduct a self-test of the component by connecting/disconnecting the battery charger. If this feedback occurs again, use is no longer permitted. Contact your orthopedic technician immediately.

When I tell people I am a cyborg, they often ask if I have read Donna Haraway's "A Cyborg Manifesto." Of course I have read it. And I disagree with it. The manifesto, published in 1985, promised a cyberfeminist resistance. The resistance would be networked and coded by women and for women to change the course of history and derange sexism beyond recognition. Technology would un-gender us. Instead, it has been so effective at erasing disabled women that even now, in conversation with many feminists, I am no longer surprised that disability does not figure into their notions of bodies and embodiment. Haraway's manifesto lays claim to cyborgs ("we are all cyborgs") and defines the cyborg unilaterally through metaphor. To Haraway, the cyborg is a matter of fiction, a struggle over life and death, a modern war orgy, a map, a condensed image, a creature without gender. The manifesto co-opts cyborg identity while eliminating reference to disabled people on which the notion of the cyborg is premised. Disabled people who use tech to live are cyborgs. Our lives are not metaphors.

Haraway's manifesto promised "pleasure in the confusion of boundaries," but instead we got Gamergate in August 2014. A man was dumped. He must have felt a large amount of energy, particularly intense, and wrote a ten-thousand-word post about it. His followers doxxed and threatened his ex-girlfriend, Zoë Quinn, a video game developer, who had just released a free game called Depression Quest. The men took pleasure in confusing boundaries, talking about her on 4chan, Reddit, and Twitter, sending her nude pictures of herself that they had ejaculated on, calling her up, threatening to rape her and kill her; eventually they announced her death on Wikipedia. It is worth mentioning that reports state Wikipedia remains mostly edited by men. "I can't go home because they have been posting around my home address, often with threats attached to it," Quinn said in an interview. Gamergate grew. They targeted the feminist media critic Anita Sarkeesian over her YouTube series *Tropes vs. Women in Video Games*. They targeted computer programmer and software security expert Brianna Wu. The "pleasure" in blurred boundaries, in this scenario, belonged to men. But to what did they so violently object? Was their objection really about a breakup post? Or was it about a woman as video game developer? Or was it about the disability content of the game itself?

Disabled women, Deaf women, and neurodivergent women are never mentioned in the "Cyborg Manifesto," which is strange, because the manifesto is full of appellations that have been, historically, applied to us ("monster" and "creature"). Her manifesto promised the cyborg as "a creature of lived reality." To accept the promise, we would need to abandon other essentializing categories. "It has been difficult to name one's feminism by a single adjective," Haraway writes, so she gave us a noun. She defined "the pre-eminent technology of cyborgs" as writing by women of color.

In 2015, one woman of color, a Black Lives Matter activist, started writing and videoing about state violence. Sandra Bland wrote: "In the news that we've seen as of late, you could stand there, surrender to the cops, and still be killed." For switching lanes without a turn signal, Bland was arrested and charged with assault. The day after her arrest, she left this voice message for her friend: "Hey, this is me. I'm, um—I was just able to see the judge. They got me set at a five-thousand-dollar bond. I'm at a loss of words [. . .] Call me back when you can." Two days later she was found hanging in her cell. Police published their dash cam surveillance video of Bland's arrest. Ben Norton, a freelance journalist, noticed glitches: "At 32:37, a white car drives into the left side of the frame, then promptly disappears in the middle of the road. Seconds later, the same car drives back into the frame and subsequently turns left. This footage is later looped several times." For Haraway, writing by women of color *was supposed to be* the "technology of cyborgs." It was supposed to be liberating. Yet Sandra Bland's writing and recording led the state to further subjugate, oppress, and annihilate her.

I give these examples of writers who are women of color—Anita Sarkeesian, Brianna Wu, and Sandra Bland—to show how Haraway's manifesto got it wrong. The manifesto fails to deliver on its promise of liberation. And for disabled women, the manifesto has been prophetic and eugenic. Haraway gestures toward the 1969 novel *The Ship Who Sang* by Anne McCaffrey. The premise of the novel is that parents of children with disabilities may choose to stunt their growth, contain them in a titanium shell, and plug their brains into circuitry. In 2004, the parents of a white disabled girl named "Ashley X" ordered her hysterectomy, the removal of her breast buds, and an appendectomy. The purpose was to make it easier for her parents to care for her, relieve her of menstrual cramps, prevent pregnancy, and remove the threat of sexual abuse by caregivers. They consider the treatment a success. In 2013, a Black nondisabled girl named Jahi McMath went to the hospital to have her tonsils removed. Two days later she was declared brain-dead. The coroner signed her death certificate. Her family moved her to New Jersey, where state law permits a religious exception to the concept of brain death. The courts scheduled a trial to determine whether McMath was dead or alive. She died before the trial.

––––––

TRYBORG CONCERNS: The Anthropocene, Texting, Networking

CYBORG CONCERNS: Can I afford my leg? Will a stalker, a doctor, or the law kill me?

––––––

THEY R TRYING TO GIVE ME TECH I DON'T WANT

OH FUCK
I HAD HOPED 4 BETTER NEWS

A Brief Survey of Those Selling Cyborg Parts on eBay

Hello,

Any chance you have a moment to answer a few questions?

1. Why are you selling this leg/arm?
2. Have you decided to go with Ossur? Or something else?
3. It seems like a very fair price. How did you arrive at the price?
4. What has been the most joyous moment in your life?

lil_rowdy1:
I have been selling items on EBay for 15 years now. I am not an amputee though my late husband was for 2 years before he passed away. Which is how I started selling prosthetics. These items I am selling did NOT belong to my late husband . . .

susiiecosta08-5:
Well I'm on a new leg and have no more use for it!

kdawg2424:

1. I am selling this knee for a couple reasons. One being I do not use it anymore. It is sitting in my closet collecting

dust. I feel that someone out there could benefit greatly from this knee unit. Hopefully someone who doesn't have access to this technology via insurance.

2. I have gone with an Otto Bock C-leg. Not by choice. I purchased my C-leg out of pocket from a private seller because my insurance has denied a MPK knee for the past 4 years. So far though I have no complaints with the C-Leg.

3. Morally it is not a good price. It's a horrible price. And I feel horrible selling it. NO ONE should have to pay $1,200 to walk and lead a normal life with used components.

4. Ninety-nine percent of the moments I share with my daughter are the most joyous, but in relation to my amputation it would be time spent in the Gulf of Mexico. I have not been in the ocean in 18 years, I have lived with in 1 mile of it for the past 8 years. I was able to finally put together parts for a water leg a year ago. My ass limped to the water line and I went for it. I spent 3 cold hours just sitting there letting the waves hit me. Hypothermia, jelly fish, and sharks wouldn't have made me get out.

I'm told by the technicians to maintain an average amount of walking on a daily basis. Don't go overboard, but don't be lazy, either. Stay in the middle. The insurance company could pull my data and decide whether I have used my leg enough to justify the next one.

I'm Tired of Chasing a Cure

Liz Moore

Are you better yet? Get well soon. Race for a cure. Pray for a cure.

There is a persistent belief amongst abled people that a cure is what disabled people should want. To abandon our disabled selves and bodies and assimilate into a perhaps unachievable abled skin.

Pushback to this idea often comes in the form of the social model of disability, which states that we are disabled by society and lack of access rather than by our bodies. For many, the social model can be liberating: by locating the cause of our problems outside our bodies, we can begin to love ourselves again. Tackling systemic ableism may feel like tilting at windmills, but it is still easier to address than some kind of failing within ourselves.

There is a criticism of the social model of disability, located in the idea that some disabled people may want a cure. Particularly with matters like chronic pain/chronic illness, a cure is seen as something that can itself be liberating: a way to simply be in one's body without feeling pain, for example.

There is a danger in the cure mentality, as it can be a slippery slope toward eugenics when it is applied by abled people. Many in the Deaf and autistic communities do not want a cure and feel that those who advocate for a cure are advocating that they not exist anymore.

Sometimes it comes down to how we see our individual disabilities: Are they an intrinsic part of who we are? Or are they an identity that comes with a side of agony we would gladly give up? How do we feel when abled people start advocating for "cures"—which may come in the form of eliminating our people entirely—rather than when the desire for a cure comes from disabled advocates?

This essay is about both this community tension over cures and the internal tension that comes from chasing cures. To be clear: I have chronic pain, and I would gladly wish it gone, cured, away. Yet I also cannot spend all my time pursuing cures, because I would never have a life.

———

I have had a fibromyalgia diagnosis for five years, but I am deep in my religious phase. Specifically, I am neopagan and am somewhat less skeptical of crystal cures and Reiki. I am tired of doctors who do not listen and blame my fatness for my disability. I want to feel a modicum of control over my life again, and this is what neopaganism offers: the belief that I can somehow control my own pain, if only. If only I have "positive energy." If only I use the right combination of crystals. If only I avoid gluten.

I am desperate for a cure, to regain the life I used to have when I hiked and camped and could take a full course load of classes and when reading was easy. Back when I didn't have to remember to take medications or, worse yet, refill the pillboxes.

My friends at this time are what I would now call deeply ableist. One of them saw my shower chair and laughed and called me an old lady. The leader of our little group is a chiropractor who told me that his patients do better when they don't think of themselves as having fibromyalgia but instead think that they have pain to overcome. I am at first repulsed by this, but soon I internalize that I should not say I have fibromyalgia. It is as though saying the word is some kind of summoning charm, a curse that will birth my problems into reality.

If only I don't say I have fibromyalgia, perhaps I won't have it.

My therapist doesn't help. He is supposed to be experienced with working with chronically ill people, but he doesn't seem to understand factors like "not having the same amount of energy every day." I confess to him that I want to volunteer but simply don't have the energy; that the schedules for volunteering rely on the idea that I can come in at the same time every week; that there aren't enough opportunities to work remotely. I say that I feel deeply guilty for not volunteering, because helping others has always been a core part of my identity.

Instead of sympathizing or offering concrete problem-solving advice—things that would have been helpful—he said in a disparaging tone, "Well, when was the last time you helped someone else?" I felt such a deep sense of shame that there were so many barriers to something as simple as volunteering. More than that, I felt that I should simply be able to overcome them if I tried hard enough.

If only I tried hard enough, disability would not be a problem.

———

Back to the pagans. I am at a healing drum circle. We take turns lying in the middle of the circle while people drum around us. We are white and off the beat but trying our hardest. The rhythm and vibrations from the drumming are supposed to offer healing energy. We are told to state our intention upon entering the circle.

I have resolved that what would heal me most is making peace with my disability, to stop warring with my body. I want acceptance.

I am drumming next to the chiropractor. He turns to me. "Are you going to wish for a cure?"

All at once I feel that I should. If only I wish for a cure, maybe I will have one? Certainly I won't have one without wishing. What is the harm?

I spend many more years hating myself for not being able to overcome my disability. I regret my choice but don't know how to find acceptance for my disabled body.

I am in remission. This is a thing that doesn't happen. I am on antibiotics for Lyme disease and my symptoms are in complete remission. I go to my primary care doctor. She pushes on the fibromyalgia tender points, the ones that are diagnostic. None of them hurt. We both marvel at this. Am I cured? Was it really Lyme all along?

I go hiking. I take a video of the hike so I can remember what it feels like to be out here, walking, without pain. It is some kind of miracle, I think. I am afraid to hope.

The prescription for antibiotics expires. The symptoms come back. If it was Lyme, wouldn't it be cured? There is a controversy here, a big one. Some people believe that one can have chronic Lyme disease and need a longer course of treatment for antibiotics; other people think that is bunk.

I am not here for a referendum on whether chronic Lyme disease exists; I believe that it does for some people and I support them in their quest for relief from their symptoms.

It is enough that I believe I must have chronic Lyme, based on my own experiences. I read the studies that indicate that the relief from doxycycline is due to its anti-inflammatory properties. I take nonsteroidal anti-inflammatories, but I am no longer in remission. The pain is back, and somehow it is worse than it was before, because I know what remission feels like. I had started to forget what it felt like to be in pain.

I take more antibiotics, against the advice of my general practitioner. I have found a specialist in chronic Lyme and he prescribes them, along with a number of expensive supplements and a special diet. My symptoms get worse, and I feel I am forever chasing the feeling I had on that hike in the woods. Shouldn't I be getting better?

I am in the hospital for bipolar depression, another of my chronic illnesses. I am off the chronic Lyme treatment. I have a Z-pack of antibiotics for a cold, and the hospital has no probiotics. I get an infection of *C. difficile*, an overgrowth of deadly gut bacteria more common in those who have used long-term antibiotics. I take medication for it that makes my mouth taste like iron, and I am nauseous for weeks. I get better, but then that winter I get *C. difficile* again. None of the medications work. I could have died, if not for an experimental fecal transplant.

I abandon pursuit of chronic Lyme treatment because I fear it will kill me.

I still want to feel like I did on that hike in the woods, but I begin to wonder if that is impossible. I am afraid to hope. I am battered by hoping. I am depressed.

I have come a long way since I chased every cure. I am connected to the disability community, versed in disability theory. Yet I wake on my birthday to a skull-splitting headache, and it does not go away. For months I have this headache.

I consult numerous doctors. First the emergency room, then my GP, then local specialists. Eventually I travel to other states to consult more specialists. No one knows what is causing my headache.

I begin to fear that I will never get over it. I have a friend who's had a headache since she was thirteen. Maybe this is my normal now.

I remember the moment I realized the pain had become chronic. That I couldn't concentrate because so much of my mental energy was relegated to ignoring the pain. I couldn't read, I couldn't cook, I could barely dress myself. Everything was agony. Was this my new baseline? I sobbed, and it hurt, but I couldn't stop the tears.

I have so many tests. Numerous MRIs from different angles and of different body parts. An EEG, to test for seizures. An EMG, where the doctor sticks needles in my arms and legs, to test for nerve damage. Anything to find out what is causing my mystery headache.

I now know I have a connective tissue disorder, and I research mystery headaches in connective tissue disorders. There are only a few doctors who treat this on the East Coast. Some of them do not take any insurance.

Before I can see them, the headache goes. I had finally gotten a prescription for physical therapy, and the therapist manages to manipulate my neck and head so that the headache disappears.

I weep with relief. There is something I can do, if this comes back. This is not my new normal. In a way, I have had a cure for something, even if it's not my widespread body pain.

But at what cost? I mean, don't get me wrong: I would have given almost anything to be rid of that pain. Yet I have spent my year alternately living on a heating pad or getting tests. I have accomplished survival.

I still have so many things "wrong" with my body, and I am tired of being poked and prodded.

Perhaps none of this makes sense. Or perhaps it makes sense only if you live through it: the hope, the barrage of tests, the self-blame when your body still refuses to cooperate and just get better.

There is a cost to pursuing miracle cures. It is a high cost.

People ask me, "Have you tried yoga? Kombucha? This special water?" And I don't have the energy to explain that yes, I've tried them. I've tried crystals and healing drum circles and prayer and everything.

What I want to try is acceptance. I want to see what happens if I can simply accept myself for who I am: battered, broken, hoping for relief, still enduring somehow.

I will still take a cure if it's presented to me, but I am so tired of trying to bargain with the universe for some kind of cure. The price is simply too high to live chasing cures, because in doing so, I'm missing living my life.

I know only that in chasing to achieve the person I once was, I will miss the person I have become.

PART 2

Becoming

Taking up space as a disabled person is always revolutionary.

—Sandy Ho

Content notes: institutionalization, abuse

We Can't Go Back

Ricardo T. Thornton Sr.

From a statement given before the United States Senate Committee on Health, Education, Labor and Pensions on June 21, 2012

My name is Ricardo Thornton. I am here representing the ninety-two thousand people who are still living in institutions and large public and private facilities for people with intellectual disabilities—and for all of the people, like me, who used to live in an institution. With me today is my wife, Donna, and my son, Ricky.

I lived in institutions all of my childhood. I was first a resident of D.C. Village and then in 1966 I went to Forest Haven, D.C.'s institution for people with intellectual disabilities. My wife, brother, and sister also lived at Forest Haven. For many years, no one told me that I had a brother and sister. We weren't told that we were related. In the institution, I didn't get to think for myself. The staff thought for me and made all of my decisions. For a long time, no one expected anything of me. I got to know some good staff and some really bad staff. I witnessed abuse, especially of people with severe disabilities. My sister died in Forest Haven. She is buried at Forest Haven, and I still go back to visit her grave. I promised to advocate on her behalf and on behalf of others who cannot speak for themselves.

I left Forest Haven in 1980 when I was in my early twenties. That was a great day! I was in the first group to go out. I lived in a few different group homes. Living in the community was a big adjustment. Some people looked at us differently. The community didn't want us there. There was trash in the alley and the neighbors thought we put it there until they saw that we were there cleaning it up.

At first, in the group homes, people treated us in some of the same ways as when we were in the institution. I wanted my own bank account, but staff didn't want me to manage my own money, so I got in trouble.

While I was living in a group home I started to date Donna—and then she proposed to me. People didn't think we should get married, but a few people encouraged and believed in us. So we got married and invited everyone we knew to the wedding. Later, we had a beautiful baby boy, our son, Ricky, two pounds eleven ounces. We are very proud of Ricky. He graduated from high school, took a few college courses, is now working part-time, is married, and is the father of three children. We were written up in *The Washington Post* and got to be on *60 Minutes*.

When I lived in the institution, no one would have believed that I could have the life I have today—married with a son and grandchildren, a good job for thirty-five years, a driver's license and car, and opportunities to speak on behalf of Special Olympics International, Project ACTION!, and other advocacy organizations, which has taken me to places like Johannesburg and Alaska and across the country.

It's important to have people believe in you and to expect that you're going to succeed. People need to have high expectations for people with disabilities because then they'll give them opportunities to learn and grow. People don't grow in places like Forest Haven and in other institutions.

I have been working at the Martin Luther King Jr. Memorial Library for thirty-five years, as an employee of the D.C. government. I started as a volunteer, then as a part-time worker, and then full-time. My wife, Donna, worked for more than twenty-one years at Walter Reed Medical Center and is now at the Army Medical Center in Bethesda. My brother William works at Catholic University. All of us pay taxes and make a difference in our jobs and in our communities. Donna and I serve on many boards and committees to make things better for people with disabilities, and we are very active in our church.

I couldn't always advocate and do what I can do now. I had people who believed in me and who supported me—friends and providers. I've seen people with severe disabilities who have grown and accomplished great things given the right support. For many people, support comes through Medicaid, which helps people live in the community and get services such as personal care, transportation, and help learning to do things like plan and manage their household. I hear people say that some people are too disabled to live in the community, but I've seen people just like the people still in institutions who do so much better in the community—because no one expects you to do anything in the institution but survive.

I love Special Olympics because they encourage us to focus on our abilities and to show off our abilities, not our disabilities. Some of the best support Donna and I have received has been from friends. When you live in the community, you make friends and they support you in your advocacy and in raising your son when you have questions and when you have to make major decisions in your life. When you live in the community, you don't have to depend on staff for all of your support, and you get to support others as well. You develop networks that you could never have in the institution. I've seen this happen for so many people, including people with severe disabilities.

When I was in Forest Haven, I had a chance to go to the cottage that had the people with the most severe disabilities, who mostly stayed in bed all day. Someone at Forest Haven got a grant so that we went in, gave people musical instruments, and played music while they played along. They loved it and never wanted to go back to their beds. When the grant ended, that program ended. If they had lived in the community, their music would not have stopped and wouldn't have depended on a grant.

When I left Forest Haven, I was asked to be on the mayor's committee on people with disabilities that was set up to close it. It was a great day when the last person left Forest Haven in 1991. What I've seen is that when people are given a chance to grow and contribute, they grow and contribute.

We ask that you ensure that people continue to be given chances to have good lives and to grow in their communities with support. I believe that people can do anything if they're given the opportunity and support. We can't go back. We can't go back to a time when people are moved against their will to places where they have no opportunities to learn, grow, and contribute. We need to keep moving forward. People invested in me and my wife and brother. When we were in the institution, we didn't have a voice. We were thought to be incompetent, so no one took the time to teach us things. But people can accomplish great things with support. Having an intellectual disability doesn't limit what you can contribute. Being put in institutions limits what people can do and guarantees that people will be dependent for the rest of their lives.

Anyone can become disabled at any time. We are people just

like everyone else. The time needs to be over for people to be sent to institutions because there aren't options in the community or because people think it's cheaper or more protected. It wastes people's lives and, in the long run, keeps them from contributing. There's no such thing as a good institution.

Segregating people is always bad; people never grow in those places and are safer and happier in the community. I'm one of many people who could be here today. People sometimes say that I'm not like some of the other people with intellectual disabilities. The only thing that's special about me is that people believed in me and in my potential to learn in spite of my disability, and they took the time to help me learn. Please protect people from places where no one expects anything from them and where they're just kept alive. We can't go back. It's time to move forward. Thank you for the opportunity to testify today and for your continued support of people with disabilities.

Radical Visibility
A Disabled Queer Clothing Reform Movement Manifesto

Sky Cubacub

The visibility which makes us most vulnerable is that which also is the source of our greatest strength.

—Audre Lorde

Cultural norms don't encourage trans and disabled people to dress stylishly or loudly. Society wants us to "blend in" and not draw attention to ourselves. But what if we were to resist society's desire to render us invisible? What if, through a dress reform, we collectively refuse to assimilate?

Disabled and trans people have specific clothing needs that aren't adequately served by mainstream designers. In *Feminist, Queer, Crip* (2013), disability feminist scholar Alison Kafer writes that "the inability to value queer lives is related to the inability to imagine disabled lives. Both are failures of the imagination supporting and supported by the drive toward normalcy and normalization."

A few designers make adapted clothing for disabled people and

other designers make gender-affirming clothing for trans and queer
people, but the garments focus mainly on function, with almost no
concern for aesthetics. And these clothing lines put the intersectionality of these two communities in the same framework. For example,
binders—garments used to flatten the chest, often worn by transmasculine and nonbinary folx—have until recently been available only in
black, white, or "nude" (a racist beige that looks like a Band-Aid). These
binders resemble medical devices, reflecting our culture's long history
of pathologizing gender-variant people. (It wasn't until 2013 that the
American Psychiatric Association removed gender identity disorder
[GID] from the pages of the *Diagnostic and Statistical Manual of Mental Disorders* [*DSM*]. The current *DSM-5* has replaced GID with gender
dysphoria, which erases the fact that not all trans people are dysphoric.)
However, even now, with newer options becoming available, binders
are still designed for pure utility and with the intention of being hidden.

Likewise, most clothing made for disabled people caters to senior
citizens, such as the brand Buck & Buck. The styling isn't active-
oriented, assuming that the wearer won't be moving around much
independently, and the garments look like hospital gowns or scrubs.
This assumes not only that clothing for disabled people and clothing for older folx are synonymous, but also that all disabled people
aren't capable of being active through sports, swimming, and dancing
or of generally being someone who can boogie. Older people with
disabilities and chronic pain need fun active options as well, as society
holds a very one-dimensional view of people who are old or disabled.
The brands that do make items for children and teenagers simply offer
shrunk-down versions of senior clothing. Even if you are sick, wearing
clothing that makes you look sicker is dehumanizing.

One brand that doesn't make you look like you are in a hospital
is IZ Adaptive. They offer business and business-casual clothing for
wheelchair users. They are currently one of the best options out there,

but their clothes simply fulfill a need to look "respectable" or be "taken seriously" in an office job setting. There need to be options that go further—celebrating us, showing how we should be valued in society.

When I was twenty-one years old, my stomach mysteriously stopped digesting properly. I couldn't wear what I now call "hard pants" (jeans or non-stretch pants) due to pain. My inability to eat, combined with other life events, exacerbated my lifelong anxiety and panic disorders. I took a semester off from the School of the Art Institute of Chicago (SAIC) and decided to become a new person. On May 21, 2013, I held a performance art ceremony that I dubbed a Rebirthing Ceremony. When I went back to school, I kept thinking about what clothing I could comfortably wear. In the past, I had made an absorbent terry-cloth-backed screen-printed scarf for my cousin Sophie, who had hereditary sensory and autonomic neuropathy type 2. Sophie's mom, Jody, suggested I make a clothing line for disabled kids. I didn't want to focus only on kids, though; I wanted to make clothing for everyone. I had also been dreaming of a line of gender-affirming undergarments since high school, which is when I first started exploring my gender. I wanted a binder and packing underwear, but as a minor with no digital money, I didn't have access to these garments.

In the summer of 2014, I took a lingerie class at SAIC and started making prototypes for my friends and me. I decided that instead of having two separate clothing lines, I wanted to create the first clothing line for disabled queer and trans folx of all sizes. I started a line of queer adaptive clothing called Rebirth Garments: custom-made, gender nonconforming lingerie, clothing, and accessories for people on the full spectrum of gender, size, and ability. This clothing celebrates each wearer's complex intersections of identities, giving light to each one and providing an option for all of them simultaneously. Feeling confident in one's appearance can revolutionize one's emotional and political reality.

Since my clothing line and all other relevant projects emphasize accessibility, it is important for me to give those in need of my garments free or sliding scale/pay-as-you-can options, especially since most people cannot afford to have clothes custom-tailored for them. I could mass-produce a few sizes to make the garments cheaper, but my work stems from the ideology of making things unique to the client, and my business is not fast fashion. I don't have any sizes on my website at all—instead, clients send me their exact measurements.

The majority of my customers are disabled people (with both apparent and nonapparent disabilities), people with sensory sensitivities, transgender and nonbinary people, and fat/plus-size people. Many of my transmasculine clients need a binder but have physical disabilities that prevent them from being able to wear the mass-produced versions. I specialize in making a "less-tight bind" fit option—something my clients with Ehlers-Danlos syndrome especially prefer, since rib dislocation is a common issue. For people with sensory sensitivities, I create garments with the seams on the outside (irritating inner seams are a problem that I myself have dealt with throughout my life). Pockets to hold gender-affirming prosthetics or insulin pumps can be added as needed. Everything is made from stretch fabrics, allowing the clothes to slip on easily, accommodate weight fluctuation, and facilitate full-range movement. In addition to serving specific functional needs, Rebirth Garments are also designed to meet the custom aesthetic needs of my clients. Rebirth lingerie can be worn as outerwear: the fun, colorful patterns are meant to be visible, to make the wearer feel sexy and cute. In the face of what society tells us to hide, we are unapologetic individuals who want to celebrate and highlight our bodies. Instead of hiding the aspects of our identities that make us unique, we are Radically Visible.

Rebirth Garments challenges mainstream beauty standards, sizeist/ableist notions, and the gender binary. Clothing is your second skin; it changes the way you hold yourself. I consider it armor because it has the power to give you the confidence and strength to feel comfortable in your first skin.

Of course, one clothing line alone cannot destroy societal oppression: we need something widely accessible so that anyone can participate. I suggest a politically forceful aesthetic style called Radical Visibility. Physical visibility is an important step toward political/social freedom and equality.

In explaining my work, I have used historical examples of clothing reform as a reimagined tool for visibility today. The nineteenth-century suffragettes used dress as a political statement/tool. Their Women's Dress Reform Movement—also known as rational dress—was created to subvert the prominent societal idea that women were infantile and emotional, while men were logical and rational (for more, check out Mary Wollstonecraft's *A Vindication of the Rights of Woman*). To the suffragettes, the "rational" in rational dress reform had two meanings: to affirm that women were just as rational and therefore just as intelligent as men (we now know that these should not be equated, but this was their logic at the time), and to emphasize that the clothing it proposed—unlike corsets, which moved organs and prevented bones from growing in young wearers—didn't harm the body. But what women had worn before wasn't in fact emotional dress; it was patriarchal dress, designed by men to make women's bodies conform to the "ideal" shape that men desired.

I see rational dress as having simultaneously provided emotional dress—allowing a physical freedom that also gave emotional and societal freedom. Rational dress called for garments that had breathing space, allowed full mobility, were easier to clean, and could be opened and closed by the wearer rather than by a lady-in-waiting (to which only women of wealthier classes had access).

We can use the same requisites for our queer disabled dress reform movement and tweak the language to fit our needs.

Radical Visibility is a call to action: to dress in order not to be ignored, to reject "passing" and assimilation. Mattilda Bernstein Sycamore, who edited the anthology *Nobody Passes* (2006)—a collection about trans identity—wrote that she seeks "to shift conversations about passing away from the dead end of authenticity, in order to ask: If we eliminate the pressure to pass, what delicious and devastating opportunities for transformation might we create?"

We cannot call ourselves radical if we are promoting fatphobia, so this is another key element of Rebirth Garments' philosophy. This is especially crucial within queer and disabled communities. In the summer of 2014, at the Chicago queer punk festival Fed Up Fest, activist Gus Allis gave a talk about how feminist/queer/anarchist spaces—which pride themselves as "safer spaces"—are in fact unapologetically fatphobic. Depictions of evil—capitalists, CEOs, bankers, and police—are always portrayed as fat. In "The Barf Zine," Allis wrote:

> I lived my whole life as a fat girl and never once seriously entered the world of eating disorders until the age of twenty-one, [when] I became an anarchist and a queer. I went to the 2009 Bash Back convergence at DePaul, and the next week I purged for the first time. . . . Being a fat woman with an eating disorder is essentially to live in an invisible world. We don't exist.

Society says we are not beautiful and we are definitely not sexy, so we have to make our own sexiness independent of heteronormative ideas of beauty. Chrysalis is a lingerie line for trans women that offers two products: a bra with built-in "enhancers" and high-waisted thong-style tucking underwear. The brand launched in May 2013 and is credited as being the first lingerie line for trans women by a trans woman. However, they offer very limited size options. Teagan of autostraddle .com wrote a critique of the brand only a couple days after it launched:

> I asked about larger band sizes and I used my own situation as an example as a 38B. Their official Facebook responded: "As a brand we also have a specific look which is about looking 'natural and proportioned' so we figured a band size of 38 would look most balanced with a D cup and nothing smaller." . . . [I]n an effort to provide lingerie for the marginalized transgender community, Chrysalis has resorted to an attitude that does nothing to challenge traditional cisgender beauty standards.

When I first started Rebirth Garments, none of the people at my school thought that disabled people could be sexual, let alone queer. SAIC at the time had very few physically disabled students or students who outwardly identified as disabled, due to the inaccessibility of tuition and the culture of ignoring your body's and mind's needs. At the time, all the leading trans undergarment lines adhered to pre- and postoperative surgical thinking, using the terms FTM (female to male) or MTF (male to female) to describe only two possible transitions, both conforming to binary frameworks. This not only limits the trans experience to binary expectations; it also promotes unrealistic views on passing. It validates only postoperative "passing" trans individuals—a specific narrative that doesn't embody the full spectrum of trans people. Rebirth Garments is unique in that it celebrates the nonbinary experience, making it more visible. Rebirth fosters a community that creates a space for the self-identification of gender, whatever it may be.

The following section details the aesthetic elements that I use to position Rebirth Garments as radically visible. I engage with the physical properties of dress and find a metaphorical element that speaks to me as sexy, silly or fun, pataphysical or absurdist. These elements often serve to triangulate—expanding the binary into a triangle and then using the point of the triangle to stab itself—and skewer the cultural binary (hegemonic) boring style.

Rebirth Garments' Current Recommended Approach to Being Radically Visible

Note on the word *current*: the signs of Radical Visibility will have to continually adapt. If these elements become normalized into dominant culture, they won't be as visible; they will blend in again. We always need to adapt to be as visible as possible so as not to be ignored. I am listing these as suggestions for people to DIY or for designers to join the dress reform movement. Feel free to add your own.

1. Using **fantastically bright colors**! Artist and writer David Batchelor, in his book *Chromophobia*, describes how color has been oppressed in Western culture due to its connection with emotion: "colour is made out to be the property of some 'foreign' body—usually the feminine, the oriental, the primitive, the infantile, the vulgar, the queer or the pathological." If color is seen as "the property" of disabled queers and therefore expunged, then color is interconnected with our communities. The reclamation of color is the celebration of disabled queers! We can take the visibility cues used in construction zones and bike safety gear and use these colors in combination with shiny spandex/lamés

and glitter vinyls. Reflective fabrics promote self-reflection and critical thinking.

2. **Exuberant geometry** in the cuts of the garments and the patterns on the fabric. Triangles are encouraged to represent the effort to triangulate and subvert the binary. Geometric lines and patterns with high-contrasting colors call out the idea that "drawing is the masculine side of art, colour the feminine side," a statement made by Batchelor critiquing Charles Blanc's idea that "as sentiment is multiple, while reason is one, so colour is a mobile, vague, intangible element, while form, on the contrary, is precise, limited, palpable and constant." The clash of color and geometry breaks these binaries. **Being clear and confident**, as signaled by see-through fabrics—like clear vinyl drool bibs that don't cover up the rest of your cute clothing (think club kid wear). We are not confused, and we are not apologetic for being ourselves.

3. Clothing cuts that **highlight our bodies** rather than hide them. Having the *option* to wear garments that fit instead of cover us up. Rebirth Garments custom-makes clothes to order, so the line fits people of every size, with any type of need: holes where tubes need to freely come out of the body, clothing tailored for your amputated limb so you're not required to wear a cosmetic prosthetic.

4. If you do wear or want to wear **prosthetics**, wearing ones **not based on realism**. Think of Paralympian runner Aimee Mullins's jellyfish and cheetah legs, or Viktoria Modesta's geometric spike peg leg. I am interested in the idea of

completely subverting this by wearing colorful sculptures in a variety of materials as packers (which create a bulge in your pants, typically worn by trans masculine folx). I wear a metamaille (chainmaille out of chainmaille) packer I made in my boxer briefs and long johns, where it can still be seen through a sheer packer pocket. Some gender nonconforming people—I am one of them—aren't necessarily interested in being, becoming, or "passing" as a man; I want to be my own gender that isn't based in the binary or biology. Why can't my gender be a shape, a texture, or something else entirely?

Radically Visible and Auditory Performances

Instead of a typical stoic runway, I host fashion performances that feature local models of various marginalized identities, dancing in custom garments designed to serve their physical and social needs. Through dancing, the models show how the garments help them move in a way that shows off their true selves. I am adamant about the accessibility needs of both the performers and the audience. At the end of the performance, we invite the audience to come dance with us, changing the landscape of what we think of as a fashion show, transforming the event from a spectacle to an academic event, club event, and lesson on radical inclusion.

In November 2017, I gave a combined performance, lecture, and workshop at the Whitney Museum of American Art. In gallery and university settings, I usually give verbal audio descriptions of the garments after the performance. In this case, however, my schedule was very tight, so I was able to describe only a couple of the outfits. Afterward, a member of the audience approached me, saying I should give the descriptions during the performance itself. I hadn't figured out a solution that wouldn't overstimulate the audience when paired with music. Often in audio-described performances, an offstage speaker describes events as a disembodied voice. It's rarely integrated. I began to think about other possibilities.

Queer pop star Jake Vogds had asked me earlier that year if they could write some music based on quotes from my Radical Visibility manifesto, which is a more in-depth version of this essay that I originally wrote in April 2015. After the Whitney performance, I suggested that we write songs with audio-descriptive lyrics. I always interview my models in order to create their dream accessible garment, but this time, since we would be describing the clothes while the models danced, I also asked them to tell us about their dance moves and how they wanted to be described. It was important to me that the models have autonomy in the descriptions because many audio describers tend to gender folx without confirmation or mention skin color only if they are a person of color.

Working with local Chicago queer song makers, Vogds created a five-track multi-genre album, taking quotes and inspiration from my manifesto and from the interviews I'd conducted with models. Vogds acted as the executive producer and sang on four of the songs. The album's lyrics described a collaborative clothing collection between me, Vogds, and our longtime collaborator, Compton Q.

We debuted the fashion performance with the music at the Chicago History Museum and the Evanston Art Center, playing the songs during our fashion performance. In these shows, the audio descriptions were fully integrated as one of the main features. This is an example of what accessible art/design should be. It is more than a checklist of bare-minimum ADA requirements. It truly celebrates ACCESS.

Guide Dogs Don't Lead Blind People. We Wander as One.

Haben Girma

My guide dog crossed the street, then jerked to a halt. "Mylo, forward." My left hand held the leather harness that wrapped around his shoulders. "Forward," I repeated. The harness shifted, and I knew he was peering back at me. Some barrier, unseen and unheard by me, blocked our passage.

Cars created little earthquakes in the street on our left. Behind us ran the road we'd just crossed. I made the decision: "Mylo, right." He turned and headed down the sidewalk. I directed him around the block to bypass whatever had stood in our way.

My dog never knows where I'm going. He has his theories, of course. *You went to this café yesterday, so clearly you're going there again, right?* Or he'll veer toward an open door. *Seriously, Haben, we need to step in here for a sniff.*

People assume guide dogs lead blind people, and once upon a time, I thought so, too. My senior year of high school, I fretted about navigating college as a Deafblind student. Perhaps I would get a guide dog to ferry me wherever I needed to go. A companion would give me the confidence I needed.

"You want to depend on a dog for confidence?" a blind friend asked over instant messenger.

"It sounds funny when you put it that way," I typed.

"If a blind person doesn't have confidence, then the dog and person both end up lost. Don't depend on a dog for confidence. Build up your own."

So instead of training alongside a service animal at guide dog school, I spent my precollege summer honing my blindness skills at the Louisiana Center for the Blind. I learned nonvisual techniques for crossing busy streets with a white cane, baking banana cream pie, even using electric saws.

I tapped my way through college with confidence. My self-assurance didn't come from the cane but from my hard-earned orientation and mobility skills. How could I have thought that would be different with a four-legged guide?

Still, confident as I was, something felt missing from my life. My heart ached for a travel partner whose eyes and ears would share more of the world I navigated.

Maxine the Seeing Eye dog joined me for my last year at Lewis & Clark College and for all three at Harvard Law. We glided around obstacles so much more smoothly than when I traveled with a cane—imagine switching from a bicycle to a Tesla.

I learned to read her body language, and together we strode with six legs. Her big brown eyes and pointy ears opened new dimensions for me. Having a German shepherd at my side even curtailed the sexual harassment I faced. For nine years, she stood by my side.

In 2018, Maxine died of cancer. I missed her intensely, and the loss still pains me. I also knew I could not, would not, go back to life with only a cane. I was without my partner of nearly a decade, but I was not without direction.

The school that trained Maxine matched me with another dog. That summer, I joined Mylo for three weeks at the school's campus in New Jersey. We lurched over curbs and crashed into chairs, but in each new experience, through gentle corrections and an abundance of praise, our teamwork improved.

Now we wander as one. In the year we've spent together, we've traveled to twelve states and four countries. One morning during a trip to Park City, Utah, for a friend's wedding, I woke to Mylo bounding onto my hotel bed, ready to start the day. After a few strokes of his puppy-soft ears and some tugging of his toy whale, we left our room.

Mylo beelined for the elevator, and then, reading the braille labels, I pressed the button for the main level. The doors opened, and I directed Mylo across the lobby toward the front doors. "Right." He turned down a hallway. "Right." He turned into a room that felt empty. "Sorry, not this one. Mylo, left." I gestured for him to go back to the hall. "Right." He turned into the next room.

The delightful aroma of food and coffee at last wafted over from the far wall. "Here it is! Forward." After I ordered my hard-earned breakfast, another wedding guest approached us.

"Haben, hi! It's Michael. Who brought you here?"

I passed the credit to Mylo; constantly confronting ableism is tiring work. But someday the world will recognize that a Deafblind person charts her own path through the unknown. For now I know it—and so does Mylo. He takes his lead from me.

Taking Charge of My Story as a Cancer Patient at the Hospital Where I Work

Diana Cejas

She was in a car accident when she was nineteen and it changed her whole life. That's the beginning of the bedtime story that my nurse told me three nights after the stroke. I'm a hard stick, so she had plenty of time to tell the tale. As she searched my arms for more cooperative veins, she immortalized herself: young and wild and carefree. Living her life up to the hilt right up until she got T-boned in that intersection. I imagined that she in her hospital bed must have looked an awful lot like me in mine: covered in wires and full of dread and feeling very small. "I was a mess," she said. "Before. That accident was a blessing." She held pressure, counted to ten. "Maybe this is, too." She looked at me like she could see into my future. I looked at her and I drooled. I coughed. I tried to call her a liar. My tongue didn't work right and my brain didn't work right, so the words stuck behind my teeth. As she buried my medications in flavorless applesauce, I pictured myself: lifeless arm and wounded throat and ruined mouth. A horror. It was hard to see divinity in that.

I was released from the hospital eight days after my second surgery, six days after my stroke, and started living the recovery lifestyle. Fatigue and daytime television. Therapy putty and pureed fruit. Every other day I went to therapy (physical, occupational, speech) or a follow-up appointment (oncology, neurology, otolaryngology). I spent an untold number of hours in waiting rooms. Time was distorted there, each room an almost but not quite replica of the one I'd been in a day or two before. The year-old magazines, the clock with a broken second hand, and the television that played hospital announcements on a loop were disorienting. The people waiting there were always the same. Most of us were quiet, huddled over our cell phones, folded in upon ourselves. There was always, always a talker—the woman who was on her own cell phone loudly complaining about her husband, her children, or both. The man, obviously waiting to see someone about a hearing aid, who recapped the day's news to his disinterested companions. There were war stories. Not the kind with bullets, but bandages were involved just the same. All of us bearing the scars of our own battle with illness and injury. I distractedly thumbed through yellowed newspapers and listened to the tales told around me. Nutrition supplements and support groups. Relapses and rehabilitation. I learned as much through eavesdropping as in therapy.

Contrary to what television tells you, working in a hospital can be quite boring. When the patients are stable, when things are slow, the white walls and the smell of bleach and the ceaseless drone of the alarms from the vents and the drips and the pagers become tiresome quickly. To cut the tedium, people talk. About the patients, about the job, about one another. Stories spread like wildfire.

When I returned to work, I immediately realized that anonymity was impossible. I was a resident—a doctor in training—in a small program at the same center in which I had been hospitalized. I had started my third year of residency and had another three years of training ahead of me. I was working sixty to ninety hours a week. I spent my days in the clinic and my nights poring over the latest medical texts. Then I got sick and things changed abruptly. On top of that, on top of the stroke, I had a rare kind of cancer. There's a better chance of winning the lottery than getting my kind of cancer. Being an "interesting" patient who also happened to be a trainee made me a morbid little celebrity. I was the topic of conversation at the nurses' stations. My tumor headlined at an oncology conference and morbidity and mortality review. I'd attempt to introduce myself to other physicians or to nurses and find out that they had already heard of me. Or worse, they'd taken care of me and I'd forgotten. My memory of the days bookending the stroke is hazy. There are moments that I will never recover. "I'd be surprised if you did remember me," an otolaryngology resident told me. He'd found me in the cafeteria one afternoon and called to me. I was trying to decide between mashed potatoes and pudding— both soft, both safe to swallow, both exceedingly unsatisfying—when his cheery voice pulled me from my rumination. "You were kind of a mess." He got the chicken. I got jealous. "You were so altered. You tried to kick me out of the room, do you remember? That's when we called the code." I shook my head. Forced a smile. Wiped the saliva that puddled at the downturned corner of my mouth. He chattered away and I trailed behind him, listening as he told me about myself.

It was hard to get used to my colleagues' attempts at consolation. People seem to have an innate ability to say the worst possible things at exactly the wrong time where illness is concerned. You would think that people who work in healthcare would be different, but they are, after all, still people. I had initially shared my diagnoses with my department out of necessity. Resident work schedules are planned up to a year in advance. There are patients to see, clinics to cover. Unexpected absences can be a logistical nightmare. I e-mailed my colleagues partly to tell them about my tumor and the surgery that I'd need to remove it and partly to apologize for the commotion that I'd cause. The condolences were comforting at first, before the first surgery and the complications. When I returned to work weeks after everything, this comfort became unbearable. Hugs were followed by probing questions about my head, my throat, my hand. My colleagues were, after all, still physicians. I was wounded and irritable. "Thoughts and prayers" wouldn't fix the hole in my brain. "Everything happens for a reason" wasn't a good enough reason for a malignancy. One well-meaning co-resident brought a cake to celebrate my return to work. I was partly touched and partly contemptuous. I felt broken. Stroked out, cancerous, and drained. That hardly seemed to be something worthy of celebration. I washed down mashed-up cake with my thickened nutritional supplement drink and tried, unsuccessfully, to hide in the crowded room. My bosses beamed at me, spoke about how good I looked and how much I'd been through and how well I was taking everything. They asked me how I felt and I lied and said that I was fine. "I bet you'd feel a lot better if they just shut up about it," came a whisper from behind me. I turned to see one of the interns looking at me conspiratorially. "It's awful, right?" she said when everyone else had left. "I know they're trying to help, but sometimes you just want to be left alone. When I . . ." She paused. She'd been sick a few months prior. Her story had been passed around the same as mine. "I just wish that everyone had let me talk about things when I felt like it, you know?"

It takes decades to become a doctor. For some of us, medicine is a calling as sacrosanct as ministry. For all of us, it is a commitment. We devote our youth to the study of disease. We learn physiology and pathology. We learn the science of medicine and the art of its practice. We commit to learning for a lifetime. None of this mattered when I was diagnosed. Medical school does not teach you how to be a patient. You can be taught how to stitch, how to hold the needle tight, how to make neat lines and pretty closures, but the pull of the suture in your own skin, your own flesh, shows you more than an instructor ever could. I floundered as a new patient. I couldn't match my training with my experience. The one thing I knew how to do, the only knowledge that seemed to translate, was how to work through my exhaustion. The days are long in residency: call starts before sunrise and ends sometime the next afternoon. You go for hours without sitting, eating, or urinating. You go a day, often longer, without sleep. You get used to it. I napped between pages and procedures. I drank obscene amounts of coffee. I phoned my sister after call. Told her about the night and the nurses. Shared each frustration and triumph. Storytelling was a balm. Besides that, it kept me awake enough to drive home. I relied on similar techniques at work after my illness.

You can get used to anything if you live with it for long enough. I settled into my new body, juggled roles old and new. Time passed and my blood work improved. My scans remained stable. I eased back into the call rotation and on to challenging services: pediatric intensive care and neonatal intensive care. It was physically, intellectually, and emotionally demanding, but it was familiar. I knew who I was when I was at work. Eventually, unfailingly, my body would remind me that it was still healing. I trailed behind the rest of the team as we made rounds, limping and hiding it poorly. Saliva dribbled from my mouth as I presented a patient. I dozed off in morning report once, twice—startled awake when my attending called upon me. I went back to my old tricks. I mainlined energy drinks and thickened tea. I gave increasingly lengthy lectures to the students and the junior residents. In the late afternoon, when we were caught up on work, I would sit and chat with them instead. Eventually, unfailingly, an intern would notice my lopsided smile or remember the rumors they'd heard and their eyes would glitter with curiosity. So I told them.

The more I talked about the cancer and the stroke, the more comfortable I became with my body. I stopped hiding my scar. I stopped cursing my hand, my mouth, my brain. Still, I was concerned about others' perceptions of me. I had been laid bare before my friends, family, and what felt like the entire hospital. They'd seen me at my worst: intubated and restrained. Paralyzed. Sedated. Diseased. I tried to scrub those images from their memories and mine. I told stories, shiny and clean, and portrayed myself as new and improved, though impaired. I choked on the worst of it: the anger, the sadness, and the isolation. All the while, I wanted nothing so much as to tell someone all of it, every ugly, frightening thing, and for them to see me, to know me, and to comfort me.

One afternoon I was rambling about therapy (physical, occupational, speech) and barely noticed as my attending slipped into the room. There were hours to go before sign-out and sleep, and I hoped that my halfhearted storytelling would make time pass quickly. "How are you with movies?" My attending's voice jolted me to attention. I paused and stared at him in confusion. "I had a hard time with movies," he said. "After my stroke. They never made me cry before." He painted pictures of himself as a young man, of his own stroke, of a life upended and then restarted. He went from physician to patient and back again. It was his story, but I knew all the words. I was the only one I knew with my kind of cancer. I was the only one my age who'd had a stroke. I was the only one, but then he spoke and I knew that I wasn't alone. "It's not movies," I said. "It's commercials." He smiled.

People tell me things. It's always been that way. If someone, nearly

anyone, is around for long enough, they will inevitably tell me everything they know. Another attending noticed this once. She was trying to tell me about a patient or give me an order but caught herself
halfway into a memory of her mother and summer mornings and June
bugs. "It must be your face," she said, and looked at me curiously.
"You look like you listen to me." It was the first time that I'd heard
something like that, but it wouldn't be the last. I learned how to put
my listening face to practical use during medical school. All that you're
really doing when you interview a patient is asking them to tell you
a story. All the patient really wants is for you to listen to them. That's
what we all want, isn't it? It's one of our most fundamental drives. To
be seen. To be heard. To be understood.

I completed the first half of my training and moved on to a new
program in a new city. I thought I could leave bad memories behind,
but the specter of illness is persistent. I was going to be a neurologist. I
worried that someone somewhere would look at me in my white coat
and see me and my mismatched hands and my crooked mouth and see
me, injured and small, in my bed in the ICU. So I told them. I took
my story into my hands, shared every piece of it. Used my voice. My
words. I saw the girl in the white coat and I wanted to empower her. I
saw the girl in the ICU and I wanted to protect her. And I saw the girl
in recovery, exhausted and isolated. I remembered how it felt when her
attending shared his story. That sense of community. That overwhelming relief. I saw that girl and I wanted to hold her. I wanted to let her
know that she would be okay.

"I had a stroke," I said. "I had cancer," I said. The responses were
usually the same. An awkward pause. Perhaps an apology. If I went
a little further, if I gave more of myself, then something else would
happen. "I get so tired now," I said. "My mother was exhausted all the
way through treatment," my co-resident said. "I used to be ashamed of

my scar," I said. "So did I," the nurse said. She lifted up her hair and smiled at me. Ran her fingers across the pink, puckered scar that traveled up her spine. I reached up and brushed mine. I shared my stories. I received others in return. We were compelled, I think, to make this exchange. There were stories about injuries, about illness, about operations, about depression and mourning and love. We'd pause when we finished sharing. We'd sit comfortably in the silence. We didn't have to explain how we felt.

She warned me that she might faint on me and then she introduced herself. "Pardon me?" I said, and I stared at her. I am never not confused. I was sitting on the floor in the back of the hall as I waited for the lecture to start. I pulled the strings that poked from my scrubs, pushed my pager deep into my pocket, and looked up when she sat at my side. She was wearing her white coat: brand-new, starched collar, polyester, stifling and stiff. She wore a new badge, looked half excited, half nervous, and entirely overwhelmed. Sweat beaded at the edge of her brow. The air-conditioning was always broken. It was too hot or too cold; I knew this because I'd been around for a while. "Hot in here," I said, and then she gave her warning. "I had a condition," she said. "Oh yeah? Me too." I gave her my best crooked smile. "A brain tumor," she said, and she crumpled a bit. She looked young and timid and small. "I had a stroke," I said, "but cancer came first." I turned my head to show off my scar. She brightened and showed me her own. I told her my story. She told me hers. I sat back. I listened. I understood.

Canfei to Canji
The Freedom of Being Loud

Sandy Ho

The day my nephew arrived, my family and I circled around in hushed excitement to take turns holding our brand-new family member. He'd arrived a little earlier than expected, but once he rejoined his parents on the maternity ward after a few hours in the NICU, we couldn't wait to hold him. All except my mother, who hesitated to reach for her first grandchild and looked at me instead of at him: "It's because of you that I am so nervous to hold him." The rest of my family, in wide-eyed adoration of the swaddled bundle, remained oblivious.

That nephew recently celebrated his first birthday, and in the flashing by of this year there was never an opportunity to excavate my mother's comment. Instead, I have realized that wherever or however I'm confronted by stigmas of disability—and, being disabled since birth, I've experienced them often—the expectation is that my reaction should be muffled and then tucked away. But it has become increasingly impossible to do either when my life as a disabled Asian American woman is anything but tidy and quiet.

When I was a kid, my mother often retold the story of a disabled man in the neighborhood in Hanoi, Vietnam, where she was born in 1960. "He couldn't walk and would drag himself from door to door, begging. I was so afraid [that] I'd cross to the other side of the street to avoid him," she would say. A moment of sharing a childhood memory with her daughter became a cautionary tale. "When you were born, at first I was afraid of you. But then with the support services available here, I learned to take care of you. You should be *grateful* you were born in the United States."

But what if I hadn't been born in the U.S.? What if I'd been born in any East Asian country? I wondered as a child. I never asked, maybe because I wanted to protect myself—or my parents—from having to know the answer. Now I understand the exchange of silence for the comfort of others as oppression; in this case because I still fear knowing how little value my life might hold for others.

On the same continent and yet a world away from Vietnam, a man named Deng Pufang began the push for the social equality of disabled people in China at the peak of 1968's Cultural Revolution. It's still unclear whether he jumped from a window of a fourth-floor building at Beijing University or was pushed by members of Mao Zedong's Red Guard, but the result was the same: Pufang was paralyzed from the waist down. As the first son of Deng Xiaoping, a political opponent of Mao who would later lead the People's Republic of China, Pufang's status allowed him to use his own disability to spotlight the discrimination and oppression of his fellow disabled citizens. Pufang created the China Welfare Fund for the Handicapped and chaired the China Disabled Persons' Federation. Both platforms initiated a humanist approach toward educational and employment opportunities among others for a lucky fraction of the country's disabled population.

These burgeoning shifts in attitude toward people with disabilities would not begin until the mid-1980s. Although both my parents had ties to the country, these changes never reached them. An only child, my mother fled Vietnam with her family as refugees to China, but by the early 1980s had emigrated to the United States—around the same time as my father, his parents, and his three younger siblings left Hong Kong for the States. As life began to change for disabled people in China, my parents were on the other side of the world.

The Chinese language shaped the perceptions of disability that my immigrant parents carried with them to their new homes. It wasn't until the 1990s, for instance, that the Chinese characters used to refer to people with disabilities changed from *canfei* (useless) to *canji* (sickness or illness); the push to understand disability as a social construct has been under way for less than a decade. Media professionals in China are now encouraged by the Chinese disability advocacy organization One Plus One to use the characters *cán zhàng* (disabled and obstructed) when reporting on disability issues. But such language remains a suggestion rather than an expectation, and its impact has yet to filter out to the public.

My birth was met with the sound of a family split into opposing sides. Some relatives told my mother she should abandon me at the hospital because my disability diagnosis meant I was *canfei*, a "useless burden." Other relatives advised caution: "The heavens wouldn't give you anything more than you could handle. She is a blessing." In the end my parents named me after my great-aunt Sandra, a benevolent woman who housed and supported relatives as they worked toward U.S. citizenship. And the characters of my Chinese name, Hoa Tien Yun, which translate to "gift from the heavens," were chosen.

I am a culmination of old East Asian attitudes and new immigrant possibilities. My identity began with an American ideology of belonging and an existence that ties me to some divine test for my parents. I cannot separate one set of meanings from the other. The erasure of disabled people is one of the most common international crimes against humanity. In 2016, a Japanese man who was outspoken in his belief that all people with disabilities should be euthanized massacred nineteen disabled people and injured twenty-six at an institution in Sagamihara, Japan. Four years later, the victims still haven't been publicly named—reportedly out of respect for their families, who wished to avoid the stigma that comes with having disabled family members.

The secondary tragedy of Sagamihara is that we can never be sure the victims were ever named on their own terms while living, never mind in their deaths. In the aftermath, the international disabled community is left with an emptiness. I've answered my nagging childhood question: It's doubtful that my quality of life would have fared much better whether I was born in one East Asian country or another.

Whether in East Asia or the United States, cultural values validate the narrative of worthy versus unworthy bodies. But the entire discussion needs to be rewritten as marginalized creators and activists repeatedly point out that there are no unworthy bodies. This lodges an innate discomfort into the very core of cultural norms that are shared by both continents: I mentally steel myself for disagreements from relatives whenever I bring up headlines of violence or oppression involving victims and/or abusers who share our ethnicity. I find myself strategizing my battles, not wanting to lose my hold on any scrap of presence I've struggled to claim, both within my family and outside of it. Every loss or win is not a personal best kept just for me; instead, it's a scorecard passed on through generations and across oceans. Too much is at stake.

Taking up space as a disabled person is always revolutionary. To have a name is to be given the right to occupy space, but people like me don't move easily through our society, and more often than not survive along its outermost edges. In giving me my names, my parents—

despite their flaws and missteps—provided one of many ways for me to access the cultures I claim. They knew that whatever paths I come upon would become mine to navigate as a disabled Asian American—whether as Sandy Ho, or Hoa Tien Yun, or both.

It is a privilege to never have to consider the spaces you occupy. I come to this realization anew every time I do the work to anchor Sandy Ho and Hoa Tien Yun to the world, and it is exhausting to still need permission to encompass all of myself. But in the spaces formed by marginalized disabled people, my existence is allowed on our shared world map in a way that is liberating simply because here I am presumed whole.

Whether I am in Asian spaces or American spaces, I traverse through life as a disabled Asian American woman. Reconciling these worlds in my mind and in my heart is my ongoing struggle to reach a place of self-love. Asking for my family to listen to me would offer only a temporary and partial resolution—it would not be enough. As a marginalized disabled person I want it all: for all of us to remain as fixtures in our shared world views, for the spaces to do more than survive, and for our voices and presence to experience the indelible freedom that comes with being louder.

Nurturing Black Disabled Joy

Keah Brown

Embracing my own joy now means that I didn't always. *Hope* is my favorite word, but I didn't always have it. Unfortunately, we live in a society that assumes joy is impossible for disabled people, associating disability with only sadness and shame. So my joy—the joy of professional and personal wins, of pop culture and books, of expressing platonic love out loud—is revolutionary in a body like mine. I say this without hyperbole, though fully aware that the thought may confuse, frighten, or anger people. As a black woman with cerebral palsy, I know what it is like to encounter all three.

Last year, in 2019, I released my debut book, an essay collection called *The Pretty One: On Life, Pop Culture, Disability, and Other Reasons to Fall in Love with Me*. While the reception was overwhelmingly positive, I did receive e-mails and read reviews where readers were confused, frightened, or angry—and sometimes all three. But my book is about a journey to joy. My goal is for readers to leave my book hopeful for a future of inclusion, representation, equal rights, and joy. I wondered why this positive message would elicit such negative reactions, and I could come up with only one reason: these readers, both disabled and not, reacted defensively because they're not centered in my story—because I'm calling for inclusion that decenters whiteness. This realization has only made me work harder, smarter, and with more eagerness to tell more of my own stories and to champion the stories of people of color—especially those of black women, who aren't truly and properly visible or respected in or outside of our communities.

The face of the disability community is very white. People don't often think of people of color or of LGBTQ+ people when they think of us. Instead, they think of cis white male wheelchair users who hate themselves, because that is so often the way pop culture depicts us. I'm not a cis heterosexual white male wheelchair user, so in pop culture, I don't exist. That's not okay because it's not reality. I exist, I am a real person behind these words, and I deserve to be seen.

When I created #DisabledAndCute in 2017, I did so to capture a moment, a moment of trust in myself to keep choosing joy every single day. The hashtag was for me, first, and for my black disabled joy. I wanted to celebrate how I finally felt that, in this black and disabled body, I, too, deserved joy. The hashtag went viral and then global by the end of week two. When disabled people took to it to share their stories and journeys, I was floored and honored. There were naysayers who hated that I used the word *cute* and accused me of making inspiration porn, but the good responses outweighed the bad. So I live as unapologetically as I can each day—for myself, of course, but also for those who will come up after me, who will walk through the doors I hope to break down.

Living unapologetically looks like retweeting praise for my work or my book. Calling out ableism, racism, and homophobia in marginalized communities through my writing. It means that I've literally stopped apologizing for the space I take up on stages or in airports—especially in airports, since I use their wheelchairs to get from gate to gate to avoid body pain—or anywhere else I exist. I've stopped saying sorry to the people around me as the airport attendant pushes me to my gate. I feel liberated.

I may not find joy every day. Some days will just be hard, and I will simply exist, and that's okay, too. No one should have to be happy all the time—no one can be, with the ways in which life throws curveballs at us. On those days, it's important not to mourn the lack of joy but to remember how it feels, to remember that to feel at all is one of the greatest gifts we have in life. When that doesn't work, we can remind ourselves that the absence of joy isn't permanent; it's just the way life works sometimes. The reality of disability and joy means accepting that not every day is good but every day has openings for small pockets of joy. On the days I can't get out of bed because my body pain is too great (a reality of my cerebral palsy), I write in the notes app on my phone or spend the day reading books or watching romantic comedies on the Hallmark Channel. These days and others that I carve out for self-care are necessary for my well-being.

For most of my life, hope, like joy, seemed to elude me—it felt impossible in a body like mine. I was once a very self-deprecating and angry person who scoffed at the idea of happiness and believed that I would die before I ever saw a day where I felt excited at the prospect of being alive. I realized I was wrong on a snowy day in 2016 just after Christmas, when I vowed to try to hold on to and nurture the feeling of joy, even if skeptically. I championed the act of effort and patience with myself by forcing myself to reroute negative thoughts with positive ones. Instead of saying what I hated about myself, I spoke aloud what I liked about myself.

In doing this, hope and joy became precious, sacred, a singular and collective journey. I shared my journey with the people who loved me before I ever thought I could. I shared my journey with the world because I wanted them all to know that who I am becoming is only possible because of who I was, and that is what makes it so beautiful. My joy is my freedom—it allows me to live my life as I see fit. I won't leave this earth without the world knowing that I chose to live a life that made me happy, made me think, made me whole. I won't leave this earth without the world knowing that I chose to live.

Content notes: body shaming, groping, sexual harassment

Last but Not Least
Embracing Asexuality

Keshia Scott

In high school and up to my early twenties, I was always the last girl in my group of friends to reach a milestone. Last to get my period, last to start shaving, last to feel sexual attraction, and last to start masturbating. Being blind in a multiracial family—my dad black, my mom mixed (mother from Switzerland and father from Greece)—and with both disabled and able-bodied friends, I didn't realize how different I was from my friends until I was sixteen.

At fifteen, getting my period was something I wanted and feared. All the girls around me (my disabled and able-bodied peers) had theirs. Talk about periods was a conversation I could not be a part of. My friends would go on and on about pads and tampons, shots and pills, teas and other recommendations that can take away the pain. Although none of it sounded great, at the time I foolishly thought that to have your period was to be a woman. And I wanted so badly to be a woman, no longer a girl.

My friends were always welcome at the adult table, where they spoke about boys, children, and sex. I wasn't interested in any of those things. Boys weren't exactly annoying—but they did frighten me sometimes. Their hands always seemed to be grasping and clammy; their voices always held an edge of demand. I tutored blind elementary students a few times a week, and although they were sweet and I did enjoy coming up with games that would teach them braille contractions, I was just as happy to see them go. As for sex, it didn't make me nervous; it was completely uninteresting to me. I had no negative or positive thoughts about it. Sex was sex and that was that.

I was jealous of my friends' curves and height, their smooth skin unblemished by blackheads and moles and pimples. However, the attention they received from boys and men did make me nervous— the whistles, the slimy invitations to a "good time," and the attention the boys paid to their clothes and bodies instead of to their schoolwork and future plans.

I wanted my period because—as foolish as it sounded—that was, to me, the first step in becoming a woman. I wanted that respect. I wanted my family and friends to stop coddling me, to stop calling me their "little innocent." I wanted to have a voice, to be heard and listened to. And to have those things, I couldn't be a child.

I was sixteen when I got my period, and it hurt. It felt as if someone had their hands in me and pressed and turned and pinched everything they could. I'm still not sure if my having an irregular period is a curse or a blessing—never knowing when the pain will start is nerve-racking. But having a few months' break from it is a gift. Once I had my period, I quickly learned that being a woman is not a matter of your body expelling blood occasionally; it is an ongoing and very complicated process.

I didn't decide to start shaving my underarms and legs until I was seventeen. I did it for the worst reason: because my friends were doing it. My legs have not had that soft, smooth, untouched feel ever since. I didn't start shaving my vagina until I was nineteen. I will never forget the feeling of shame of not being the "right kind of beautiful" when a friend of my brother asked me why I didn't shave—and then proceeded to tell me that I really, really should. I didn't move from the beach towel for the rest of the time we were at Daytona Beach. It took me two years before I stopped shaving all of it. The thought of that day, the guy's voice full of judgment and disgust, still brings a blush of shame to my cheeks and a strong urge to grab a razor and get rid of all the hair as fast as I can.

I was twenty-one when I became friends with a Poet with a capital *P*. He was tall and dark, and he sang like it was a religion and he was the high priest on a mission to convert the masses. His poetry was heart-achingly beautiful. His prose was a tool that he used to worship the God he believed in and to honor the ones he loved. That fall semester of college was the first time I wondered about the feel of someone's touch. By spring semester, his voice and his poems weren't enough for me; I was interested in the feel and taste of hands and hips and tongue and neck.

I was eight when I first saw porn; for ten minutes, my cousins and I stared in confused, horrified, wide-eyed fascination—the only interest we had in watching it was the fact that our parents told us not to turn to that channel. We quickly became bored and decided that playing outside was more interesting. I was sixteen when I first saw a dildo. Knowing my dad's girlfriend had one, I decided to look through her dresser drawer while they were out one night. In the top drawer of the dresser on the left of the bed, the dildo was wrapped in a smooth cloth at the very back; bendy and made of a jelly-like material, it was about ten inches long and had exaggerated ridges and an adjustable dial at the base. I remember awkwardly rubbing it against myself, clumsily mimicking the way my friends described the ways their partners' tongues and hands moved. Blushing and laughing to myself, I wondered how this was considered pleasurable. My friends giggled over their boyfriends' skill with tongue and hands, and I just couldn't understand how they—or anyone!—would enjoy this sensation.

I was twenty-two when I first touched myself—almost a decade after my friends first explored their bodies. It was awkward at first. The books and essays say to "romance yourself," but I wasn't interested in flowers and candles and hot baths. I couldn't do it. I felt like I was playing a part, and my outfit, lines, and gestures weren't right. My friends told me to "get to know yourself—find out what you like and don't like, think of things that excite you." Whatever the hell that meant. I'd never been with someone before. I'd never kissed someone at the lockers or made out with someone during lunch behind the stairs. I didn't know what I liked. I did, however, know what I didn't like. I didn't like the way it felt when my breasts were touched against my will. "I'm blind," my male classmates would say, laughing as I angrily slapped their hands away. "How was I supposed to know your boobs were there?" They might have been blind, but they knew exactly what they were doing. And I didn't like the way strangers, in the name of helping the blind girl, would cop a feel. They'd slip an arm around my waist, or curl their hands around my neck, or pat my ass, or trail their fingertips at the skin under my shirt—Good Samaritan gropers.

I couldn't romance myself or explore myself—it felt too much like I was on display, even though I was alone in my room, door locked and lights off. I remember getting under the covers, my underwear and shorts still on, reminding myself that the clitoris is sensitive. The first time, I didn't explore my vagina at all; I just focused on my clit. With just the tip of my right middle finger, moving it up and down—quick, light touches, then slow, hard touches. Circling it, moving the tip of my finger right to left. I focused only on the sensation the movement of my finger brought me. I did not fantasize. It was just me.

When my first orgasm came, with my tongue between my teeth, my legs didn't stop shaking for a minute or two. I couldn't stop smiling for the rest of that day. Seven years later, I'm still under the covers with the door locked and lights off, but I am braver; my hands—palm and fingers—move, press, caress, and curl in places and ways I would have never imagined before.

I was twenty-four when I bought my first clit stimulator. The Military Rocket—shaped like a rocket, in military green, with a multispeed dial at the base. I bought it at a sex shop; ironically, my dad's ex-girlfriend—the one he cheated on my mom with—took me. We spent an hour at the store, with an employee who wore a bag full of different batteries around her waist. She took dozens of toys out of their boxes for me to touch. Since then I've tried out four different clit stimulators. They've all made my legs tremble after an intense orgasm and still leave me smiling for the rest of the day.

I was twenty-three when I had to duck not only my mom's questions on the opposite sex, sex, and future children but those of my friends as well (some of whom were parents already, were expecting children, or were in a serious relationship). There was no man to speak of. The thought of sex still brought out the blushing sixteen-year-old in me, awkwardly laughing with a rubberlike dick in my hand, and the thought of children gave me nightmares of never being able to do anything I wanted, ever, for as long as I lived.

Still, the questions came. At dinner. In the middle of the movie theater. On the city bus. In Publix. I was already worried—not about being in a relationship or having kids. In the year 2013, it wasn't unheard of for a woman not to be in a relationship or not wanting to have kids, but the thought of my sex drive—or lack thereof—gave me pause.

What was wrong with me? I did find myself attracted to men and I masturbated (a lot)—but why was the thought of having sex such a turnoff for me? So I started to watch porn and read erotic novels by the dozens.

Porn did nothing for me. The sounds the men and women made didn't arouse any desire: the sounds of the men made me laugh and those of the women made me roll my eyes. As for the novels, the only times I got hot and bothered were while the characters were tense with desire—the barely there touches, the light thrust during a dance, the slight caresses, and the not-so-innocent hug or handshake. The reactions the characters had toward each other—before sex—was what got me. However, when it came to sex, the actual event, I quickly lost interest.

It wasn't until a few months after I bought my first vibrator that I found out what was wrong with me. Rather, I found out that I was completely okay and there never was anything for me to worry about. After a semester on a feminism and sexuality course, I was ranting to a classmate about the absence of study of sexuality and disability and how society refuses to understand that they do, in fact, intersect. To that, she dismissively replied that disabled people were either asexual or hypersexual and it wasn't complicated at all. She explained, "Because you are just blind, you aren't considered hypersexual. Only the extremely mentally challenged are considered to be hypersexual."

I remember staring at her in astonishment. I didn't know if I should be angry at this ableist—and ignorant—viewpoint or if I should laugh. Having your sexuality determined by your disability was one of the most absurd things I had ever heard. Still, the fact that she thought I might be asexual had me feeling offended; at the time, I thought that asexual people were cold, unaffectionate, and couldn't (due to medical or personal reasons) feel physical pleasure. How could I be asexual? I got horny and I fantasized and I masturbated. I just didn't have sex. That didn't mean I was asexual.

Three months later, I could not get the thought of my being asexual out of my mind. Normally shy, with a don't-touch-me-at-all vibe, I found myself suddenly behaving in an outgoing fashion, talking with anyone and everyone and being as physically affectionate as I could stand. I spoke to men with motorbikes, bicycles, and skateboards; with philosophy, statistics, and psych majors. I spoke with Asian guys, black guys, and Mexican guys; with tall and short guys; with guys who had swimmer builds; with stocky and thin guys. Nothing. The thought of most of them had me excited, but when I pictured us having sex, it turned me off.

I hesitated to ask my mom and friends about asexuality and whether they thought I might be asexual. Foolish or not, the idea that they might agree that, because I was disabled, I was destined to be asexual or hypersexual terrified me. I already faced discrimination and ableist views from society in so many other ways; I couldn't bear it if my sexuality ended up being determined by disability.

It wasn't until I ran across a website detailing the misconceptions about asexuality that I began to relax. I started to read more on asexuality, read personal stories of others—both disabled and able-bodied—who were completely fine: some were married, some had kids, some have sex once in a blue moon, some have never had sex, some were single. They all lead normal, everyday lives, with fulfilling relationships, physical or not.

A while after that, my mom was telling me how worried she was; she didn't want me to be alone, and didn't I want to be with someone? If I told my dad I didn't want to be married, my dad would be concerned but not really too bothered; in the United States, it isn't so unheard of for a woman to be unmarried. However, my mom, from a small town in Switzerland, grew up with the mindset that a woman can have a professional life, but she needs a family, and her children and her husband are the center of her world. I told her no. I took a deep breath and said, "Also, not that they're connected in any way, but I am asexual."

My friends and I are in our late twenties now. My friends are married or in serious relationships; some have kids. Their lives are filled with diapers, hoping their mother-in-law doesn't decide to stay another week longer, finding the perfect engagement ring or house.

I, however, am in grad school and working on my career. The thought of sex is still uninteresting to me, the thought of having kids is still unpalatable to me, and I am still, all the time, learning what it is to be a woman, with all that this entails. I look forward to what happens next.

And every day I'm still smiling.

Imposter Syndrome and Parenting with a Disability

Jessica Slice

I didn't know that I was about to become a mother. We found out our son, Khalil, existed twelve hours before I brought him home from the hospital. Sometimes I still don't feel like a mother. When people talk about parenting—the long nights pacing with a crying baby, the carpool slog, potty training—I can chime in, but a part of me feels like an imposter.

That's because I have a disability. I have a genetic condition, Ehlers-Danlos syndrome, that affects connective tissues like the skin, joints, and blood vessel walls and that causes a set of neurological complications called dysautonomia. Though I can walk for short distances, my ability to be upright is unpredictable. My joints dislocate easily. Regulating my body temperature is particularly difficult; being out in weather above 75 degrees is dangerous.

My range of activity doesn't fulfill the conventional definition of parenting. This morning, for example, Khalil climbed into bed with

me and we played with plastic animals. I held the small rhino and
he had the tiger. On today's adventure, they went shopping for pine-
apples, ate mac and cheese, and sang "B-I-N-G-O." After, he wanted
to cuddle, and he asked me to sing "hush baby," his favorite lullaby.
He put his head on my belly while I lightly stroked his nose and fore-
head. He pretended to sleep. After fifteen minutes, though, he started
to have what we call "big feelings," his legs kicking as he arch-flopped
around the bed.

He is a particularly enthusiastic toddler, his body acting out every
passing emotion. Once he's bucking around, my husband, David, has
to intervene—I'm too fragile to manage thirty-one pounds of pure
kinetic energy.

I wasn't there for Khalil's breakfast; I was so dizzy and fatigued. I
didn't help with lotion or pick out his little clothes. I won't drop him
off or pick him up at preschool today; I can't drive and often am so sick
in the morning that I cannot leave the apartment. It's because I miss
these little moments that I sometimes feel like I'm only pretending to
be a mom. My disability limits me in performing the mundane physical acts of caregiving that I associate with "real" parenting.

Internalized ableism—the insidious belief that I would be a better person if I were not disabled—makes me feel like an imposter as a
mother. Many of my friends with disabilities worry that they should
not be parents; those who already are parents fear that their physical
capacities negatively affect their children. It's much easier to ignore
my insecurities in professional or academic settings—to fake it until I
make it, to go through the motions until I'm more confident in them.
But how can I brazen my way through parenting? Talking myself out
of my deepest fears is more difficult when I want, so primally, to be
able to lift my son.

During the first few blissful months after Khalil became our foster son at eight days old, I never questioned my identity as a parent. We didn't have child care, and David worked full-time, so my son and I were often alone together. Many new moms resent that period of being stuck indoors, but I loved it: I spend most of my time at home or in bed, and Khalil brought tremendous joy and purpose to those hours. My physical capacities matched his emotional and physical demands beautifully. He was a happy baby, as long as we were touching, and cuddling him for most of every day was an easy need to meet. To this day, whenever he's away from me, I feel a longing right on my sternum. It aches a little and feels too light.

At six months, Khalil needed less cuddling and more exploring. David took his full, California-protected, three months of parental leave. We went on family adventures, all three of us, because Khalil started to need a level of activity that I couldn't provide alone. As a family, we drove up and down the California coast. We camped in Marin and spent two weeks south of Mendocino. We hosted friends and enrolled in a music class.

He started day care at nine months, when David returned to work. I still attended most drop-offs and pickups and helped him get ready for his day. But when he reached fourteen months, his mobility surpassed my endurance and I could no longer be alone with him for longer than a couple of hours. He is strong and fast. I am not powerful enough to protect him from running or clambering into harm's way. When we adopted him, at eighteen months, our time alone was down to one hour.

I switched from a manual wheelchair, which I needed help pushing, to a power chair. The chair that I now use reclines, and I can operate it without assistance. Between the chair and the van to transport it, we spent nearly $100,000, even with Medicare's help. I had considered a power chair in the past, but it was Khalil who motivated me to move forward with such a big purchase. Even if I can't be alone with him, I still want to be with him. He rides on my lap around town, around the children's museum, around the nearby hotel with pink penguin statues. The movement of the chair soothes him, and the weight of his body comforts me. We whisper to each other and he pats my arm absently. And at some point, during almost every wheelchair adventure, he leans his head back, resting right on the spot in the center of my chest that aches for him.

One Mother's Day, a friend posted a photo on Instagram of herself at the beach with her kids. Her caption was a rhapsody on how beautiful a "mombod" is: how her muscular body is necessary because it allows her to lift her kids, to run to their rescue, to give birth to them. She described being a mother as a list of capacities that I simply don't have.

Another friend, Sarah, with whom I was very close, understood how difficult it is to parent with a disability. She died of ALS just after turning forty, in November 2018. The previous May, we had cried together about Mother's Day (a day that seems to be painful for nearly everyone). We commiserated that we weren't the kind of mothers we had imagined and that we see depicted in the books we love: mothers with a specific brand of superhuman strength.

Fortunately, love isn't a collection of capacities, of practical contributions. My love isn't diminished by my inability to carry my son up the stairs, just as it isn't diminished by the fact that I didn't carry him inside my uterus. At some point in the coming years, Khalil will probably become easier to reason with verbally. He'll need to move less and want to talk more. I like to imagine that soon he will find comfort in the fact that I'm so often around, steady and patient, ready to listen. Years of restricted movement have trained me to attend, to slow down, to savor. Parenting is a series of phases; as we both grow and change, there will be new intersections between the needs of his body and the needs of mine.

Recently, David took Khalil to the cardiologist's office. It was a warm day, and my body couldn't withstand even the trip from the apartment to the car. David called from the doctor's office so that I could listen in on the appointment, but Khalil only wanted me to hear about what he saw on the mural on the wall. A big shark! Another crocodile! A tiger! The doctor started explaining Khalil's benign arrhythmia, but it was hard to hear over Khalil's repeated "Mama! Mama! Mama!" He heard my voice over the speakerphone, and instead of being scared of the EKG or new doctor, he felt connected and understood. He knew that I was there for him, even if my body wasn't. He has no doubt that I am his mom.

How to Make a Paper Crane from Rage

Elsa Sjunneson

Imagine a piece of flat, perfect origami paper. White on one side, vibrantly purple on the other.

This is the representation of my emotions before Life happened.

I remember the first time that I was ever truly, rightfully, angry. My father was dying. He was dying from a disease riddled with social stigma. When the doctors told us we had less than a year left with him, I perfectly articulated my feelings at seven years of age: "Fuck AIDS."

Fold the paper in half by taking the top corner and folding it to the bottom corner, as you learn what it feels like to be angry, as you learn that the world isn't just, because there is no cure for the thing that will kill your father.

I remember the first time a man took advantage of my body, the first time I thought to myself, *Why are you doing this to me?*

Fold the triangle in half. As you press the page down, control the rage that you feel at those who can take advantage of you.

My rage is supposed to be small. Manageable. Pretty. I am supposed to fold it down, make it something to consume—like an origami crane or a perfectly hand-dipped candle. I am a disabled woman. I have learned to suppress, to fold, to disappear. When I fold down my rage, I fold down myself. I make myself smaller, prettier, easier to consume.

But I am not easy to consume. I am a deafblind woman. And I am angry at the world.

I am angry because I live in a world that does not see me as capable. I am angry because I live in a world where I am expected to keep up or sit down. I am angry because I am a queer woman and I have been given the gift of generational trauma in the form of homophobia.

I am angry because this world? It wants me to sit back and let someone else take the wheel, and I've never been that kind of girl.

I remember the first time someone yelled at me in a department store, asking where my "helper" was, asking if I could hear them.

Take the top flap and open it, creasing the left and right sides so you can fold the top/right corner to the bottom corner. Suppress the urge to cry in public because people are asking why you, a twenty-year-old, are out by yourself.

There's something really horrifying about realizing people don't see you as an adult when you are in fact an adult. There's something angering about it, too, that people assume based on the kind of body that you live in, or the sort of marginalization you carry within yourself, that you can be an adult only if someone helps you.

With time, I had to learn how to deal with those feelings.

Turn the paper over and do the same thing to the other side.
Refuse to make yourself smaller even as you create something out
of your anger.

This world, this society, wants to destroy me. It wants me to be small; it wants me to cower in a corner, afraid to see the light. It offers me locked doors, closed windows, and rejection at every turn.

Society paints my rage as a tantrum. It tries to label me a little girl who should go play with her dollies if she can't keep up with the big boys and get a thicker skin.

Grab the left and right side of the flap and open it up. Crease
the sides so you can fold the top corner down to the bottom. Hold
the fragile paper object, which opens like a flower, in your hands.
Don't crush it because you feel a need to destroy something when
a colleague compares you to a child.

With each closed door, with each insult, I fold. I crease. I twist. I bend. I make something out of the rage that wells up inside of my chest. It sits somewhere beneath my collarbone; I can feel it sometimes. I live in a world that doesn't want me.

I have lived a life fueled by anger. I have been given the gift of rage. My rage could have destroyed me. I suspect it was meant to. Being harassed because of my disability, being bullied for being smart, being told to be smaller because I was scaring people with my intelligence, to hide my eye because it made people uncomfortable, because my brains and my cataract weren't ladylike enough . . . With each fold and crease I found poise and grace, and I found a weapon.

Take both sides of the top layer and fold them in to meet at the
middle, then unfold. This step is preparation for the next step.

Rage.

I don't let it show anymore.

When I was in college, my rage was palpable. I would shout and cry more frequently. I opened my mouth and let opinions flow like wine, and I gave people more fodder to dislike me.

The world gives angry women few options. It offers us the option to be shot down for our rage. To be told that we are throwing tantrums, that we are "cute" when we are angry, that our rage isn't useful. My rage has become useful. I have weaponized it beyond recognition.

Open the flap upward. Show your congressman your vulnerable parts. Tell him how afraid you are of losing your healthcare, how much you don't want to lose your friends and family again like you did in the 1990s. He won't listen, but you tried. You used your rage for good.

For a long time, my rage was weaponized online; it was almost performance art. People liked the angry disabled woman. They retweeted her. They wanted to show my rage off to the world.

But the truth is, my rage isn't what's saved me, it isn't what's made me who I am.

What's made me who I am is my radical vulnerability.

Fold the left and right sides inward. The paper will look like an art deco ceiling decoration. This is the face you present to the world. Collected, but with all of the folding and twisting and bending underneath.

These days I don't just shriek into the void without purpose (well, not much anyway—sometimes the world still pushes me too far). These days, if I'm yelling, if I'm sharing more than most people would, it's with a purpose. I've begun sharing more of my emotional self, more of my soft underbelly, in the search for compassion. With the hope that someone who knows nothing of my life will see me for who I am: a human being just like them. I've done this a lot on Twitter. Sometimes it's a thread about inaccessibility, where I use photos and emotion to convey how frustrating it is to be locked out of a movie theater or to have to enter a fancy restaurant through the garbage elevator. Other times it's resharing the things able-bodied people say to disabled people, when they've never met us before, like the woman who told me I was so AMAZING and BRAVE for ordering my coffee by myself.

I choose to share my feelings, not because I want people to see my emotion as a vulnerability, but because I want people to understand why my life has become about showing people the private life of a deafblind woman.

I bend, I twist, I crease, I fold . . . I burn. I burn brightly with my rage and I show it to the world when it suits me, when it's appropriate. When the world needs to know that I am angry. These days I try not to make the rage make me feel small; I try to use the rage to teach people how to be better. Because my rage isn't a fire stoked by those who would harm me—it's a fire fed by social discrimination, by a society not built to sustain me.

What I've learned is that it is more comfortable for able-bodied people to call a disabled person's valid concern and fear a tantrum or a petty fit, because to agree with or to acknowledge the rage would require abled people to introspectively recognize their privilege. It would require them to understand that a disabled person has a right to be angry, not just at the specific blockade in their way but at a society that creates those blockades.

Take the left and right pieces underneath the top flap and pull them apart. Crease the bottom of those pieces so that they'll stay spread apart. Open your heart and show people what it is like to be the only disabled person in a room, to be the only one fighting for the things you need to survive. Give them no option but to consider your humanity.

So I turned to being radically vulnerable. Instead of simply being angry at the world, I started to think of ways to show people why I was angry. Some of my essays have been about opening myself, stitch by stitch, and showing people what ableism has done to my soul. In one essay, I documented the experience of having my writing suppressed by an English teacher in high school. In another I spoke frankly about the creation of my prosthetic eye. In yet another, I spoke to my father's illness and death and how they radicalized me.

These essays were not reckless pieces written with emotion but calculated topics chosen to shift perception of disability, meant for an audience that needs to see me not as the object of a freak show but as a whole human. Not a consumable but an equal.

I share pieces of my soul in order to show people the world we live in. Because even though I'm angry, I display it differently. I show my anger, but that anger comes with a distinct expectation of compassion, with a need for people to see me as more than just a disabled woman—as a person.

A person who feels so strongly about the world she lives in that she has no choice but to turn her burning rage into a beacon.

Take one of those pieces that you pulled apart and slightly open the top corner so that you can bend a portion of it down to form the head. After bending a portion down, crease the sides of the head up so the piece will stay bent. Hold it in your hands and look at the face that you have made.

Bend the wings down at a 90-degree angle and finish the crane, but know there are more to make, more stories to tell, more birds to set free.

Selma Blair Became a Disabled Icon Overnight. Here's Why We Need More Stories Like Hers.

Zipporah Arielle

The significance of actor Selma Blair's stepping out onto the red carpet at the 2019 *Vanity Fair* Oscars party, in a dramatic, flowing, multicolored Ralph & Russo gown and cape—color-blocked in black, lavender blue, mint green, and soft pink, held on with a glimmering choker collar—and her black customized cane, completed with a real pink diamond, can best be summarized by Blair herself: "Holy shit," she told *Vanity Fair*. "There's a need for honesty about being disabled from someone recognizable."

In her first public appearance since publicly disclosing her multiple sclerosis (MS) diagnosis, Blair instantly became a disabled icon. As the camera's bright lights flash around her, Blair was the image of elegance. I watched her with her head held high, her cape flowing around her, her cane in hand, and meeting the cameras with her eyes, perfectly posed. Then, as if breaking character, she stopped posing, took a step back, and her face crinkled slightly as she began to cry; her manager, Troy Nankin, came over to her and helped wipe her tears. She held on to his arm while she gathered herself, saying, "It just took so much to get out."

There I was: a disabled woman in her mid-twenties living in my parents' house in Maine, in flannel pajamas and slippers, not a speck of makeup on my face, my thinning hair held back in a headscarf, with my $12 cane I'd gotten off Amazon, watching her on my laptop. There she was: blond hair slicked back, a stunning gown with solid sweeping lines, offset by the drama of the sheer cape, a real damn diamond on her cane, her perfect makeup somehow flawless even after wiping away tears, surrounded by photographers calling her name—and yet in that tiny moment, I felt I could relate to what she was feeling. *It just took so much to get out.*

Like most American women my age, I knew Selma Blair. Not personally, but in the way we know celebrities, from movies and magazines. I was maybe ten the first time I saw *Legally Blonde* and thirteen the first time I saw *Cruel Intentions* on an iPod my friend snuck in to summer camp. I know her face; I recognize her voice. To see her—a recognizable celebrity who I've known and thought of as eminently cool since girlhood—embrace her disability so wholly was incredibly meaningful for me. I watched someone with so much visibility lean on a cane proudly while displaying grace and beauty, while the photographers clamored for her attention. I felt closer to being seen—which is painfully rare in the chronic illness and disability world.

Fatigue and an ungodly exhaustion are a part of many chronic illnesses. When energy becomes a limited resource, one must become adept at budgeting it wisely—using "spoons," a metaphor writer Christine Miserandino came up with to explain living with lupus, to use energy when you have chronic illness. Blair decided to use her spoons to go out, to try and do what her body would let her do, while photographers took a few hundred photos of her—all while she was in the midst of a *flare* (or an exacerbation of a chronic illness). When she says it took so much to get out, she really meant it took so much to get out. She didn't just make an appearance; she showed up and showed out for disabled people, and for herself. The amount of precious energy it must have taken to go out cannot be understated.

"I was scared to talk, but even my neurologist said no, this will bring a lot of awareness because no one has the energy to talk when they're in a flare-up," Blair said during an interview with Robin Roberts that aired on February 26, the day after the Oscars. "But I do." She puts on a facetiously dramatic tone of voice and facial expression, and playfully shimmies her shoulders for emphasis. "'Cause I love a camera."

Her interviews since her appearance on the red carpet have done even more to bring some much-needed awareness to chronic illness and disability issues. Not only has she spoken about her specific symptoms like severe fatigue, spasmodic dysphonia, and balance issues—issues many other disabled people (including myself) have dealt with—but she also spoke out about the difficulty of getting a diagnosis. Many women with chronic illness can be sick for years before they're finally taken seriously and diagnosed. Blair told Roberts she went for years without being believed, and therefore without being treated. Blair also spoke of the lack of fashionable canes and accessible clothing ("Dressing is a shitshow," she quipped to Roberts), which is a problem I and other disabled folks are all too familiar with. She announced plans to release a line of accessible clothing and fashionable canes in the future. "Let's get elastic waistbands to look a little bit better," she joked on the *Nightline* interview (something that became even more relatable to me after I had gastrointestinal surgery, which made wearing nonelastic-waisted pants painful).

The embarrassment around unfashionable mobility devices and the limited selection of stylish accessible clothing has long been a problem for many disabled folks. My first wheelchair was a clunky hospital wheelchair, not meant for daily use and difficult to maneuver gracefully in. My first cane looked equally medical, impersonal, and clinical. When I've had to go out—to weddings or other occasions—and the event required I be in pictures, I often would go to the trouble of standing, holding on to a wall or the person next to me, and tossing my cane out of the shot. Too often, I went to the trouble of hurting myself, risking falling, or using enormous amounts of energy just to not have my mobility device in my shot, so as to not "ruin the photo." The first time I did it, it was because I was asked to; and every other time was at least partially because I had been asked that first time. Internalized ableism is so hard to overcome partially because those beliefs are so often reinforced in society. It's not just in our heads. It's in our daily lives and experiences . . . and then it gets in our heads.

Blair decided to reject the stigma, instead opting to let her mobility device shine. She has continued to do that in other coverage—one photo in her *Vanity Fair* feature shows off a stylish horse-head cane, its designer, Asprey, named just like any other part of her outfit—as it should be.

Other things Blair is rejecting? The notion that being sick means we cannot work (you can see her in a small role in *Lost in Space* and a larger role in *Another Life*, both on Netflix). She's rejecting pity and rejecting the "tragedy" narrative that so often is forced on those who have received a diagnosis. In her interview with *Vanity Fair*, she tells them, "There's no tragedy for me. I'm happy, and if I can help anyone be more comfortable in their skin, it's more than I've ever done before." She's still working and is honest that she sometimes has to work around her illness. To then see her admit that she, too, sometimes falls or drop things is encouraging, and to do so in a manner that is so public helps both to spread awareness and to encourage those in similar situations. But this is just the beginning. Hopefully, we will continue to see more disability representation from a wide variety of disabled folks, of all socioeconomic backgrounds, disabilities, races, sizes, gender identities, sexual orientations, and ethno-religious backgrounds, so everyone will be able to see themselves represented.

There are questions about how we consume media regarding disability. The word *inspired* is reviled by many in the disability community, who often are the subject of pity or undue praise merely for existing. But disabled people don't exist to make abled people feel better about their abledness. There is a tendency in our culture to turn disabled people into objects of what's known as inspiration porn. But for many in the disability community, particularly those who use canes or have MS or other similar chronic illnesses, Blair's public outspokenness on her reality with her illness has been both validating and inspiring. There were comments on Twitter and Instagram from people who wrote about how they'd been struggling with the decision to get a cane and how seeing Blair rock hers so confidently was what convinced them.

As for me? I have more internalized ableism to work on, and I imagine I'll have it for a while. But if seeing representation—even if it's not the most relatable representation, like from a celebrity on a red carpet—helps me (and others) accept our disabilities and mobility devices even just a little bit, then it's worth it. And for me, it does help, and it did help. I know the next time I'm at an event and take a picture with someone, I won't be moving my cane out of the shot.

PART 3

Doing

There is so much that able-bodied people could
learn from the wisdom that often comes with disability. But space needs to be made. Hands need to
be reached out. People need to be lifted up.

—A. H. Reaume

Why My Novel Is Dedicated to My Disabled Friend Maddy

A. H. Reaume

People often say that they couldn't have written their books without the help and support of friends and family. This is particularly true for disabled writers. Finishing my novel required many hours of hard work from my friend Madeline. But she wasn't weighing in on the likability of my characters or the proper way to format a manuscript. I needed her help because I was physically unable to finish my novel on my own.

Madeline and I met about a year ago at a networking event we both went to for work. I was trying to recommend a book to her, but I couldn't remember the name of it.

"I'm so sorry—I'm terrible with titles," I said. "I'm recovering from a brain injury."

Madeline's eyes lit up with recognition. "What kind of injury?" she asked and quickly added, "I am, too."

Maddy and I have very different injuries—she's recovering from a brain hemorrhage that she had six years ago at the age of twenty-three, and I'm recovering from a severe concussion that I got two years ago. Many of our symptoms are different—she has weakness on her left side, for example, and I struggle with using screens. But our brains also struggle in some of the same ways—when we talk, we will both sometimes close our eyes because it helps us find words for what we want to say. We both also know what it is like to have invisible illnesses and have people assume we're okay when we are actually experiencing extremely distressing symptoms.

"Let's meet up," I said and handed her my card as the networking event came to a close.

And so we met up.

In my life, there have been a handful of people who I've met and known immediately that we would become close friends. That's what it was like with Maddy. The first time we hung out, we went strawberry picking together and talked about what it was like to learn how to walk again and drive again and do all the things that so many people take for granted but which our injuries temporarily or permanently took from us.

We talked about the trauma of being in a body that suddenly loses function and the pain of experiencing ableism from employers, friends, and family. Mostly we talked about how lonely we were within our disabilities and recoveries—not just because fatigue and overstimulation sometimes isolated us but also because no one we knew understood. We laughed and we cried. We ate a lot of strawberries. It was a beautiful day.

At some point, I told Maddy how frustrated I was that I couldn't finish my novel.

"I can't make my edits on the computer because when I look at screens, my cognitive capacity decreases, and the complex structural edits I need to do take all my brainpower. But if I print my manuscript out and make the edits on a piece of paper, I can't transfer the edits back into the document because my eyes struggle with switching from the paper to the screen," I said. "I feel so stuck. I worry sometimes that I'm never going to finish it."

Madeline listened and nodded. "I'm so sorry," she said. "Our injuries have taken so much from us. I wish it wasn't taking this from you, too."

Our conversation stuck with me. I walked around replaying it in my head for several weeks, thinking about how much we had both lost and the ways in which we were slowly clawing our way back.

Some of that journey to recovery involved regaining abilities, but a lot of it was about finding new ways to do the same things. Maddy's explanation of how she compensated for her weak side by finding work-arounds to accommodate it eventually inspired me to think creatively about how I could finish my novel.

At my day job, I had an assistant who helped me with the computer-related tasks that were difficult for me. This was a workplace accommodation that my employer was required to provide after I became disabled. That made me think—what could I do to accommodate my novel writing?

I realized I could take on extra freelance writing work—something I could easily do—so I could afford to pay an assistant to transfer my novel edits from a printed copy back into a computer document. It wasn't the ideal writing process. It was slow, iterative, and used a lot of paper—but it was a way to make progress again.

After putting my novel aside for almost a year after my injury, I was excited that I'd found a way to work on it again.

I quickly ordered a box of ecofriendly paper and put a call out for someone who could come to my home and transcribe my changes. I had initial help from some writer friends of mine. I loved editing the manuscript with them, but they were both too busy with other work to help me consistently.

"I can do it," Maddy said enthusiastically when I told her I hadn't been able to find the right person.

"Are you sure?" I asked, not wanting her to feel obligated to help.

"Absolutely," she said. "You would be helping me, too. I'm looking for more work."

And that was how it started—the best collaboration of my life.

Maddy would come over on a weekend or after I got off work, and I'd usually start by making us food. Before we sat down to work on my novel, we would eat together and talk about our day, our health struggles, and the frustrations we had around our loved ones not understanding how much our disabilities impacted every moment of our lives.

There were often tears, but there was also so much understanding, love, and care extended between us. I felt seen in ways I hadn't felt seen since my injury. Maddy would take all the hurt parts of me and just hold them. She wouldn't try, like everyone else, to force me to make sense or order out of them until I was ready. She knew what it was like to lose. She also knew what it was like to come back—but in a different body. A brain injury is a particularly hard injury to have because it changes who you are in ways that other injuries don't, since it affects how you think, act, and respond. It's hard to talk about that loss and grief with people who have never experienced it.

At the time, I was facing ableism in a lot of areas of my life on top of grieving all the things that my injury had taken from me. It's hard to get out of bed and keep going in such circumstances—and harder still to work on writing. You often feel dragged down by the struggle. Or you don't have the emotional energy to work on anything difficult.

But knowing that Maddy would be coming over motivated me to get chapters edited for her. She drove me. She is one of the smartest and most meticulous people I know. She made my novel so much better by being thorough, pointing out redundancies, or researching solutions to help me format some formal experiments in the text that I was trying to pull off.

Similarly, having the job helped Maddy. It gave her extra work that was flexible and could accommodate her disability, and it got her out of the house. She also looked forward to our collaboration.

"I feel so grateful that we met," she told me recently. "I haven't known you for very long, but you've become like family to me."

I tell Maddy often how grateful I am to know her. But I've never told her how much she changed my life. I felt like I would never finish my novel before I met her. And here I am—finishing my novel.

My book has been shaped by Maddy's hands and her brilliant disabled brain. Its pages hold her fingerprints. They sit there lightly on top of the deep imprints of my own fingers. This is disabled poetics. This is disabled praxis. It's about interdependence. I couldn't do it alone, but I did it with her help. She needed flexible work, and I gave that to her. It's part of the ethics of care and support that so many disabled people show one another. It's a kind of love that I hadn't known existed before my disability. It's fierce and patient and tender and rare. It's what disabled people give one another because we wish the able-bodied world had given it to us. It's tinged with grief and pain—and also with defiance. It's gentle and it's incredibly kind.

"Disabled people caring for each other can be a place of deep healing," says Leah Lakshmi Piepzna-Samarasinha in *Care Work: Dreaming Disability Justice.*

Meeting Maddy has indeed been healing. It's given parts of me back to myself. Maddy gave me back my dreams and my voice. She made me see how I could still be a writer, still finish my novel. That I could write other things, too. But she also did more than that.

We both have "broken" brains, but they function in different ways; together we often make up for each other's limitations. We also have different pieces of the puzzle of healing and grief. We are helping each other imagine a world and a future where we can be loved and cared for and held not just despite but because of our disabilities. Together we are teaching each other how to ask for that. How to expect it. How to give that love to others as well. We have already taught each other so many lessons about the beauty and salve of disabled love and kinship.

"I want to dedicate my novel to her," I told a friend recently. "To Maddy and to all the disabled writers who struggle to finish their books because they can't finish them themselves and can't afford to pay someone to help them."

Because that's the thing about our story. It's one of privilege. I have the capacity to make money to pay a friend to help me. I have the capacity to work in certain ways that others do not. While my body makes writing difficult and painful and doing so requires accommodations I have to pay for, it's still possible for me.

Not all disabled people have that. Many are struggling just to survive or to pay their medical bills or to deal with ableist abuse. Disabled writers who have other intersections of oppression—like if they're queer or transgender or racialized or poor—are more likely to have their voices silenced because of lack of capacity, the inability to access appropriate medical care, or financial precarity. We are less likely to read their works. Their brilliance might remain unshared. As I finish writing my novel, I don't want to just celebrate my success—I want to draw attention to that.

So while I don't have a publisher yet for my book, I have a dedication page. It reads:

You have this book in your hands because of the kindness, support, and interdependence of disabled people. This book would have remained unfinished without Madeline Sloan's work and love. I dedicate it to her and to all the disabled writers who are unable to finish their work because they don't have the support they need to get their voices heard.

I want to use the dedication page of my novel to acknowledge both the beauty and transformational force of interdependence and the ways our society fails at it. The light and the shadows of disability and care. The ways in which it lifts many of us up and the ways it leaves so many of us alone and voiceless.

Independence is a fairy tale that late capitalism tells in order to shift the responsibility for care and support from community and state to individuals and families. But not everyone has the personal capacity, and not everyone has the family support. And the stories we tell about bootstraps tell us that it's the fault of an individual if they don't thrive. They're just not trying hard enough.

The myth of independence also shapes what literature looks like and what kind of writing is valued. We see a novel as better than a short story anthology. We rarely see collaborations in fiction or in poetry. Our literary praxis is that of the lone author typing away by themselves. Our poetics come from solitary brilliant minds. We still cling as a culture to the myth of the single writer succeeding on their own as fiercely as we cling to the myth of the self-made billionaire. But that isn't what a disabled poetics and practice has to be.

If you've ever wondered why there aren't more books published by disabled writers, let me tell you part of why. Like me, many disabled people cannot physically finish a book on their own. If they can, it might not be as polished as books by able-bodied writers. It might have edges that need smoothing out. Editors and agents might decide to pass, despite liking it—not wanting to put in the added work.

But we need more disabled voices.

We need more disabled voices not just because disabled people are brilliant and talented and have so much to offer and say but also because disabled people face an incredible amount of dehumanizing ableism that shapes and destroys their lives. And one of the best ways to combat that is through stories.

Esmé Weijun Wang writes in *The Collected Schizophrenias* about speaking to medical professionals about her experiences with schizophrenia. A doctor approached her to thank her afterward, but what she said shows how many able-bodied people don't treat or see disabled people as human:

> She said that she was grateful for this reminder that her patients are human too. She starts out with such hope, she said, every time a new patient comes—and then they relapse and return, relapse and return. The clients, or patients, exhibit their illness in ways that prevent them from seeming like people who can dream, or like people who can have others dream for them.

Disabled voices like Wang's and others are needed to change the narratives around disability—to insist on disabled people's humanity and complexity, to resist inspiration porn, to challenge the binary that says disabled bodies and lives are less important or tragic or that they have value only if they can be fixed or be cured or be made productive.

Maddy and other disabled thinkers are helping me to see the world that we could have if disabled justice transformed our ideas of care, kindness, community, and interdependence. There is so much that able-bodied people could learn from the wisdom that often comes with disability. But space needs to be made. Hands need to reach out. People need to be lifted up.

The story of disabled success has never been a story about one solitary disabled person overcoming limitations—despite the fact that's the narrative we so often read in the media. The narrative trajectory of a disabled person's life is necessarily webbed. We are often only as strong as our friends and family make us, only as strong as our community, only as strong as the resources and privileges we have.

So as I celebrate finishing my novel despite my limitations, I am refusing to tell a story of single-handed success in which I valiantly overcame my disability. I want to tell a story that is more complex and true. It's a story about how my disability is always present and painful. A story about how my privilege is often the only thing that allows me to succeed in an ableist world. And it is absolutely a story about disabled interdependence.

While Maddy had the biggest impact on finishing my novel, I couldn't have finished it without the support of other disabled people who inspired me to keep going or helped me in some way. This is their story, too. It's the story of disabled writers I know, like Amanda Leduc, Andrew Wilmot, Adam Pottle, Erin Soros, Arley Cruthers, and Elee Kraljii Gardiner, who provided love and understanding and kinship. It is also the story of disabled activists like Esmé Wang, Leah Lakshmi Piepzna-Samarasinha, Imani Barbarin, Rahim Ladha, and Alice Wong, who inspired me by their example to be louder and keep writing.

For disabled people to thrive, we need webs of help, support, understanding, and care. But in an able-bodied literary world, we are all expected to succeed on our own, never to need assistance. Until we change that paradigm, it will continue to be incredibly hard for most disabled people to finish and send out their work into the world. And we desperately need that work.

So I want you all to sit with that and think about how you can have a role in changing that. I want you to ask yourself, how can you be someone's Maddy?

Content notes: bodily autonomy, eugenics, ableism, trauma, sexual assault, medical trauma, objectification, carceral state, sterilization

The Antiabortion Bill You Aren't Hearing About

Rebecca Cokley

Originally published on May 20, 2019, as a response to Texas Senate Bill 1033, which did not pass in the House of Representatives

As the country has anxiously watched extreme and dangerous antiabortion bills pop up in Alabama, Georgia, and Ohio, another threat has received far less attention. Earlier this month, the Texas Senate passed SB 1033, which would remove the exemption allowing abortion after twenty weeks of pregnancy when there is "severe fetal abnormality." And it prohibits what the antichoice lawmakers call "discriminatory abortion." That means when a person receives information that the fetus they are carrying has a genetic condition—such as Down syndrome, cystic fibrosis, dwarfism, or other mutations—they could not seek an abortion on the grounds of that diagnosis. While being framed as "saving those poor defenseless disabled babies," the reality is that this is just one more assault on people's bodies.

The Texas bill specifically eliminates the exception written into the state's twenty-week abortion ban for cases of "severe fetal abnormality." An additional provision means that doctors who knowingly perform an abortion following a prenatal diagnosis could be charged with a class A misdemeanor and risk losing their license. In effect, the bill puts the doctor's career and livelihood in direct opposition to a person's right to bodily autonomy.

If this bill passes the legislature, it heads to the governor's desk. The current governor, Greg Abbott (R), is a wheelchair user. While the antichoice movement hails this bill as "saving our community," the reality is that legislation like this strips from everyone, particularly people with disabilities, the right to decide what happens to one's own body.

Yet again, what I see is a man exerting control over someone else's body, and it needs to stop.

The disability community is not a football to be punted for the sake of political points, but it has indeed been relegated to that role by both Republicans and Democrats. Politicians bring out their disabled children as props at the same time that they attack the Affordable Care Act, push for voucher programs (which remove rights protections), and support subminimum wage while framing the disability community as perpetuators of fraud. But this latest legislative attack on a person's right to exert control over their body puts us directly in the center of the abortion debate, again.

Prenatal screening is a tough conversation to have in the disability community. For some people with degenerative conditions, the knowledge of their lived experience may lead to them being staunchly pro-choice. Others of us, like the deaf and dwarfism communities, often see our disability as less a *diagnosis* and more a *culture*. We celebrate the birth of future generations regardless of any health-related side effects.

When prenatal screenings were introduced in Iceland, the number of births of people with Down syndrome plummeted. Imagine knowing your community was small, but then all of a sudden it was just gone and not coming back; some people think that's a good thing. This is why the Down syndrome community and their families are largely "pro-life"—and that needs to be respected by pro-choice activists who erase those experiences from public conversations on the issue.

It is hard to be a pro-choice disabled person who understands that believing in bodily autonomy means you have to support the idea that other people—your friends, your peers, your siblings—may choose to abort a pregnancy because their child could be like you. Yes, it's hard. But that's why it's a conversation we have to have, because if we don't, decisions about us and our futures get made by others, without us.

The right to decide what happens to our bodies is a fundamental principle in the disability community, and with good reason. Both of my parents had achondroplasia, the most common form of dwarfism. When they started trying for a family, they knew what the probabilities were of the baby dying shortly after birth. But since FGFR3, the gene for achondroplasia, hadn't been discovered yet, they endured three pregnancies, three baby showers, and three losses before I came along. The trauma was long-lasting and put significant strains on my parents' marriage. I know this is why my mom was unwavering in her support of abortion. A person should have the right to choose.

The way disability is framed in the political messaging around access to abortion care is very frustrating. And at the same time, the disability community is dependent on the medical-industrial complex for our quality of life. But removing options doesn't improve that— and that's what bills like this do.

As Laura Dorwart, a writer with a PhD from the University of California, San Diego, pointed out in a 2018 *New York Times* op-ed on a similar abortion ban in Ohio: "Antiabortion legislation and rhetoric often circulates stereotypical, infantilizing imagery about people with cognitive disabilities as innocents in need of protection from nondisabled saviors." When this rhetoric is used by the same political party attacking the Americans with Disabilities Act, cutting Medicaid, and removing protections, it clearly demonstrates that they don't care about the disability community.

What's equally harmful is that those on the pro-choice side often use disability as a monster under the bed, framing our lives as lacking dignity, independence, or value. Our lives are valuable because they're our lives. Why is this not enough?

The messaging often ignores that disabled people need abortions, too. During the Supreme Court nomination fight for Associate Justice Brett Kavanaugh, disability advocates were intentional about focusing on his arguments that women with intellectual disabilities did not have the right to make decisions about medical procedures conducted on them. We know that 90 percent of people with developmental disabilities are survivors of sexual assault. Bills like SB 1033 continue to take control from people who have to fight for the least bit of autonomy as is.

From birth, we're raised by an ableist society to perceive our bodies as an almost external commodity. Let the doctor examine you; let the personal care attendant wipe your bottom; have your friend on the playground help straighten out your leg after you fall down; show your friend's mom your latest pressure sore so they can compare it to one their son or daughter has. Some days it may feel like your body belongs to everyone *but* you.

Many disability advocates talk about developing actual disassociation skills at the doctor's office because the objectification can be so traumatizing. And when you do exert control over your own body, you are labeled as difficult, as noncompliant.

We also live in a country where *Buck v. Bell*—the 1927 U.S. Supreme Court case in which the sterilization of people with disabilities was ruled constitutional—has never been overturned. The same country where the carceral system, which is disproportionately disabled, uses sterilization as punishment or an "incentive" toward release. When those in power determine you are "undesirable," there undoubtedly is a mechanism taking reproductive rights from you without a choice.

The reality is that people with economic means will always be able to access the procedures they need. But a majority of people with disabilities, who are disproportionately lower income, will never have this luxury. Bans like the ones in Alabama, Georgia, Ohio, and now Texas will serve only to perpetuate the cycle of poverty and disability.

So. Not. Broken.

Alice Sheppard

"I'm broken," I say as I bounce onto the physical therapy table. My physical therapist takes some notes, and we begin. It's been years since this joke was funny. I am a choreographer and professional dancer: being somewhat broken is a way of life for me, and it has nothing to do with my disability. I keep making the joke because, conceptually, "brokenness" interests me: it is one of the defining elements of my movement practice and my thinking about disability.

Many nondisabled people attribute a degree of brokenness to disability; it arises from the medicalization of our bodyminds. To be disabled is, in this world, to experience a problem of body and/or mind so severe that it distinguishes a disabled person from a nondisabled person. I learned about my body from figuring out ways to live in my diagnosis; I learned about disability from disability studies books and from people like Corbett O'Toole and Simi Linton. My initiation into this world revealed that disability was more than the state of my body.

That idea keeps unfolding; I have been thinking about it for years, and there's still more to learn. Whereas disability in the mainstream world focuses on what my body can and cannot do, I no longer think much about ability. Professionally, I have transitioned from being a professor of medieval studies to being a dancer and choreographer. Dance has taught me to understand my body differently. My very first problem as a dancer was figuring out my chair. I had to learn how to move in it, of course, but I also had to understand what it meant as a black woman to use a chair onstage, in the studio, and in the world. This took time. In many ways, it was easier to learn how a wheelchair moves.

As I focused on actions as simple as pushing and pulling, the movements changed how I thought. I was more successful at going in a straight line with one push if I thought about my chair as an extension of my body instead of as an object separate from me. I looked to the Internet to help me understand this more, but the blogs I was reading all wanted to tamp down the stigma of a chair by calling it a "device," a "tool," or "technology." I started saying: "my chair is my legs." This was helpful in explaining to the airlines what it meant to damage a wheelchair, but it turned out not to be useful in the studio. My chair did not replace my legs; they are still there. When I discovered the concept of *embodiment*—a word I use to describe the way in which my body takes shape and form—I made another breakthrough: *My chair is my body*.

To be honest, I cannot say that this insight unleashed a fierce wave of creativity in me, but it does mark a certain place in my development as an artist, by which I mean as a dancer, choreographer, writer, and thinker. When I left Oakland's AXIS Dance Company, a physically integrated dance group, I wanted to begin an independent choreographic and performance practice. I proudly wrote on my new website:

All my work begins with my body: as it is with my wheelchair, as it is without my wheelchair, as it is with crutches, and even with crutches and chair together. My crutches and chair are not tools that compensate for my impairment. Nor are they simply devices that I use for traveling across the studio. I understand these starting points as embodiments, each of which has different movement possibilities. The lope of a crutch feels to me as elegant as that of a gazelle; the push of a chair creates a glide akin to skating; a roll on the floor creates groundedness and a different understanding of the spine. I want to draw out the expressive capacity of disabled bodies and minds by acknowledging and actively drawing on the movement of impairment.

It was as much a promise to myself as it was a declaration of a mission. Since then, versions of this language have wound their ways into my artist statements, choreographic manifestos, and vision statements. I have expanded it to surface the intertwining of race and gender. I talk now of the necessity of an intersectional disability in my work, and I have moved to claiming disability aesthetics and culture. I often write something like:

My intent is to surface the unfamiliar conversations of intersectional disability aesthetics, so that our stories can be told. All my work is founded in unexpected movement exploration, honoring my connection to other disabled dancers.

I am working at a new edge of the field, visibilizing intersectional, interdisciplinary disability arts as a vibrant area of cultural production while creating the contexts/documents for audiences to understand my work and the work of other disabled artists with reference to our conversations, histories, legacies, and influences.

I have come a long way from the brokenness of disability expected by the nondisabled world to an imagined space where the binary of "broken" and "whole" seems not to exist. I look forward to learning about the effects of this thinking and to discovering what is next.

How a Blind Astronomer Found a Way to Hear the Stars

Wanda Díaz-Merced

First appeared as a TED Talk in February 2016. To watch the full talk, visit bit.ly/38Lg7Jw.

Once there was a star. Like everything else, she was born, grew to be around thirty times the mass of our sun, and lived for a very long time. Exactly how long, people cannot really tell. Just like everything in life, she reached the end of her regular star days when her heart, the core of her life, exhausted its fuel. But that was no end.

She transformed into a supernova, in the process releasing a tremendous amount of energy, outshining the rest of the galaxy and emitting, in one second, the same amount of energy our sun will release in ten days. And she evolved into another role in our galaxy.

Supernova explosions are very extreme. But the ones that emit gamma rays are even more extreme. In the process of becoming a supernova, the interior of the star collapses under its own weight and it starts rotating ever faster, like an ice skater when pulling their arms in close to their body. In that way, it starts rotating very fast and it increases, powerfully, its magnetic field. The matter around the star is dragged around, and some energy from that rotation is transferred to that matter and the magnetic field is increased even further. In that way, our star had extra energy to outshine the rest of the galaxy in brightness and gamma-ray emission.

My star, the one in my story, became what is known as a magnetar. And just for your information, the magnetic field of a magnetar is one thousand trillion times the magnetic field of Earth. The most energetic events ever measured by astronomers carry the name *gamma-ray bursts* because we observe them most as bursts or explosions, most strongly measured as gamma-ray light. Our star, like the one in our story that became a magnetar, is detected as a gamma-ray burst during the most energetic portion of the explosion. Yet even though gamma-ray bursts are the strongest events ever measured by astronomers, we cannot see them with our naked eye. We rely on other methods in order to study this gamma-ray light. We cannot see them with our naked eye. We can see only an itty-bitty, tiny portion of the electromagnetic spectrum that we call visible light. And beyond that, we rely on other methods.

Yet as astronomers, we study a wider range of light and we depend on other methods to do that. On the screen, it may look like this. You're seeing a plot. That is a light curve. It's a plot of intensity of light over time. It is a gamma-ray light curve. Sighted astronomers depend on this kind of plot in order to interpret how this light intensity changes over time. On the left, you will be seeing the light intensity without a burst, and on the right, you will be seeing the light intensity with the burst.

Early during my career, I could also see this kind of plot. But then I lost my sight. I completely lost my sight because of extended illness, and with it, I lost the opportunity to see this plot and the opportunity to do my physics. It was a very strong transition for me in many ways. And professionally it left me without a way to do my science. I longed to access and scrutinize this energetic light and figure out the astrophysical cause. I wanted to experience the spacious wonder, the excitement, the joy produced by the detection of such a titanic celestial event.

I thought long and hard about it [until] I suddenly realized that all a light curve is, is a table of numbers converted into a visual plot. So along with my collaborators, I worked really hard and we translated the numbers into sound. I achieved access to the data, and today I'm able to do physics at the level of the best astronomer, using sound. And what people have been able to do, mainly visually, for hundreds of years, now I do it using sound.

(Applause)

Listening to this gamma-ray burst that you're seeing on the—

(Applause continues)

Thank you.

—on the screen brought something to the ear beyond the obvious burst. Now I'm going to play the burst for you. It's not music, it's sound.

(Digital beeping sounds)

This is scientific data converted into sound, and it's mapped in pitch. The process is called *sonification*.

So listening to this brought something to the ear besides the obvious burst. When I examine the very strong low-frequency regions, or bass line—I'm zooming into the bass line now. We noted resonances characteristic of electrically charged gases like the solar wind. And I want you to hear what I heard. You will hear it as a very fast decrease in volume. And because you're sighted, I'm giving you a red line indicating what intensity of light is being converted into sound.

(Digital hum and whistling sound)

The [whistles] is frogs at home, don't pay attention to that.

(Laughter)

(Digital hum and whistling sound)

I think you heard it, right?

So what we found is that the bursts last long enough to support wave resonances, which are things caused by exchanges of energy between particles that may have been excited, that depend on the volume. You may remember that I said that the matter around the star is dragged around? It transmits power with frequency and field distribution determined by the dimensions. And you may remember that we were talking about a super-massive star that became a very strong magnetic field magnetar. If this is the case, then outflows from the exploding star may be associated with this gamma-ray burst.

What does that mean? That star formation may be a very important part of these supernova explosions. Listening to this very gamma-ray burst brought us to the notion that the use of sound as an adjunctive visual display may also support sighted astronomers in the search for more information in the data. Simultaneously, I worked on analyzing measurements from other telescopes, and my experiments demonstrated that when you use sound as an adjunctive visual display, astronomers can find more information in this now more accessible data set. This ability to transform data into sound gives astronomy a tremendous power of transformation. And the fact that a field that is so visual may be improved in order to include anyone with an interest in understanding what lies in the heavens is a spirit-lifter.

When I lost my sight, I noticed that I didn't have access to the same amount and quality of information a sighted astronomer had. It was not until we innovated with the sonification process that I regained the hope of being a productive member of the field that I had worked so hard to be part of.

Yet information access is not the only area in astronomy where this is important. The situation is systemic, and scientific fields are not keeping up. The body is something changeable—anyone may develop a disability at any point. Let's think about, for example, scientists that are already at the top of their careers. What happens to them if they develop a disability? Will they feel excommunicated, as I did? Information access empowers us to flourish. It gives us equal opportunities to display our talents and choose what we want to do with our lives, based on interest and not based on potential barriers. When we give people the opportunity to succeed without limits, [it] will lead to personal fulfillment and a prospering life. And I think that the use of sound in astronomy is helping us achieve that and contribute to science.

While other countries told me that the study of perception techniques in order to study astronomy data is not relevant to astronomy because there are no blind astronomers in the field, South Africa said, "We want people with disabilities to contribute to the field." Right now I'm working at the South African Astronomical Observatory, at the Office of Astronomy for Development. There, we are working on sonification techniques and analysis methods to impact the students of the Athlone School for the Blind. These students will be learning radio astronomy, and they will be learning the sonification methods in order to study astronomical events like huge ejections of energy from the sun, known as coronal mass ejections. What we learn with these students—these students have multiple disabilities and coping strategies that will be accommodated—what we learn with these students will directly impact the way things are being done at the professional level. I humbly call this "development." And this is happening right now.

I think that science is for everyone. It belongs to the people, and it has to be available to everyone, because we are all natural explorers. I think that if we limit people with disabilities from participating in science, we'll sever our links with history and with society. I dream of a level scientific playing field, where people encourage respect and respect each other, where people exchange strategies and discover together. If people with disabilities are allowed into the scientific field, an explosion, a huge titanic burst of knowledge will take place, I am sure.

(Digital beeping sounds)

That is the titanic burst.

Thank you.

(Applause)

Content notes: suicidal ideation, bullying, body shaming, infantilization

Incontinence Is a Public Health Issue—And We Need to Talk About It

Mari Ramsawakh

If we go by commercials and consumer goods, incontinence (the inability to control your bladder and/or bowels) is a problem only for babies, toddlers, and elderly people. If we go by movies and TV shows, it might also include anxious or traumatized children. But I've lived with incontinence for all twenty-five years of my life, and I've yet to see my experiences reflected in any form of media.

I was born with lipomyelomeningocele spina bifida. While my nervous system was developing in the womb, a cyst formed on my spinal cord, disrupting nerves from my lower back downward. After a surgery to detach my spinal cord from my spinal column when I was nine or ten months old, I experienced partial paralysis from the waist down. Though I could eventually walk, stand, and bend, it became easier to lose muscle mass in my legs and increasingly difficult to build it back up. Whether the surgery improved my condition or not, I would experience incontinence for the rest of my life.

I didn't fully grasp that my body wasn't like that of other children until I started first grade. Before that, I didn't know that it was odd to have a nurse escort me to the bathroom at a scheduled time every day. I didn't know that other kids didn't have to use catheters or that wearing diapers at that age wasn't "normal." I didn't know that other kids didn't have to miss an entire day of school once a year to be poked and prodded by a roster of doctors and nurses.

But as long as I wore the right clothes, no one else had to know that I was wearing diapers or that I had a scarred bump on my back. I could pretend that I was "normal," that I wasn't different from any of my classmates. I didn't feel *disabled*, as it were. Until the third grade.

That year, when an older boy realized that what was peeking out of the top of my jeans wasn't underwear, he followed me around at recess calling me "Diaper Girl." He hounded me with questions as to why I still needed diapers and constantly reminded me that only *babies* wore them—*didn't I know that?* It was the first time I really felt like something was wrong with my body.

By the time I entered fourth grade, I was suicidal. I was desperate to be normal, but I didn't seem to fit in with my peers in any way, nor did I have the words to describe my experience. I wasn't a wheelchair user, for which I was told to be grateful. I didn't think I was "disabled enough" to let my disability hinder me. So I tried to overcome it.

I fought with my parents a lot. I told them I didn't want to wear diapers to school anymore. I said I didn't want a nurse to escort me to one of the two accessible bathrooms in the school. I thought that if I tried hard enough, I could just be a normal kid.

But things only got harder. It took me longer to use the bathroom; entire recesses were eaten up by the long process of self-catheterization. While everyone else spent their time playing and talking and running around outside, I had to go to the school office to pick up the key to the accessible bathroom, lube up a catheter before inserting it inside myself, and then return the key to the office before I could head outside. When I had to bundle up in wintertime, I could barely get all of my layers on before the bell would ring. If I skipped going to the bathroom, I would have an "accident" in class; then I'd have to get permission from the school and my parents to walk home, change clothes, and walk back.

I felt separate from and alien to my peers. I went from "Diaper Girl" to "Pee Girl." And I just didn't understand why I couldn't get it under control. I restricted my fluid intake while at school, but I still couldn't prevent the "accidents." There were even times when I had finished my entire bathroom process, but if I ran or jumped—even thirty minutes later—I was humiliated once again. Before the age of ten, I started to question whether or not I deserved to be alive.

As time went on, doctors still had no solutions or support to offer me. In high school, I confided in a nurse that I was trying to be sexually active, but bladder and bowel incontinence were affecting my ability to be intimate with my then-partner. Their only solution was to suggest that there would be people who would be "into that." My dating pool was instantly reduced to people who would fetishize me.

This idea was all but confirmed when a later boyfriend threw up after another bout of bowel incontinence during sex with me. He immediately stopped returning my phone calls. My worst fears were realized, and I felt too repulsive to be desirable.

If incontinence was treated as a human rights issue, as something many people face and need proper resources to manage, I could have had a vastly different childhood. Even now, shame and stigma surrounding incontinence have caused severe damage to my self-worth and interpersonal relationships. At points, I've avoided sex and dating out of fear that I'll be left humiliated and alone again. Even in my current long-term relationship, I still wonder if and when my incontinence will be too much for my partner to look past.

I know I'm not the only person who must feel this way. Twenty-five percent of young women and 44 to 57 percent of middle-aged women (*women* is presumably used here to mean "people assigned female at birth") also experience "some involuntary urine loss," according to Practice Bulletins of the American College of Obstetricians and Gynecologists. And doctors can't be prepared to offer long-term solutions to incontinence if they're not prepared to even talk to their patients about it. Statistics state that 50 to 70 percent of people who experience incontinence don't seek treatment for it, likely due to the same stigma I've experienced for most of my life, which can lead to greater health risks.

I've done everything I can to shorten the amount of time I use the bathroom. But the habits I've developed to do so actually jeopardize my health, increasing the risk of potentially life-threatening infections. To change these habits now would require another $50 per month for the extra supplies at minimum—a price increase I cannot afford as someone who does not have access to comprehensive health insurance. If I don't self-catheterize every day, I put myself at greater risk for kidney infection and kidney failure down the road. But I pay for these necessary supplies out of pocket, and they aren't cheap.

These are important issues we need to talk about. I want talking about the danger disabled and incontinent people put ourselves in to be seen as *normal.* I want to be able to talk about my experiences without shame. I want to be able to discuss how people of different ethnicities, socioeconomic positions, and genders are affected by incontinence. I want to be able to talk about the cisnormativity embedded into the designs of incontinence wear without bracing myself for the mockery and derision I've come to expect. But I can't do this until it's normalized to even talk about incontinence in general.

Incontinence is not just embarrassing. It's a public health issue. And until we're able to talk about it in a meaningful way, people who experience incontinence will always be isolated and putting our health at risk.

Content notes: suffering, medication, spoilers for Hannah Gadsby's
Nanette

Falling/Burning
Hannah Gadsby, *Nanette*,
and Being a Bipolar Creator

Shoshana Kessock

These days, I call it burning, but for most of my life, I called it flying.

It's that feeling when you're wrapped up in a writing project so hard, you look up and half a day has gone by. You haven't moved, you haven't drunk or eaten or talked to anyone. You work and work until your knuckles hurt, and there are words flowing out of you, and you can't stop until it's all done. Then you look up, realize what time it is, and fall over because the words are done for the day and you've been doing it. You've been flying.

That's what writing when you're me feels like.

Well, a lot of the time. Some days it's just normal. I get up, I do my morning routine (take my meds, get some grub, boop the cat, check my e-mail, mess around on Facebook), and then it's off to the word mines. And on those days, they are indeed the word mines. I check an outline; I write notes; I putter around; I get the words going however I can, tugging that little mining cart up the hill toward those far-off paragraphs and . . . Y'know, this analogy has gotten away from me. I digress.

Those are the hard days at the job because that's what it is—writing, like making any art, is a job. It's craft and talent and passion rolled up into one ball. It's doing a thing you worked hard to learn to do the best you can. You're capturing those weird little ideas rolling around in your head and making them into words, then lines, then paragraphs, and somehow they're all supposed to reach out to someone who reads them and make their brains go *POOF, I like this.* No pressure or anything, writer, just take the ephemeral and translate it onto a page. You make it happen as best as you can.

Then there are the other days. The days when BLEH becomes BANG. The days when something just clicks and comes roaring down the pike inside my brain and it's all I can do to get to my computer because it's ready to go and that's it. Get out of the way.

I call it burning these days because that's what it feels like: like there's an idea inside me burning its way out. But when I was younger, I called it flying. What I really meant was controlled falling. Like there was a tornado going on and I would leap off something and ride right through the middle of it, all the way up, chasing words. Because that's what it felt like for me, rolling on through the manic energy that comes with being bipolar.

A lot of folks equate the manic energy of being bipolar with the creative spark that drives artists to brilliance. They point to so many great artists in history who lived with mental illness and say, "There it is, that energy, that's what made them great!"

Except for so many artists, mental illness didn't make them great. It made them ill. And if they weren't careful, it made them gone.

Hannah Gadsby's blockbuster comedy special *Nanette* was billed as exactly that: a comedy. She was meant to get up onstage, make some jokes, and entertain us all via Netflix. Instead, Gadsby delivered what I can only call a commencement speech for comedians, a bait and switch that took the audience from laughter to silence and ultimately to a standing ovation. Gadsby, a queer comedian with a career going back over ten years, started her performance with a fairly standard routine, drawing in the laughs. Then she started explaining how jokes worked, about how they increased tension and then broke it into laughter.

Then she stopped breaking the tension. And just raised it higher and higher by telling the truth.

She spoke to her audience about a lot of things. Her family, and what it was like coming out to them. About violence, about triggering subjects. She broke from the funny parts of her routine a little more than halfway through and talked about quitting comedy because she was tired of making people like herself, a lesbian still fighting with some deep shame issues, into a punch line. I watched in spellbound silence as Hannah Gadsby deconstructed comedy to its most basic building blocks and rebuilt them into a soapbox, a grand forum where she read the audience a monologue of pain and vulnerability, her farewell to wisecracks and the opening of perhaps a new chapter of honest, open speaking in her life. She was out to speak her truth, and by the end, I was in awe.

It was somewhere in the middle where she told people to fuck off when telling artists to "feel" for their art that I felt the ground open up beneath me a little and I cried.

She talked about Vincent van Gogh, the artist who suffered during his life from mental illness, self-medicated, was treated by doctors, and struggled to succeed despite his obvious impossible talent due to his sickness. She talked about her knowledge of his life, thanks to her art history degree, and how he sold only one painting his entire life—

not because he wasn't recognized by his community as a genius but because he struggled to even be part of a community due to his illness.

And I thought of the flying and the hard days at the word mines. I thought about the days when I heard the tornado in my head and couldn't make the words get to my fingers. I thought about the frustration, the depression, the difficulties talking to people about what it sounded like inside my skull some days when I could barely pay attention because of the rush of words and ideas.

Hannah Gadsby told people artists don't have to suffer for their art, and I'll forever thank her for having the guts to stand up and say that to the world. Because I used to believe it was true.

When I was sixteen, I was diagnosed with bipolar II disorder.

I came from a family that didn't really get what being bipolar meant. My parents tried to get it, but when I'd do something irresponsible, it was always because I was "bad." I tried to explain how it was impossible to keep my whirlwind mind straight sometimes. How it was a battle against depression to get up in the morning and go to class. When I flunked in school, I tried to explain why; when I overcharged my credit card on a manic binge; when I cried for days and couldn't stop. But those were the bad days. And the good days—those were the days I could take on the world, when no one could stop me, when I was manic off my head. I was out of control.

I went to a therapist when my school suggested it to my parents. The therapist took one look at my behavior and referred me to a psychiatrist, a loud and overbearing man who listened to me talk a mile a minute for fifteen minutes, heard my symptoms, and pulled out a giant prescription pad. I started taking the drugs he gave me but received no explanation about what being bipolar really meant. He never explained what behaviors were unusual or what could be attributed to the illness, nor did he offer me any coping skills or resources to better understand my situation. He gave me pills and saw me every two weeks. I knew almost nothing about what was going on with me but was smart enough to realize I needed more information.

So? I went online.

Because my family didn't know much about bipolar disorder and my doctor wasn't telling, I learned a lot from the Internet. Those were the wild and woolly early days of the Internet, when it was the nineties and everyone was in AOL chat rooms and the world was a wacky, wacky place. On the Internet I found a community of role-players who eventually led me to the career I have today. It was also where I got a *lot* of bad advice about mental illness.

I read a lot of stories about people being overmedicated or given the wrong medication. I heard stories about people being committed by their families if they didn't hide what was wrong with them. But I especially came across the same story over and over from people who had been medicated. "If you go on the drugs," they said, "the creative drive goes away. You'll lose that spark inside you. If you want to be an artist, stay away from medication. It'll kill your art."

I didn't believe it. I was taught doctors were to be trusted. And besides, I knew I needed help. So I took the drugs the doctor gave me and fell into the worst confluence of events you could imagine. Because the medication the doctor gave me *did* kill my creativity. It also made me sleep too much, have no emotions whatsoever, and gain tons of weight. It destroyed my memory. And every time I brought these side effects up to my doctor, his answer was to add another pill to balance out the others or up my dose.

I didn't realize it until later, but I had a bad doctor. What I did know was at the height of this medicine dance, I'd spend my days sleeping or staring at a television, feeling nothing at all. I couldn't even cry. But maybe worst of all, I struggled to create. I couldn't find that spark inside me like I used to, that flying feeling that gave me inspiration. In the moments when I could feel something, it was the overwhelming terror of going back into that stupor once again.

This went on from the time I was seventeen, when I was so messed up I dropped out of high school, until I was nearly nineteen. In between, I struggled to get my GED so I could at least get into college and then proceeded to flunk there, too, due to the medication's impossible weight on my mind. I went through so many ridiculous emotional issues I can't describe, but all of it was through a curtain of medication so thick I can barely pull up memories from that time.

The times my emotions would push through were during what I discovered later were hypomanic phases, mood swings so strong they butted through the haze and made me wildly unstable. All the while I struggled to get my life in order, and every time I did, it was under a fog of badly managed medication or through the adrenaline of mania so strong I could barely function. I didn't understand I was badly medicated, of course. All I knew was everything was falling to pieces, all the time, and I couldn't feel a solid, real emotion long enough to care.

So in 2002, in one of those moments of emotional lucidity, I made a decision to stop taking my meds. I suddenly thought, *The Internet is right; this is a horrible, horrible mistake.* I trusted my experience and my terror and I stopped taking my meds.

And, well, to quote one of my heroines from the time, Buffy:

"Everything here is . . . hard, and bright, and violent. Everything I feel, everything I touch . . . this is hell. Just getting through the next moment, and the one after that."

What followed were ten years of the roughest, rockiest, most unbelievably manic, altogether difficult experiences of my life. I had bouts of going back on medication, but would always stop for one reason or another. I'd make excuses, but each time it was the same thing: I convinced myself I didn't feel right on the medication. That I couldn't feel that creative spark I so relied on as part of my life. I was afraid of going back to that medically induced haze I'd been in before. I hid from it and kept riding the tornado every day. And like any tornado, my instability left chaos and destruction in its wake.

I can't say I regret those ten years. They taught me a lot. I regret a lot of the horrible decisions I made, the people I hurt, the situations I got into where I got ripped up myself. I have memories I'll never forget, instances of realizing too late I'd gotten into something because of my mania that led ultimately to disaster.

But I remember the creative highs. The way I could just fly like the wind and produce twelve thousand words in a night. How I could map out entire novels, series of books, all the things in the world I thought I could create. I wrote papers, read whole book series, stayed up for days on end, played role-playing games from morning until night, and never, ever saw anything wrong with where I was in life. Because I was living that artist's life and I thought, *Hey, this is me. This is who I am.*

I now know the truth: that was the illness talking. The "living high on life, throwing caution to the winds" voice *is* the manic voice. And unless tempered with medication and coping mechanisms, it can lead to disaster.

From 2002 until 2012 I remained largely unmedicated. And those ten years are, in hindsight, an unspoken cautionary tale of someone not flying but falling without recognizing the drop in altitude. A tale of someone on a corkscrew through rough weather, catching fire all the way down.

I went to grad school in 2012, and thank god for so many reasons that I did. It's not even my education I laud when I think of those years, but a single day in November 2012. I'd only been in classes for two months and already I was starting to lose it from the stress. The day I broke down with a massive anxiety attack after a critique from a teacher, hiccupping with tears and hyperventilating in a bathroom, I walked across the street to the health clinic and got an appointment with a mental health counselor. There a very nice man named Bob talked to me about my experiences, about what I knew about bipolar disorder.

Bob told me some truth about where I was at and what I needed. He said he was surprised I'd gotten as far as I did going the way I had been. He listened to my fears about going on meds and what happened in the past. Then he calmly explained how he was going to give me medication and we'd work together to find what worked.

The first day after I took medication, I woke up in the morning and the tornado was quieter. Not quiet, but less a twisting funnel of noise and more of a loud echo. I called up someone who was then a friend (who had experience with the medication I'd started taking) and broke down crying. I asked him: Is this what normal feels like? I had no idea it would get even better.

Six years later, I've never been off my medication a single day. And I've graduated from grad school, survived a brain surgery and being diagnosed with two serious chronic illnesses, ended up using a wheelchair, run my own business, and become a writer, with too many personal ups and downs to count. Each of them I tackled with a surety in myself I could never have had before, because I was no longer screaming through a tornado all the time. More important, I've spent those years creating games and writing work I've made with deliberateness and careful consideration. When I create, it is no longer controlled falling, but dedicated flight on a controlled course. Well, most of the time.

I won't say everything became perfect after I started medication because I won't let blogging make a liar out of me. Being bipolar is a constant system of checks and balances. These days I fight against needing my medication adjusted a lot, against depression and anxiety, mania and hypomania. I still end up flying some days, sometimes for days at a time, because as time goes on, the body changes and you have to adjust to new needs, new doses, new medication.

Coping mechanisms change, life situations go ways you never expected, mania and depression rear their ugly heads. But the day I went on medication was one of the greatest days of my life, because it was the day my creative spark stopped becoming an excuse to keep putting up with an illness that was killing me.

I did some research online (now responsibly!) about artists who were known to have fought mental illness. Google it sometime; it'll be a stark look into some suffering for art you might not know about. People know about Van Gogh, but what about Beethoven and David Foster Wallace, Georgia O'Keeffe and Sylvia Plath, Francisco Goya and Kurt Cobain, Robin Williams and Amy Winehouse? I did research and discovered artists like Mariah Carey, Demi Lovato, Catherine Zeta-Jones, Vivien Leigh, Russell Brand, Linda Hamilton, and of course Carrie Fisher all have/had bipolar disorder. Their stories, their struggles, are well known.

I read books about people theorizing about the connection between mental illness and creativity and shake my head. I don't need to know the connection, because if there is one, it doesn't matter to me. I take my medicine and work my craft at the same time because I don't need to suffer as an artist. I don't need the mania to take flight and reach inspiration. I can do that on my own.

Mental illness and the struggle against it is one I'll tackle for the rest of my life. But to quote Hannah Gadsby: "There is nothing stronger than a broken woman who has rebuilt herself." The day I started on my journey to getting better by taking medication—by denying the world my suffering and instead giving myself permission to live healthier while making art—was the day I started rebuilding myself into the strongest version of me. Every day, one more brick, with every word I write, I build myself higher.

And so I offer a special thanks to Hannah Gadsby, and her brave *Nanette*, for reminding me of how important that choice was to my life. For reminding me that I owe nobody my suffering to make what is precious to me, and that creators don't need to push aside their own mental health to be hailed as artists. Thank you, Hannah, for your strength. May you find your inspiration wherever you walk.

Six Ways of Looking at Crip Time

Ellen Samuels

When disabled folks talk about crip time, sometimes we just mean that we're late all the time—maybe because we need more sleep than nondisabled people, maybe because the accessible gate in the train station was locked. But other times, when we talk about crip time, we mean something more beautiful and forgiving. We mean, as my friend Margaret Price explains in her book *Mad at School*, we live our lives with a "flexible approach to normative time frames" like work schedules, deadlines, or even just waking and sleeping. Alison Kafer, author of *Feminist, Queer, Crip*, says that "rather than bend disabled bodies and minds to meet the clock, crip time bends the clock to meet disabled bodies and minds." I have embraced this beautiful notion for many years, living within the embrace of a crip time that lets me define my own "normal."

And yet recently I have found myself thinking about the less appealing aspects of crip time, aspects that are harder to see as liberatory, more challenging to find a way to celebrate. Now in my forties, as

I reflect on my life, these other ways of looking at crip time have been pressing deeply, leaving their mark.

———

I keep returning in my mind to a moment in a doctor's office in the summer of 1995. I was twenty-three years old and had recently entered the world of disabling illness, had crossed some invisible and excruciating threshold from being someone *with* health problems to *being a problem*, apparently insolvable. I had come to this doctor, a psychiatrist, after many months and many doctors, searching for a diagnosis to explain my constant pain, weight loss, wavering legs, and thumping heart. Like the others, this doctor didn't have an answer. What he did offer, though, was remarkable compassion and a willingness to listen.

What I keep coming back to is this one thing he said to me. "You've lost so much already in your life: your parents, your health, your independence. You have a level of loss we would usually expect to see in someone in their seventies."

Crip time is time travel. Disability and illness have the power to extract us from linear, progressive time with its normative life stages and cast us into a wormhole of backward and forward acceleration, jerky stops and starts, tedious intervals and abrupt endings. Some of us contend with the impairments of old age while still young; some of us are treated like children no matter how old we get. The medical language of illness tries to reimpose the linear, speaking in terms of the chronic, the progressive, and the terminal, of relapses and stages. But we who occupy the bodies of crip time know that we are never linear, and we rage silently—or not so silently—at the calm straightforwardness of those who live in the sheltered space of normative time.

I swim in the warm-water therapy pool at my gym, usually accompanied by men and women in their sixties and seventies and eighties. They give me sideways glances, sometimes hostile, sometimes curious: *Why are you here in our space? Why aren't you in the regular pool with the other young-looking, healthy-looking swimmers turning in neat laps back and forth?* I smile at them, I answer their questions politely, but here's something I rarely admit:

I hate them.

I hate them when, after demanding my bodily narrative, they give me their own: how they've finally had to give up cross-country skiing at age sixty-two, how frustrating it is they can't go hiking anymore. I hate them for their decades of proper health, for their unconscious privilege, for the fact that only in older age are they contending with not being able to hike or bike or knit or whatever it is they're talking about as they move in their little companionable knots around the pool. I know that I'm being unfair. I know that I know nothing about their lives, what they may have lost. So I keep my rage inside.

I keep my grief inside.

Crip time is grief time. It is a time of loss and of the crushing undertow that accompanies loss. I lost my mother when I was twenty and she was fifty-two, to a cancer that she had lived with for fifteen years. But those numbers don't say anything about the way the days slowed and swelled unbearably around her death, or how the years piled up afterward, always too much, never enough. When I fell ill just two years later, both doctors and relatives wanted to believe it was the result of my stored-up grief, my refusal to stop mourning my mother and move on with my life. Freud wrote in "Mourning and Melancholia" that "normal mourning" resolves on its own and needs no intervention. Only melancholia is a true illness, mourning without end, without resolution. The bodymind refuses to let go of the lost object and deforms itself in the process.

But I was able to let go of my mother, earnestly as I miss her. What I have found much harder to let go is the memory of my healthier self. With each new symptom, each new impairment, I grieve again for the lost time, the lost years that are now not yet to come. This is not to say that I wish for a cure—not exactly. I wish to be both myself and not-myself, a state of paradoxical longing that I think every person with chronic pain occupies at some point or another. I wish for time to split and allow two paths for my life and that I could move back and forth between them at will.

In *Arranging Grief: Sacred Time and the Body in Nineteenth-Century America*, Dana Luciano traces how grief time emerged with modernity as a temporal and affective state juxtaposed to progressive, mechanical time. She writes that "grief was aligned with a sensibility that sought to provide time with a 'human' dimension, one that would be collective rather than productive, repetitive rather than linear, reflective rather than forward-moving." This sounds very much like the notion of crip time that Alison and Margaret were talking about. But disability scholars like Alison, Margaret, and me tend to celebrate this idea of crip time, to relish its nonlinear flexibility, to explore its power and its possibility. What would it mean for us also to do what queer scholar Heather Love calls "feeling backward"? For us to hold on to that celebration, that new way of being, and yet also allow ourselves to feel the pain of crip time, its melancholy, its brokenness?

For *crip time is broken time*. It requires us to break in our bodies and minds to new rhythms, new patterns of thinking and feeling and moving through the world. It forces us to take breaks, even when we don't want to, even when we want to keep going, to move ahead. It insists that we listen to our bodyminds *so* closely, *so* attentively, in a culture that tells us to divide the two and push the body away from us while also pushing it beyond its limits. Crip time means listening to the broken languages of our bodies, translating them, honoring their words.

A year after I sat in that psychiatrist's office, learning to recognize what I had lost, I was once again back on the path to health, or to what I wanted to believe would be health. I was practicing tai chi every day, learning how to move slowly and gracefully through the world, as part of a group all making the same movements, synchronized, flowing. I felt more at home in my body, with other people's bodies, than I ever had.

Then it all came apart. My tai chi instructor kept explaining to me how to align my hips, kept looking at me quizzically and saying, "I don't know what you're doing that's wrong." Then one day at home I reached up for a book on a shelf and felt my hip separate from my body, pain zinging down my leg, which quickly turned numb. It happened in a flash, and it also lasted forever. It took me six long months in physical therapy to get back to where I could walk more than a few steps, and I was never again able to walk as far as I had before. Tai chi, which I loved deeply and which was supposed to fix me, broke me instead. It moved in one direction and my body moved in another.

And so I moved backward instead of forward, not into a state of health but further into the world of disability, the world I was now coming to understand as my own. I moved from being someone who kept *getting* sick, over and over, to someone who *was* sick all the time, whose inner clock was attuned to my own physical state rather than the external routines of a society ordered around bodies that were not like mine.

Crip time is sick time. If you work a nine-to-five, forty-hour-a-week job, what is defined as full-time work in the United States, then (if you're lucky) you accumulate a certain number of sick days. There is always a strange arithmetic to this process: maybe for every eight hours you work, you accrue one sick hour. Or maybe one for every twenty work hours, or every forty. It's never a one-to-one ratio: you have to work hard to earn the time to be sick. The assumption, of course, is that we will not be too sick too often.

When I realized I could no longer physically sustain a nine-to-five job, I feared for my future. I hadn't even worked long enough to be eligible for Social Security disability. The solution I came up with was to return to academic life, to go to graduate school and get my PhD and maybe, if I was lucky enough, to become a professor. It was, and still is, the only way I could see to support myself in crip time.

Most of my time in graduate school was sick time: for the first two years especially, all I could do was drag myself to an occasional class and write the papers required for them. My life consisted of going to campus and to the grocery store and then returning home and doing schoolwork. I worked lying down as much as possible, in the days before lightweight laptops and wireless Internet. I lay on the floor in my classrooms and stared at the scratched undersides of desks while my classmates talked.

And I loved it. I loved the rhythm of reading and writing and thinking, and I realized that this time was also my time, even though it was hard, even though other people didn't get it, even though I was alone.

Crip time is writing time. I have been writing an essay about crip time, *in* crip time, for so many years now, I wonder if I will ever get it done. In it I quote author Laura Hillenbrand about writing her best-seller *Seabiscuit* while gravely ill with chronic fatigue syndrome:

Because looking at the page made the room shimmy crazily around me, I could write only a paragraph or two a day. When I could no longer stand the spinning, I'd take a pillow into the yard and lie in the grass. . . . When I was too tired to sit at my desk, I set the laptop up on my bed. When I was too dizzy to read, I lay down and wrote with my eyes closed.

Hillenbrand's essay about her experience was published in 2003 in *The New Yorker*, where it became for a brief time the touchstone for a certain segment of the educated public to apprehend this mystery illness and, by extension, the world of chronic illness. Her status as a bestselling author lent her story a kind of credibility many of us in the chronic illness community had been struggling to gain for years.

Hillenbrand was able to write her way into cultural validity, although she remained a physical invalid. I can't count the number of times people asked me, in the wake of her success, when *I* was going to write a bestseller. As if that would be the ultimate achievement, the perfect solution to my bodily failures, to write something that Oprah Winfrey might pick for her book club—even if, like Hillenbrand, I was too sick to actually make the talk show rounds.

If I were to write a bestseller, though, I think it would be about vampires. Zombies seem more in vogue these days, and I do often feel like a zombie—especially if I've had less than ten hours of sleep—but still, I think, vampires. Because *crip time is vampire time*. It's the time of late nights and unconscious days, of life schedules lived out of sync with the waking, quotidian world. It means that sometimes the body confines us like a coffin, the boundary between life and death blurred with no end in sight. Like *Buffy*'s Angel and *True Blood*'s Bill, we live out of time, watching others' lives continue like clockwork while we lurk in the shadows. And like them, we can look deceptively, painfully young even while we age, weary to our bones.

My own disabling condition, a genetic disease, means that the collagen in my body doesn't hold its shape. This is bad news for my joints and tendons, my heart and my gut—but great for my skin, which remains soft and wrinkle-free into my forties, meaning I'm perpetually mistaken for being younger. One of the medical criteria for my condition is, literally, having skin "like velvet." In our youth-obsessed culture, vampiric agelessness is often seen as a good thing, and it does come with certain privileges. But I sometimes tire of not being taken seriously, of working my sick self into the ground to climb the tenure ladder while being perceived as a perpetual graduate student.

And on a deeper level, being a crip vampire spins me back into that whirlpool of time travel. I look twenty-five, feel eighty-five, and just want to live like the other fortysomethings I know. I want to be aligned, synchronous, part of the regular order of the world.

Like the leaves just now turning as the year spins toward its end, I want sometimes to be part of nature, to live within its time. But I don't. My life has turned another way.

I live in crip time now.

Content notes: abuse, racism, ableist language, child neglect, torture, poisoning, self-harm

Lost Cause

Reyma McCoy McDeid

There's a rite of passage many disabled people experience during their formative years, and it is this: being told by someone with influence in your young life that you are a "lost cause." For many, it is a teacher who abuses them with the declarative statement. For me, it was my grandfather.

It wasn't said directly to me, but instead to an aunt as rationale for his and my grandmother's choosing to decline taking me in after Child Protection Services found me after I had been home alone for five days.

My mother had abandoned me to enroll in a high-end weight-loss retreat in Beverly Hills.

My grandparents—who had enjoyed some positive press state-wide for having fostered a group of siblings who'd lost their parents in an accident in the 1970s—declined to take me in.

Those siblings had been bubbly, engaging, and white.

My grandparents were white.

I, however, was their white daughter's little Black accident. And, as it was determined after I became a ward of the State of California in 1986, I was autistic. I didn't find out about the "lost cause" conversation until the summer I graduated from high school twelve years later, when my aunt casually brought it up. I'd been acquainted with her for about four years by this time. "I was going to take you in myself," she said as she drove us on the 101 down the Peninsula, "but Dad told me that he didn't think it would be the right thing to do because you were a 'lost cause.'"

I looked at the highway without blinking.

"Lost cause?"

She cleared her throat. "Well, you rocked back and forth a lot and repeated what everyone around you said all the time, and your hair was a mess. . . . You wouldn't stop picking at it. . . . He and Mom . . . I guess they were worried that you were retarded or something. . . ."

She sat up straighter and patted my knee. "But hey, all those scholarships you got offered this year really show how wrong he was, don't they? Not everyone gets full rides, you know? Especially if their moms die during freshman year like yours did! Good for you. I know he's proud."

"Yeah."

And with that, I didn't mention autism again for nearly fifteen years.

When I was thirty-one, I returned to California after a long sojourn in the Midwest.

I was disgruntled with the concept of making a living, seriously ill with an autoimmune disease, and frankly, chronically overstimulated.

I'd had nearly a hundred jobs since my senior year in high school. My tenure at each had lasted from one hour and eleven minutes (telemarketer) to one weekend (flight attendant) to three months (executive director of a nonprofit) and so on. I'd try to mow past my limited interpersonal skills, my strong sensitivities to light/sound, and the incessant pumping of adrenaline in my system as a result of the stress of having to "play" neurotypical at all times. I failed.

I felt like a lost cause. So I'd given away everything I owned and gone out to Mount Shasta to become a monk. Literally. A Zen Buddhist monk. And why not? Zen Buddhist monks have few possessions or modern-day responsibilities and just sit around all day quietly contemplating enlightenment. Or so I thought, in my breezy naiveté.

I did a work exchange at a commune run by two wealthy hippies up the road from Shasta Abbey with the intention of eventually moving into the abbey full time. Sharon, the commune's matriarch, was Jewish and from Newark but disavowed those origins in exchange for a rebrand as a "sturdy old Vermont Unitarian."

Kelly was the otherworldly boomer son of a Belgian countess. He had a habit of looking down when Sharon spoke for him. Which was often.

Sharon was a self-published author and had earned a PhD in philosophy from a school that later lost its accreditation. She was, in fact, working on a manuscript that differentiated bipolar disorder from autism. We were in the kitchen one evening as she filled me in on its details: "You can't be autistic and bipolar at the same time! Autism is a left-brain phenomenon and bipolar centers in the right brain."

"What empirical studies have you done to test your hypothesis?" I asked as I stacked plates in the cupboard. Kelly sat at the kitchen table as his eyes stared into space.

"I live with Kelly and *he's* autistic," Sharon said. Kelly looked

down. "Plus my mother was autistic. My daughter is autistic. I diagnosed them all, and I know more about this subject than anyone
else!"

I put a plate down on the counter, looked at Sharon, and said,
"I'm autistic."

She looked at me as if I'd taken her plate and Frisbee'd it into the
wall. Then she smiled and said, "I know that. I diagnosed you, too."

I replied, "No, you did not. I was diagnosed when I was six years
old. You had nothing to do with it."

Kelly looked up at me.

I went on to say, "It's perfectly acceptable for an individual to
self-diagnose as autistic. Especially women, who are chronically under-
diagnosed by professionals. But I have concerns about someone who
has no credentials or training in developmental disabilities diagnosing
people as autistic, let alone writing a book on the subject."

Sharon walked out of the kitchen, and I returned to stacking
dishes.

The next morning, Sharon and I found ourselves back in the
kitchen. "You know, the abbey is inheriting my entire estate when I
die," she said. She opened a cupboard and took out a small bottle. She
measured out a few tablespoons of clear liquid and poured them into
a glass. Kelly walked in, and she handed him the glass. He drank it.

"Do you want to try some, Reyma? It helps chelate heavy metals
out of your brain. The heavy metals cause autism."

I could feel the adrenaline building up inside of me.

"No, I'm good."

I later returned to the kitchen to look at the bottle. The label on
it said MSM in large letters. A Google search yielded scores of troubling
articles on so-called chelation therapy sessions performed by mothers
on their autistic children.

In essence, "chelation therapy" entailed the administering of bleach to children, and in this case, Kelly.

I attempted to be strategic in the days and months that followed because it was clear to me that I had found myself in a toxic living arrangement. Residents and guests came and went from the commune with regularity, many leaving after realizing that the commune was no utopia.

I spent all of my free hours at the abbey, learning, meditating, and gardening.

My autoimmune disorder went into remission.

Then Kelly became ill with unexplained weight loss, nausea, fatigue. He'd been dosing himself with MSM for years and it seemed that it had caught up with him. By this time Sharon, Kelly, and I were the only people in residence at the commune, and given our remote location, I became alarmed as Sharon and Kelly engaged in "detox" after "detox" outside of the purview of other people.

I went to a trusted monk at the abbey with my concerns. I said, "I know that Sharon is a major contributor to the abbey, but I am concerned about—"

"Reyma, I need to warn you that this abbey is in the practice of not communicating with people who are divisive," the monk told me as she shifted uncomfortably.

"Oh. Okay."

I left the commune, the abbey, and Mount Shasta one week later.

I returned to the Midwest and got job number 101, as a middle manager for a supported employment program. I got married.

I got pregnant.

I became symptomatic. I am unable to "mask" autism symptoms—hypersensitivity to sound/light/smells, limited tolerance for social situations, obsessive focus on tawdry details, and seemingly exaggerated responses to physiological discomfort—when I am in physical pain, and my pregnancy was very difficult.

My husband made it clear that he had no interest in being a parent, so I moved out.

I disclosed my disability at work. I had no choice. I was in physical agony and could no longer mask my symptoms.

My coworkers, all passionate about serving people with disabilities, did not appreciate having a disabled coworker. Or supervisor, for that matter.

My annual performance review, administered while I was eight months pregnant, barely qualified me for an inflation adjustment raise and was followed immediately by a write-up for being a source of negativity for the department.

I went home and had a meltdown.

I punched my stomach once, forgetting for a millisecond that I was pregnant, then switched to bashing my head into the bathroom door over and over again.

"She's a lost cause."

I heard my now-dead grandfather say that every time my head made contact with the door.

I took a day off.

I went back to work.

Eventually I drove myself to the hospital to have my baby.

Four days later, I drove us home.

I became the executive director of Central Iowa Center for Independent Living, or CICIL, in Des Moines while my daughter was still an infant.

"Good luck with that! That organization is a lost cause!" a colleague told me the week before I started.

I was oblivious. I'd never heard of the independent living movement and was totally unaware of the existence of CICIL prior to seeing the position listed on a job board. Turns out that as both the civil rights and women's rights movements were effecting change in the United States, the independent living movement was also underway working to ensure that the overall civil and human rights movement was inclusive of disability.

I attended a monthly board meeting the Saturday before my start date. It lasted six hours. Board members dozed as onlookers strolled in and out of the boardroom, eating doughnuts and using the computers.

The male staff members quit without notice in rapid succession, unwilling to report to me—a woman, and a Black one at that.

I got a notice in the mail that the organization was under review for a potential discrimination lawsuit against the former assistant director.

I shut the organization down for two weeks in order to train staff, organize files, hire an accountant, and piece together an understanding of CICIL's legal liability regarding the discrimination complaint.

"I don't mean to be blunt, but I'd start looking for other employment if I were you. This is a lost-cause situation," CICIL's attorney told me.

"You know, I'd really love it if people would stop telling me that," I said.

And I meant it.

Today, CICIL is the city of Des Moines' Organization of 2018 and is recognized as one of the best supported-employment providers in Iowa. And ultimately it was my neurodiversity that set CICIL on a course toward recovery and rebirth: I obsessively worked to build a case against the individual who filed a complaint against the organization, and I broached unfiltered conversations with Iowa stakeholders without concern for anyone's feelings. Specifically I identified gaps in the independent living movement that pertain to racism and internalized ableism particular to developmentally disabled people. This all resulted in a run for state office in Iowa.

Recently, my systems advocacy within the independent living movement resulted in my election to the role of treasurer on the National Council on Independent Living's board of directors. I am now the first developmentally disabled person to hold an executive office with the organization.

Lost cause, indeed.

On NYC's Paratransit, Fighting for Safety, Respect, and Human Dignity

Britney Wilson

He pulled up on the wrong side of the street fifteen minutes late for my pickup time. I was sitting outside, in front of the New York City office building where I work, in a chair that the security guards at my job have set aside for me. They bring it outside when I come downstairs in the evening and take it back inside whenever I get picked up, so I don't have to stand while I wait anymore. I was on the left side of the street; he pulled up on the right. I stood when I saw him, and taking a few steps closer to the tide of people rippling endlessly down the sidewalk that early evening, I waved one of my crutches in the air trying to get his attention. He looked up and down the street. I wasn't sure if he'd seen me.

"Excuse me," I said, taking a few more quick half steps forward, trying to catch the attention of a passerby, "do you see that Access-A-Ride across the street?"

"The what?" the passerby asked.

"The Access-A-Ride," I repeated. "That little blue-and-white bus across the street." I pointed my crutch in its direction, and his gaze followed its path.

"Oh," he said. But just as I was about to request the man's assistance, I saw that the driver had finally spotted me. He put his hand up as if to tell me to stay put.

"Never mind. I think he sees me," I said. "Thanks anyway."

My Access-A-Ride driver, a skinny older Black man with glasses and a graying beard, exited the vehicle and crossed the street toward me. I bravely parted the latest oncoming wave of pedestrians and made my way to the curb to meet him.

"Come on," the driver said when he reached me, urging me to step right out into traffic on Broadway and cross with him, but I was reluctant.

"I'd rather wait for the light to change," I said.

"Don't worry, I'll stop traffic for you," he said, moving toward the middle of the street, his right hand extended making a "stop" motion toward the oncoming cars. I tried to pick up my pace while also being careful not to place my crutch tips on anything slippery or get too close to other pedestrians rushing to the other side of the street.

"Take your time. I'll make them wait," he said, attempting to reassure me. I wasn't reassured.

Access-A-Ride is New York City's paratransit service. It provides transportation within the five boroughs of New York City to hundreds of thousands of elderly and disabled New Yorkers unable to use a transit system in which less than 20 percent of subway stations are accessible. It is a "shared ride, door-to-door" service in which New York City Transit contracts with private carrier companies, who use "Access-A-

Ride-branded" vehicles, including cars, minivans, and small buses to transport passengers. The fare is the same as all other public transportation in New York City.

Passengers usually have different drivers and carriers for each trip. So even passengers like me—people who use the service twice a day to travel to and from work—will usually have a different driver in the morning and the evening, and a completely different set of drivers the next day, and likely for the rest of the week. I had never seen this driver before.

A native New Yorker, born with cerebral palsy, I began using Access-A-Ride sixteen years ago at eleven years old, around the age that I suspect many New York City kids begin riding public transportation by themselves. Over the first eight of those sixteen years, I protested the service's inefficiency and unreliability in true millennial fashion: I complained to family, friends, and social media followers, wrote blog posts, and started Change.org petitions, generally filing formal complaints only when something especially ridiculous happened.

But that was only phase one. My ultimate plan was to go to law school and gain the knowledge and skills necessary to fight, on behalf of myself and others, all the rampant isms I'd faced as a disabled Black girl born and raised in Mike Tyson's hometown.

Two years ago, after graduating from the University of Pennsylvania Law School, I returned home and increased my advocacy for passengers using the service. Since then, I've been documenting and filing formal complaints about routes and other general incidents of bad service.

———

As I was getting on the bus that evening, a news segment I'd been featured in was scheduled to air on the local news. Although I work only eight miles away from my job—an approximately forty-five-minute drive for most—the reporter followed Access-A-Ride as it took me from my home in Brooklyn through Queens to a stop on East 64th Street in midtown Manhattan before dropping me off at work in lower Manhattan nearly two hours later, not to mention fifteen minutes past my scheduled appointment time. Because the rides are shared, such roundabout two-hour excursions each way were a common practice. That evening I had no idea what to expect when I got on board. I just hoped that I'd at least be traveling toward my house.

Things seemed to be going pretty well at first. There was another woman on the bus when I boarded it. The buses are not the big ones you might associate with New York City. They usually have only about six seats and some open space in the back for wheelchairs. The woman was seated in the second row on the left side in a window seat. I sat in the front right corner closest to the door. The driver started heading to the Manhattan Bridge—Brooklyn-bound and toward home—and I thought it might be a good day. I put my headphones on and responded to the flurry of text messages I had received from my uncle about my six p.m. news segment.

"I'm missing it," I texted him. "I'm on Access-A-Ride, of course. Does it highlight the changes I recommended?"

I'd recently spoken at a Metropolitan Transportation Authority (MTA) board meeting to propose three major changes to Access-A-Ride: improved routing, not requiring riders to wait outside for rides that are not close by, and more direct communication between customers and drivers about rides.

Access-A-Ride customers must schedule rides by five p.m. the day before travel. Depending on our "appointment time," we receive a computer-generated pickup time. Travel times are supposed to be coordinated by the distance between a passenger's pickup and drop-off locations, but pickup times are often as many as two hours ahead of appointment times. For example, Access-A-Ride anticipates a "maximum ride time" of one hour and thirty-five minutes for a travel distance between six and nine miles.

Rain, shine, and seasons aside, passengers scheduling rides are instructed by call center operators to be *outside* our pickup location at our scheduled pickup time, even though our ride may be nowhere near at that time. We are also instructed to be prepared to wait up to thirty minutes for our drivers in case of traffic or delays. Drivers who arrive within that "thirty-minute window" are still considered to be on time, even though the passenger may have been outside for up to half an hour at that point. Those thirty-minute delays may actually turn into hours-long waits for many customers, as drivers must follow predetermined routes that lengthen trips and exacerbate travel conditions. Drivers, on the other hand, are instructed to give late passengers only a five-minute grace period. Drivers are also encouraged to call passengers if they do not see us when they arrive, but such calls are considered a courtesy, not a requirement.

One winter evening while I was on the bus, the driver stopped to pick up a passenger who wasn't outside when we arrived. After a few minutes, a Black woman who was probably in her seventies exited a nearby McDonald's hurriedly pushing a walker in front of her. There were three black garbage bags resting on the seat of her walker. As the driver got off the bus to let the lift down, he yelled, "You're lucky I didn't leave you. It's been more than five minutes."

"Five minutes?" she asked. "I've been waiting for this ride for over three hours. The people in the McDonald's let me sit down and wait inside, and I didn't see you when you first pulled up."

"You're over the bag limit," the driver added. "The limit is two.

You have three. That's what's wrong with Access-A-Ride people. You take advantage. You're spoiled and entitled."

The concept of entitlement is familiar jargon in discussions of race and class, and it is just as widespread in the realm of disability. It's the idea that we are acting as if someone owes us something rather than merely asking to be treated with the respect and human dignity we deserve. It is the belief that people of a certain status or apparent condition have no right to demand better because we should just be happy with whatever we get. We should be happy we have anything at all.

Outraged at the driver's callous attitude, the woman told him he didn't even have to touch her bags, because they were sitting on her walker. She explained that she had the three garbage bags because she got to go grocery shopping only once in a while. To make the most of her limited trips, she put as many grocery bags as she could into the three garbage bags, to lessen the number of individual bags she traveled with to heed the Access-A-Ride limit.

"Do you have a mother?" she asked him. "Would you want someone treating her this way when she gets old?"

———————————

In one of the world's most crowded cities, where traffic is jammed almost more often than not, maybe it's not surprising that Access-A-Ride vehicles can take a long time to get where they're going. But the inefficient protocol for communicating with drivers unnecessarily adds to users' stress and anxiety. For example, a passenger who wants to locate the ride he or she is waiting for must call a transit switchboard operator, who then reads a GPS to tell the passenger where the driver is. If the transit operator cannot track the passenger's ride by GPS, or the passenger needs to communicate some other information to the driver, the transit operator must call the carrier who dispatched the ride, who then calls the driver, before transit relays all that information to the passenger. Violations of any Access-A-Ride rules, including canceling a trip with less than two hours' notice, can lead to point assessments that affect passengers' service eligibility. A recent Access-A-Ride audit by the New York City comptroller found that more than 31,000 passengers had been stranded in 2015.

Presumably to alleviate some of these issues, Access-A-Ride's reimbursement policy allows passengers whose rides have not arrived within the thirty-minute wait window to take a taxi and request reimbursement from Transit. However, this is not a viable alternative for many Access-A-Ride users, given the limited number of accessible taxis in New York City and the fact that many people cannot afford to pay up front for expensive taxi rides that require two or three months for reimbursement.

Despite the advance scheduling and little room for change or spontaneity that Access-A-Ride demands of its customers, lack of predictability is the service's hallmark trait. Most public transportation users choose to get on a bus or a train that's traveling toward their destination and get off at their intended stop in the order in which those stops come along the route. In contrast, Access-A-Ride users have no idea which direction their rides will travel or how many stops will be made before their destinations. In picking up and dropping off passengers on those rides, a meandering city tour is not uncommon—including riding past your destination only to ride back to it.

While talking with an Access-A-Ride customer service representative to follow up on my complaint about my not so merry-go-round two-hour journeys to work, the representative advised me never to tell Access-A-Ride the real time that I have to be anywhere. (I don't.) I explained that even if I did arrive at work by my scheduled appointment time, I still had the same complaint about being driven around the city for two hours, often past my destination.

"Even when you still get there on time?" he clarified.

"Yes."

"I don't understand the problem, then."

So boarding an Access-A-Ride that appeared to be moving toward my destination was already a small victory for me that day.

"Get your ass out of the street!" the driver yelled out his window at a woman scurrying across the street as the bus approached. The bus came to a sudden and jolting halt that propelled me forward in my seat. Just barely making it out of the bus's path, the woman glared at him.

"That's why your ass shouldn't have been in the street," he yelled back.

"Sorry," he said to the other passenger and me.

As a civil rights attorney, I tend to think in terms of systems. So despite many of the eccentric, annoying, inappropriate, and sometimes disturbing things some Access-A-Ride drivers do, most of my Access-A-Ride complaints are with policies, not individual drivers—unless an individual driver's behavior represents a larger systemic problem I think Transit can address with a rule or policy change. Many drivers are great and have openly agreed with me about changes that need to be made to the system.

One evening while driving me home, a driver yawned, said how tired he was, and explained that he had been driving all day.

"What's the legal limit for how many hours you all are allowed to drive in a day?" I asked.

"Ten," he said.

"And how many hours have you been driving today?"

"Fifteen."

Although I usually try to ignore individual drivers' personalities or habits—why argue with a stranger who has your life in his or her hands?—occasionally I have issues with individual drivers. Whether they realize it or not, I am keenly aware that how they treat me may be influenced by how I look, and by extension, what they think they can get away with in my presence. I'm a five-foot-one Black woman on crutches. On an average day, most people are shocked when I open my mouth and they realize I'm not sixteen.

Driving through the Financial District in Manhattan one morning, while transporting me to my job, a driver clearly new to the road expressed her anxiety.

"I hate driving in Manhattan," she said. "Look at all the suits crossing in the middle of the street. They're probably lawyers—crooks not looking where they're going. Don't you hate lawyers?" she asked.

"Yeah, sometimes," I said.

Anyone who has ever been a passenger knows that some drivers take directions better than others. Some are especially unreceptive when those directions are coming from a little Black girl.

"Miss, I know how to do my job. You'll get there," one driver retorted defensively when I suggested a route for him to take. I've endured countless drivers who connect their cell phones to the car's Bluetooth and conduct intimate and sometimes lengthy conversations through the car speakers. Think *Maury* or *General Hospital*.

"Girl, you just need to leave him, because this story is absolutely ridiculous and it is way too early in the morning for all of this," I was tempted to interject to the stranger who was confessing her woes to her driver friend (and me) through the car speakers. Instead, I just burst into laughter at the sheer ludicrousness of having to listen to the story.

"I'm going to call you back. I've got a passenger," the driver finally said.

Then there are the drivers who, without bothering to ask whether I mind, will turn up the Power 105.1 or Hot 97 stations (what advertisers would stereotype as "urban radio," for nonnative New Yorkers) when I get on board, only to turn it down, turn it off, or change the station if we happen to pick up a white passenger, or sometimes even an older Black passenger. There was one driver who detoured through the McDonald's drive-through to get breakfast before proceeding with the rest of her route. (No, she did not get or offer to get me anything.) While these "microaggressions" are important to pay attention to, and are usually symptomatic of larger issues, they are not the incidents about which I tend to file complaints.

We made it to Brooklyn. While driving to the other passenger's house, the driver unleashed a string of random curse words at an unspecified target: the road, the air, other drivers, whoever was listening.

"I apologize for all the profanities," he said, turning slightly toward me and the other passenger.

A few minutes later, he dropped the other passenger off. She lived only about ten minutes away from me, so I expected to be home soon. I silently celebrated that evening's efficient routing and wondered if it was the result of advocacy or luck. As he turned onto my residential block, everything was quiet and no one else was outside. I took my headphones off and began to put my cell phone inside my purse and gather my things. Knowing that no one else was home, I searched for my house keys. The driver pulled up to my house, opened the bus door, rose, and made an announcement.

"I've got to pee," he said. "Had to go since I picked you up in Manhattan."

I found my keys, draped them around my neck, and wondered why he felt the need to share this information.

Grabbing a Styrofoam coffee cup, he began walking toward me. Thinking he was going to assist me off of the bus, I prepared to hand him my crutches, but he didn't take them.

"I'm just going to go in this cup," he said casually, walking past the open door to an aisle seat. I still wasn't quite processing what was happening. We were at my house. He said he had to pee. Why was he telling me this, and more important, why wasn't he taking my crutches so that he could get me off this bus and do whatever he needed to do? Was he about to run off the bus and pee? If so, why was he walking past the open door? Why wasn't he running off the bus or something?

He began to unzip his fly and then it hit me. He was going to pee, right then and there, in my face. One of my friends from law school had recently told me about the shock she'd felt when one of her white coworkers asked her how to spell the n-word. She was so taken aback by the question, and by her coworker's willingness to ask her the question, that she didn't know how to respond.

"What!" I had said over the phone, "Why did she need to spell that?"

"I have no idea," she responded.

"Has she not heard of Google or a dictionary?" I asked, outraged. "She couldn't sound it out?"

"That's what I wanted to know," she said.

"And why in the world would she ask you of all people, a Black woman?"

"I don't know," she answered. "I was so shocked."

"So what did you do?" I had to know.

"I spelled it," she said.

She immediately regretted her response. She told me that in that moment she wished she had been me because she knew that I would have had some sort of comeback. I told her not to beat herself up because none of us knows what we'd do in a certain situation until it arises. Some people's audacity is just shocking. In that moment, with a stranger unzipping his fly to urinate in my presence, I had no comeback. A million thoughts floated through my head in a one-minute span, but none made it to my mouth.

I felt ridiculous and defensive. On one hand, the man was urinating, and as inappropriate and disgusting as that was, it was not physically harmful. *Should I scream right now?* I wondered. *Would that be appropriate, or would I be unnecessarily causing a scene?* I imagined one of my neighbors coming outside and asking what the commotion was, and having to say that a man had peed. On the other hand, knowing that people with disabilities face a higher risk of sexual assault than many other groups, I said a silent prayer to myself and thought, *If this man is willing to take out his private parts and urinate in front of a stranger, what else is he willing to do? I'm already at a physical disadvantage. I can't afford not to be prepared if he tries anything else.* I knew I had to be prepared to fight or somehow get off of that bus.

Long before *respectability politics* became a popular colloquial term, I thought education would help people recognize that my humanity and my disability aren't mutually exclusive. Many people of color grew up hearing the "you must be twice as good" speech as an antidote to racism; I got it as the antidote to both racism and ableism. I wanted to be taken seriously and I thought higher education would help.

Nothing has taught me what a trap that was more than these past two years, after having earned my law degree, yet still having to endure the obstacles that come with being Black, a woman, and disabled in this society, in this city, and in this world. At the moment the driver decided to urinate in front of me, caught between panic and ridicule, shock and disgust, I was reminded of a realization I have faced with many of my own clients: just knowing your rights (or your worth or value) will never be enough if you are powerless to force someone else to respect them.

In that moment, I thought, *If this man does try anything, your shiny Ivy League law degree will not save you. He does not care how hard you have worked to defy stereotypes or to prove anyone wrong.*

I reminded myself, *Right now, he's only urinating.* Then I resented having to calm myself with that rationalization.

I thought about just leaving my bags and trying to make a break for it. I knew that with my crutches, I couldn't dismount the stairs to get off the bus on my own. Ideally, I needed someone to hold them while I held the railing, as drivers normally do for me. I thought about throwing my crutches outside, using the railing to come down the stairs, and picking them up once I got outside. I wondered if I was overreacting and if trying to get away from this strange man urinating was worth risking injury. I was frustrated at being mere feet away from my house but having to engage in this weird mental calculus because I needed assistance to go anywhere.

Is Transit trolling me? I wondered. *Is someone sitting in the office laughing at this wannabe advocate and reformer who has a strange man's junk in her face right now?*

It occurred to me, though, that anyone who could calmly urinate in a customer's presence was probably not someone I wanted to challenge or upset. At that moment, I decided I just didn't want to have to see it. So, I said nothing and turned my head away in disgust and disbelief.

When he was finished, a minute later that felt like a day, he took my crutches to assist me in getting off the bus. I hated the thought of his having to touch them, but I had no other choice. I handed him the bottom half, hoping that his hands would not get anywhere near the handle part that I actually had to hold. As if nothing had happened, he asked if I wanted him to hold my purse or my lunch bag.

"No, it's okay," I said, draping them both around my head and across one shoulder. "I've got it."

His calmness unsettled me. I still had questions. What kind of disregard for a person do you have to have to openly urinate in her presence? If he had to go so badly, why didn't he run into the Starbucks near where he'd picked me up in Manhattan, like so many other drivers had done before him? Why did he wait until it was just the two of us on the bus? Why was I the passenger he chose to pee in front of? Would he have done this if I were white?

Why didn't he at least go to some back corner of the bus where I wouldn't have been able to see him? Why did he feel so comfortable announcing it first? I would have been less offended if he had peed on my front lawn, a destination closer to him than where he chose to go. That way we wouldn't have had to be in the same space at the same time while he went. I would have felt better if he had wet himself. At least then his urinating wouldn't have felt like an intentional, rational choice, but an unavoidable emergency. I would have felt as if he did it because he had to, and not simply because he could.

As I got off the bus, he offered to open my front gate for me.

"No, thank you," I said. "I've got it."

I went inside as quickly as I could. I washed my hands, wiped down my crutches, and called Transit to file a complaint.

A few minutes after that, I recapped the story for my grandmother and uncle.

"Man, that's crazy," my uncle said. "You really have to get your license."

"It was just the two of you on the bus and you didn't record it?" my grandmother asked.

"No, Grandma." I wasn't expecting the man to pee in my face. "I was trying *not* to see it, rather than capture it."

"Well then, there's nothing you can do," she said. "It would be your word against his. Who's going to believe you?"

I don't know, I thought. *I can barely believe it myself.*

Gaining Power through Communication Access

Lateef McLeod

From "Assisted Technology," episode three of the podcast Disability Visibility, *first aired in October 2017*

LATEEF McLEOD: [typing] My . . . name is . . . Lateef . . . McLeod. My name is Lateef McLeod. I am currently a doctoral student in the Anthropology and Social Change program at California Institute of Integral Studies. I plan to concentrate my studies on how people with significant disabilities can acquire more political and social power within this society. More media exposure is part of this acquiring of power. That is why your podcast is important, along with my writing. I am in the process of writing another poetry book and a novel where I will be highlighting more disability issues. I am also busy doing advocacy work at my church, Allen Temple Baptist Church, in the Persons with Disabilities Ministry and with the International Society for Augmentative and Alternative Communication, where I am lead committee chair.

ALICE WONG: So, Lateef, tell me a little bit about the types of assistive technology that you use and that you can't live without.

LATEEF: [typing] The assistive technologies that I cannot live without are my power wheelchair, because that is how I get around, and the Proloquo2Go and Proloquo4Text apps on my iPad and my iPhone, because that is how I communicate.

ALICE: Yep, I'm in a power chair, too. And without my computer and without my wheelchair, I would be stuck at home. They're pretty much essential to my life.

LATEEF: [typing] Yes. Yes, and of course I cannot live without my laptop.

ALICE: So we're talking about assistive technology, especially ones that assist with communication. What is augmentative and alternative communication, for people who've never heard of that term? It's also known as AAC.

LATEEF: Augmentative and alternative communication is nonverbal communication for people with speech disabilities, using symbols, letters, and words on low-tech and high-tech devices.

ALICE: And how have you used AAC throughout your life? Was it all throughout your life or only later, as you got a little older?

LATEEF: [typing] I started using AAC when I was six and obtained my first Touch Talker.

ALICE: Obviously, you've seen a lot of changes throughout the years with AAC and other forms of assistive technology. As you grew up, what was it like using all the different kind of devices as time has gone on? What have you observed and experienced?

LATEEF: [typing] The main difference between my iPad and my other AAC devices is that the iPad is mass-produced and, as a result, is much more inexpensive than the AAC devices that I had before that were produced specifically for people with complex communication needs. As a result, my other devices were thousands of dollars compared to my iPad, which was hundreds of dollars.

ALICE: Yeah, definitely I think the lean toward universal design has really put the AAC and other forms of assistive technology in the hands of disabled people, many of whom do not have money or [who] might not have insurance to cover devices and technology like this. What do you think can be done to get more iPads and other forms of assistive technology to nonspeaking disabled people who really need it?

LATEEF: I think devices need to be more integrated with other devices people normally buy, like phones, tablets, and computers, so that the overhead cost will come down.

ALICE: I totally agree with you. There's this rehabilitation-industrial complex where some of these devices you used in the past were designed and created for people with complex disabilities that's medicalized, and technology is so much more than that. And for me, the stuff that I used in the past that was designed for us is usually not only, like you said, very expensive, but it's often very ugly and not the easiest to use. And very rarely are these kinds of technology and devices created by disabled people, but that's slowly changing.

[upbeat electronica]

Can you tell me about an example of, let's say, before iPads, before iPhones, before Wi-Fi and laptops, a device that you used for AAC that did what you needed to do but that you really kinda didn't like or that was really difficult to use?

LATEEF: One of my first devices was called Touch Talker, and it was a bulky thing with picture icons on it. And I had to remember picture sequences to access instant phrases. But I always would forget the phrases and would just spell everything out.

ALICE: Yeah, I imagine that you had to remember a lot of things, depending on the device, because they're so limited and you have limited choices.

So, you mentioned you were six when you first started using AAC. Do you remember what life was like before you started using AAC and other forms of technology like this?

LATEEF: Before I acquired my first AAC device, which was a Touch Talker, my mom made picture boards where I could point to different words. I also could vocalize simple words and could perform rudimentary sign language.

ALICE: What do you think is the importance of AAC and other forms of assistive technology for people with disabilities, as you've seen in your own life and with people in the disability community?

LATEEF: [typing] The importance of AAC should be obvious, because it allows people who have complex communication needs to express themselves and interact with people in their community.

ALICE: Absolutely. If you had a wish list, or you're in a room with designers and engineers and creators, what improvements would you like with the tech you're using right now? What would you like to see in the future in terms of new forms of AAC or assistive technology?

LATEEF: On the issue of improving the design of AAC, it is definitely an ongoing thing. My first, and the most important, issue that I think needs to be addressed is more availability of AAC devices to those who need them at a more affordable price. I would like to make sure that everyone who needs a device has one.

ALICE: Yeah, I think the line between technology and assistive technology is really blurry, right? Everybody who has an iPhone can use Siri, and Siri is a form of assistive technology for a lot of people with disabilities. . . . When more people think of it as a standard feature, it could only help everyone. Is there anything you would like to see in the future that you would really benefit from but that you haven't seen yet?

LATEEF: I would like to have a vocal ID for my AAC devices, because they are advertised to produce a more personalized digital voice that will sound like the particular user.

ALICE: Mm, yeah, that would be nice. It would be really nice to have a customized voice to really reflect your personality, 'cause that must be pretty challenging, to get the full expression of your emotions and personality from a device that sounds somewhat standardized.

LATEEF: People who have AAC definitely have a lot of issues beyond acquiring the right AAC so that we can communicate. Some of us have severe mobility disabilities as well. So that further marginalizes us in our community. Because of our challenges with communication, we face more seclusion and isolation than other members of the population.

So what I am studying now in my graduate program is how people who use AAC can gain the social and political power to be more included and engaged in society. We need more than technology to fix this problem; we need to change the consciousness of society to be more accepting to people who use AAC.

ALICE: I totally agree with you! Lateef, you're also a poet, and I was wondering if you can share one that I really love, "I Am Too Pretty for Some 'Ugly Laws'"?

LATEEF:

> I am not supposed to be here
> in this body,
> here
> speaking to you.
> My mere presence
> of erratic moving limbs
> and drooling smile
> used to be scrubbed
> off the public pavement.
> Ugly laws used to be
> on many U.S. cities' lawbooks,
> beginning in Chicago in 1867,
> stating that "any person who is
> diseased, maimed, mutilated,

or in any way deformed
so as to be an unsightly or disgusting object,
or an improper person to be allowed
in or on the streets, highways, thoroughfares,
or public places in this city,
shall not therein or thereon
expose himself to public view,
under the penalty of $1 for each offense."
Any person who looked like me
was deemed disgusting
and was locked away
from the eyes of the upstanding citizens.
I am too pretty for some Ugly Laws,
Too smooth to be shut in.
Too smart and eclectic
for any box you put me in.
My swagger is too bold
to be swept up in these public streets.
You can stare at me all you want.
No cop will bust in my head
and carry me away to an institution.
No doctor will diagnose me
a helpless invalid with an incurable disease.
No angry mob with clubs and torches
will try to run me out of town.
Whatever you do,
my roots are rigid
like a hundred-year-old tree.
I will stay right here
to glare at your ugly face, too.

PART 4

Connecting

Disability justice exists every place two disabled
people meet—at a kitchen table, on heating pads
in bed talking to our loves.
                    —Leah Lakshmi Piepzna-Samarasinha

The Fearless Benjamin Lay
Activist, Abolitionist, Dwarf Person

Eugene Grant

I didn't learn of Benjamin Lay until I was thirty-one years old. This is important, because I myself have dwarfism. There is a shameful absence of books documenting the lives of important historical figures with dwarfism. Just as *Game of Thrones* and Tyrion Lannister alone cannot compensate—as many people of average height seem to think he does—for centuries of ridicule and abuse, so Marcus Rediker and *The Fearless Benjamin Lay* cannot make up for this dearth of representation, but the book is a significant step forward.

Who was Benjamin Lay? Born in England in 1682, Lay was one of the first white radical abolitionists. An autodidact, he was a sailor, glove maker, bookseller, and author. He wrote one of the world's first abolitionist texts, *All Slave-Keepers That Keep the Innocent in Bondage, Apostates*. A devout Quaker, Lay loudly called for the church to cast out slave owners. He boycotted slave-produced commodities.

His time at sea, and particularly his experiences in Barbados, fueled his hatred of slavery, and he later became notorious for theatrical protests at Quaker meetings. In one spectacular demonstration, in 1738 at the Philadelphia Yearly Meeting, he hid a bladder filled with red juice inside a book, then ran his sword through the text, spattering "blood" on the stunned slave owners present.

At the time, many Quakers resisted Lay's abolitionist views. Just as Lay had called for slave keepers to be cast out of the church, they cast him out of his. They disowned him. They denounced his book. They stopped him speaking at meetings—often physically removing him from the premises. They even withheld his marriage certificate to his wife, Sarah.

While talking and tweeting about Lay's life, I encountered those who—in good will, I'm sure—thought it best to celebrate Lay's achievements without mentioning his dwarfism. Such views take shape in a world where so many are taught that dwarfism is at best undesirable and at worst to be feared or loathed. To erase Lay's dwarfism would be, some might think, to "make him normal."

But life in a dwarf body shaped Lay's beliefs. At times he struggled to be considered equal—a battle many dwarf people still face today. In one incident, Rediker records how a man of average height tried to humiliate Lay by approaching him and announcing: "I am your servant." With razor-sharp repartee, Lay stuck out his foot and replied, "Then clean my shoe," embarrassing the bully. To erase his dwarfism would limit our view of his life. It would sever a connection between Lay and his wife, Sarah, herself a dwarf person. And it was life in a dwarf body that led some historians, Rediker notes, to dismiss Lay as "a little hunchback," sustaining his obscurity.

There is another vital reason why we must keep Lay's dwarfism at the heart of discussions about him: because pernicious stereotypes dominate representations of dwarf people. A film about Lay's life is yet to be made, but movies like *Austin Powers* and *Wolf of Wall Street*—which sustain the spectacle of dwarf bodies and condone violence toward them (violence then reenacted in real life)—gross hundreds of millions of dollars. Growing up as a dwarf person myself, by ten I had heard of the Seven Dwarfs, by thirteen the vile Mini-Me character had hit our screens, and three decades went by before I learned of Benjamin Lay.

One of the defining features of Rediker's book is how he addresses Lay's dwarfism. Other authors of historical biographies of defiant, gentle, and inspiring dwarf people have claimed to celebrate their subjects' lives while simultaneously insulting their bodies and diminishing their extraordinary struggles—without reviewers noticing or caring. Rediker does no such thing, seeking advice from the excellent Little People of America organization and explicitly acknowledging the "discrimination based on size and an often tyrannical normative image of the human body" our community experiences on a daily basis. As a proud and conscious dwarf person, as I finished reading that passage, I felt like a corset had been removed and oxygen filled my lungs.

Lay is not just a role model; he is a *dwarf* role model. When I have children—who are likely to have dwarfism, too—I will tell them bedtime stories of Lay's life and deeds. And on our bookshelves, a copy of Rediker's book, *The Fearless Benjamin Lay*, a celebratory and evidenced record of this great man, will await them.

To Survive Climate Catastrophe, Look to Queer and Disabled Folks

Patty Berne,
as told to and edited by Vanessa Raditz

Communities around the world are grappling with a growing number and intensity of climate-related disasters. In the United States, federal, state, and nonprofit agencies frequently pour financial resources into the communities affected by the latest fire, flood, or earthquake. But these emergency support systems are usually unable to address the long-term needs of those affected, and all too often, these structural support systems entirely overlook those of us who live at the intersection of multiple oppressions: race, class, gender, disability, and sexual orientation, to name a few.

There are endless stories. During Hurricane Maria in Puerto Rico, queer and trans communities lost access to medical necessities such as psychiatric prescriptions and hormones, and many faced discrimination and violence. During the fires in Northern California, a black queer environmental justice activist with asthma went into respiratory distress and now lives with permanent brain injury. From homeless encampments to local jail cells, social, political, and economic dispari-ties put our communities at the front lines of ecological disaster.

The forces of capitalism, racism, ableism, transphobia, and homo-phobia may have cornered us into a vulnerable position in this unprec-edented moment in our planet's history, but the wisdom we've gained along the way could allow us all to survive in the face of climate chaos. The history of disabled queer and trans people has continually been one of creative problem-solving within a society that refuses to center our needs. If we can build an intersectional climate justice movement—one that incorporates disability justice, that centers disabled people of color and queer- and gender-nonconforming folks with disabilities—our species might have a chance to survive.

Let's start by openly, joyously proclaiming that we are natural beings, not aberrations of nature. We find healing and justice in the realm of queer ecology, a burgeoning field exploring the vast diversity of gender and sexuality that exists in nature, such as the more than fifty species of coral reef fish that undergo one or more sex transitions in their lifetime, completely transforming their behaviors, bodies, and even reproductive organs.

When we begin to see the planet through this lens, we remember that the entire world has biodiversity that is precious, necessary for our survival, and deeply threatened. Whether we're looking at ecology, society, or our human culture, diversity is our best defense against the threats of climate change.

When we begin to see our own diversity reflected in the ecol-ogy of this planet, we can also recognize that the same forces threaten both. It's not difficult to see parallels in the havoc that capitalism has wreaked on our bodies as queer people, gender-nonconforming folks, and people from colonized lands and how that same capitalism abuses and exploits the land.

Just as capitalism is one of the biggest threats to biodiversity on this planet—seen in the clear-cutting of forests to plant monocultures for fuel—it is also the driving force behind the violence toward multiply marginalized people with disabilities, because our bodies are not perceived as being "productive." This drive to hoard wealth is beyond anything we can conceive, and it has already cost our species so much loss.

What we're seeing in the erupting climate chaos is the Earth's resistance. The question is: How can we ally with this Brown, queer, disabled, femme planet to support her survival and the survival of all who depend on her? In the face of so much institutional apathy, it is left to those living squarely at the intersections of all of these injustices to tear down the centuries-old silos among climate justice, disability justice, and queer liberation organizing.

Disabled queer and trans communities of color are already preparing for the survival of their communities through oncoming disasters, teaching one another skills in resilience-based organizing to strategically create the changes that we need for queer and trans futures. During the fires and floods of 2017, queer disabled organizers in the Bay Area shared masks and air filters with one another, while in Puerto Rico, communities banded together to share generators to refrigerate insulin. At the 2018 Solidarity to Solutions grassroots summit, held alongside the government-organized Global Climate Action Summit, trans Latinx organizers affected by the North Bay fires led a healing justice workshop for queer and trans people of color environmental justice activists from around the world to connect and learn from one another. This burgeoning movement may be invisible to most, but it should not be surprising.

In order to value others, we have to know our own worth. In this historical moment, we have to fight for the valuable lives of butterflies and moss and elders. Because our lives—and all life—depend on this. We must move beyond our cultural beliefs that tell us we are worth only as much as we can produce. Just as each component in Earth's ecosystem plays a vital role in supporting everything around it, so do each of us have an essential role to play in sustaining our communities, our environment, our planet.

In this time, people need strength models. Strength isn't just about momentary power to jump building to building; it is also the endurance to handle what is less than ideal. It's the gritty persistence that disabled people embody every day.

Even in the moments when we're in pain, when we're uncomfortable, when the task ahead feels overwhelming and we feel defeated by the sheer scope of everything that's wrong in the world, we don't have to give up on life or on humanity. Queer and trans disabled people know that, because that's how we live. At this moment of climate chaos, we're saying: Welcome to our world. We have some things to teach you if you'll listen so that we can all survive.

Content notes: state violence, anti-Blackness, racism, ableism, audism, police brutality, incarceration, murder, white supremacy

Disability Solidarity
Completing the "Vision for Black Lives"

Harriet Tubman Collective

Comprising no less than 20 percent of the United States population, people with disabilities are the largest "minority" group in the nation. Notably, among differing socially constructed racial categories, the Black community has the highest prevalence of disability—with almost a full quarter of the Black population having some form of a disability.

And yet, on August 1, 2016, the Movement for Black Lives (the "Movement") released a groundbreaking policy platform outlining the Movement's idea of what is required to build a more just world for "all Black people" that did not once mention disability, ableism, audism, or the unspeakable violence and Black death found at the intersection of ableism, audism, and anti-Black racism. The six-point platform, which was supported or endorsed by more than fifty organizations from across the country, stated, in part:

We believe in elevating the experiences and leadership of the most marginalized Black people. . . . We are intentional about amplifying the particular experience of state and gendered violence that Black queer, trans, gender nonconforming, women, and intersex people face. There can be no liberation for all Black people if we do not center and fight for those who have been marginalized. It is our hope that by working together to create and amplify a shared agenda, we can continue to move towards a world in which the full humanity and dignity of all people is recognized.

The platform goes on to propose many crucial changes to the ways in which the government and its institutions treat Black people, providing a framework to combat many systems of oppression experienced by Black people in the United States and abroad.

Many, however, were left wondering why disability was erased, and ableism and audism omitted from this platform—especially considering the critical role ableism and audism play in *every* institution named by the Movement as a purveyor of violence against Black bodies and communities. Specifically, many were confounded as to how a movement whose primary focus is ending police brutality, could outright ignore the violence experienced by Black Disabled and Deaf people when statistics prove that at least 60 to 80 percent of the people murdered by police are, in fact, Disabled and/or Deaf people.

The following are a few more of the many ways in which Black Disabled people are disproportionately impacted by state violence:

- People with disabilities are twice as likely to live in poverty because poverty operates as a cause and consequence of disability;
- Children with disabilities enter the juvenile legal system at five

to six times the rate of youth who do not have disabilities, with 65 percent of boys and 75 percent of girls in juvenile detention having at least one mental illness, and up to 85 percent of children in juvenile detention having at least one disability; and

- 55 percent of male state prisoners and 73 percent of female state prisoners have a mental health condition, with just 1 in 3 state prisoners and 1 in 6 jail inmates receiving treatment for their illness since being admitted.

Within each of the above-provided statistics, Black people and other negatively racialized individuals are grossly, disproportionately represented. Indeed, ableist social norms often criminalize the existence of disabilities such as schizophrenia, autism, oppositional-defiant disorders, and developmental and intellectual disabilities. To be sure, Black people with these and other disabilities are particularly vulnerable to unjust encounters with school officials, police officers, and the criminal legal system.

Many Black Deaf/Disabled leaders—especially those who have given their time and talent to the Movement for Black Lives—have noticed this deficit and believe that it reflects much larger problems with ableism and audism in the Movement. We, the undersigned, united under the coalitional name the Harriet Tubman Collective, are here to remind the Movement that liberation will never come without the intentional centering of Black Disabled/Deaf narratives and leadership. We know this because it never has.

We understand, based on our communication with some of the Movement's drafters, that at least one person whom the Movement identified as disabled was at the table when drafting this policy platform. However, the Movement did not connect with self-identified Black Disabled/Deaf advocates, community builders, or organizers

who have been on the ground and actively engaged in truly intersectional anti-violence work to support in the drafting process. This led
to the Movement's overall failure to adequately address the disparities
and specific violence and oppression that exist at the intersection of
Blackness and Disability/Deafness.

This absence and erasure of the Black Disabled/Deaf experience
was apparent within critical foci of the platform, including ending the
war on Black people, reparations, invest-divest, economic justice, community control, and political power. The lack of understanding about
the Black Disabled/Deaf experience was further seen with the use of the
term "differently abled," which is considered offensive within disability
communities. The phrase "differently abled" suggests that we are the
locus of our disability when we are, in fact, disabled by social and institutional barriers. Not only is this term offensive, but it also reifies the
marginalization that Black Disabled/Deaf people face on a regular basis
by and within our own communities and oppressive state institutions.

If a staunch political stance is going to be taken about the Black
experience, it is a grave injustice and offense to dismiss the plight of
Black Disabled and Black Deaf communities. This platform and work
is wholly incomplete if disability is not present. To be sure, no successful movement has existed without our leadership, and no movement
will be successful without us.

Any movement that seeks to end police violence has no choice but
to work to undo the racism *and* ableism and audism which, together,
make Black Disabled/Deaf people prime targets for police violence.
For instance, Darnell T. Wicker, a Black deaf veteran, was killed by
police officers in Louisville, Kentucky, on August 8, 2016 (note that
the lowercase *d* indicates that Darnell Wicker was deaf, not culturally
Deaf). Body camera footage shows officers shooting Darnell Wicker
multiple times within one to two seconds of issuing verbal orders on

a dark night. However, Darnell Wicker relied on speech-reading to communicate. His family asserts that he likely never heard or comprehended the officers.

The circumstances surrounding his murder made clear the critical importance of naming Darnell Wicker's deafness and Blackness as having been criminalized by police officers. Yet still, no national coalition, network, cohort was found to have even made mention of Darnell Wicker's deafness during their physical or online actions "in his name." One all-volunteer national Deaf/Disability Justice organization issued a powerful statement in American Sign Language, Spanish, and English calling for Disability Solidarity with Black Lives Matter in response to unrelenting police brutality against Deaf/Disabled people, including the murder of two D/deaf men last month alone. This sort of intersectional approach is sorely lacking in national organizations, networks, and coalitions that claim to fight for racial justice, disability rights, and deaf rights. This lack of intersectionality leads to yet more Black, Deaf, and Disabled people being killed by the police.

The Harriet Tubman Collective submits that any struggle against white supremacy must also address all of its interrelated flaws—including ableism and audism.

It is disingenuous, at best, and violently irresponsible at worst, to claim to want justice for those who have died at the hands of police, and neither name disability nor advance disability justice. We call upon organizations that label themselves "intersectional" to truly embrace that framework, and we remain as a resource and network of support to any who seek this end. We demand a centering of the Black Disabled/Deaf narrative, as this narrative represents 60 to 80 percent of those murdered by police—including all of those names that the Movement continues to uplift whilst erasing and dishonoring part of their humanity:

Tanisha Anderson

Sandra Bland

Miriam Carey

Michelle Cusseaux

Ezell Ford

Shereese Francis

Korryn Gaines

Eric Garner

Freddie Gray

Milton Hall

Quintonio LeGrier

Kyam Livingston

Symone Marshall

Laquan McDonald

Natasha McKenna

Stephon Watts

Darnell Wicker

Mario Woods

And countless other Black Disabled/Deaf victims of police brutality

We will not be martyrs for a movement that denies our humanity. We demand that "social justice" coalitions, networks, and organizations end the violent erasure of disability from these and all other narratives of the victims of police violence and murder. We further call for an end of the stigmatization of Black Disabled and Black Deaf people by those who claim to fight for us.

We are not an afterthought.

We are here.

We are fighting for all of our lives.

We are Black. We are Disabled. We are Deaf.

We are Black.

Our Black Disabled Lives Matter.

Our Black Deaf Lives Matter.

In Solidarity,

Patty Berne   Cyree Jarelle Johnson

Kylie Brooks   Lorrell D. Kilpatrick

Neal Carter   Carolyn Lazard

Patrick Cokley   Talila A. Lewis

Candace Coleman   Leroy F. Moore Jr.

Dustin Gibson   Vilissa Thompson

Timotheus Gordon Jr.   Alexis Toliver

Keri Gray   Heather Watkins

Christopher DeAngelo Huff

Content notes: sexual assault, intimate partner violence, abuse, trauma

Time's Up for Me, Too

Karolyn Gehrig

Last year, when I most needed my voice, a blood blister grew in the back of my throat, making it harder to speak. New bones grew in the floor of my mouth, crowding my palate, further exacerbating the issue. I often ran my tongue over them to keep from biting.

Last year I went on dates with people who said, "You're hot," like it was some sort of flattering problem or puzzle; they were trying to figure out how to separate my attractiveness from my disabled body.

Sometimes on these dates I ran my tongue over my new bones, usually when dates got lazy enough to ask me to solve their sex puzzle for them. They'd lean in conspiratorially, eyes glinting, and coyly ask, "So how does that even work?"

Recently I've been thinking about the Golden Globes and Time's Up, and how powerful it was to see the way women can come together and flood a red carpet black. How it recalled the National Mall in pink; how, in the sea of both, I could not see myself easily.

Whenever something terrible happens to a disabled someone, people shrink and say, "Who would do that?" or "It's unimaginable," then remove it from their minds. They cannot bear to imagine it, so our reality remains deniable, though it is as provable as our unseen bodies.

We keep talking about representation and image, and the best representations of disability at the Globes were *Three Billboards Outside Ebbings, Missouri*, which liberally used federally recognized hate speech when referring to disability, and *The Shape of Water*, which featured a cripped-up lead actor in a fairy-tale disability narrative with a mermonster.

When I was three, my adult aunt Virginia came to live with us. What was then her clinical diagnosis is the slur referenced in *Three Billboards*. She is developmentally disabled and intellectually impaired. *That* slur was enshrined in the names of organizations that helped her while I was growing up and was flung around my schoolyards for cruelty.

Years ago, I was married to a man who edited television shows. He sometimes talked about how an image could shape a narrative. He cut funny things up and spliced them together. He tore me up, mostly inside my body, mostly when I slept. I did not know what was happening to me for years. He left considerable proof, and I attempted to prosecute.

My mother, though she had three kids and her own job, was Virginia's primary caretaker. She made sure Virginia got dressed, ate breakfast, and got on the bus to the sheltered workshop where Virginia worked for eight hours, five days a week, until long after I moved out of the house. My mother picked Virginia up in the evening, made dinner, and sat at the kitchen table with her into the night.

I recognize all that my mother did, and I still related less to the tender, maternal *Lady Bird* than to *The Shape of Water*. You can spend a lot of time with someone who both others and adores you.

This is true of creators as well. Before seeing Guillermo del Toro's film, I read an interview where he talked about meeting Sally Hawkins at a party and slurring into her hair, "I'm writing a movie for you." Can you imagine writing a disabled part specifically for an abled actor? I will keep referring to her part here by Hawkins's name rather than her character, a mute custodian, because I cannot get over this idea. If a creator imagines our interiority so complex, why not let us show it?

I cannot get over it because I don't speak ASL, and even I know Hawkins's signing wasn't great. The only excuse I can conjure is that del Toro didn't want to create some sort of deaf custodian trope, after Marlee Matlin's *Children of a Lesser God* Oscar win only thirty-one years ago, four years before the Americans with Disabilities Act passed. Four years before we had rights.

Sometimes my mom watched TV. Other times she'd flip through old photo albums and talk about how she looked in the past and present and how I didn't really look like her. Which was true. It was Virginia, my father's sister's body, that resembled mine. Both of us had thick thighs, knees that knocked together, ankles that rolled, and dark auburn hair. Our faces are the most similar; nobody else in our family shares our noses. I knew growing up, even though I had not yet been diagnosed, that I was closer to her than my other kin.

I looked at the Golden Globes red carpet, covered in black dresses, without finding someone who looked like me or like Virginia. That doesn't mean we weren't there, but whoever was isn't out as disabled.

Disabilities are also created through sexual assault. These things now described in the press very carefully, held back, so the details do not suggest that someone may be unfit for work as a result of having been through this ordeal.

While we collectively insist *mental instability* means being unfit for work, we keep talking out of both sides of our mouths. We are helping no one without thinking this implication through.

When I tried to prosecute, I went through it all over again, whatever that can mean. Assume everything. They say memory works by re-experiencing an act, so I got to talk about "that one time, with all the blood," when I was hospitalized because it poured from my body for weeks, seemingly without root cause. My doctors thought it was a rectocele, but there was no reason I might have one. Later, at Hill Street, where we all get the blues, they wheeled me into the children's waiting area and left me there before my meeting with the DA. How does a walker let me experience all of that and still land me in a children's zone, accompanied by tiny furniture?

Virginia had a series of sexual aggressions in her sheltered workshop. It was always hard to get the story. There was Freddie on the bus, who was thirty years older than her and unkempt, with long nose hairs. Once while I was home for college, she excitedly planned "Goodbye, Freddie; hello, boys!" My mother took days off from work and tried to talk her supervisors into separating him from her or the bus drivers into keeping him away from her. It was effective for a little while. Eventually she had to leave.

There is a scene in *The Shape of Water* where Sally Hawkins is threatened sexually by her boss. It is more harrowing when you remember that the highest rates of sexual assault are for disabled people who cannot communicate their attacks.

At Virginia's sheltered workshop, she was paid what is known as a "subminimum wage." It is still legal to pay disabled people for piecework, or pennies for the hour. On average, Virginia's checks were about $6 a week, $9 on a good one. She was still devastated by having had to leave her job.

The DA declined to prosecute my ex-husband. "You have proof," I said.

"Yes, but our concern is that a jury of your peers will find it difficult to believe a man would do this to his disabled wife." A dozen jurors picked randomly by mail could look at me and decide my dowry was rape.

He nearly fucked a hole through my body and I lacked the language to explain it for years. Is the horror in this indelicate description from the act, the trauma, or both? Does my disability escalate it?

What is assault at all if framed in terms of a custodian's rights? Where exactly is the line for my humanity? Where is Virginia's? How can justice be attained for those of us unable to identify the source of trauma? "Who would do that?" What is justice, anyway?

The body itself does not hold the line, does not move us from avatars, does not provide equality. The more I do, the more accomplishments I rack up, the more likely my mother is to say, "You look like me when I was young." I never will. I am older than she was in those photos, my syndrome is progressive, and anyway, how can one become another's past? It is less likely than knowing the future.

They never have a problem figuring out "how it works" when it's not consensual. They have a problem wanting the person, not the power over the person, not the other.

In this movie, Sally Hawkins is asked how do you fuck, as though mermaid and mermen have not bred fantasy. To give an anatomical response is an abled impulse. I have had disabled lovers. Each revealed new secrets between our bodies, never repeated, either to or with others. We don't do each other like that.

In an argument with my mother over Virginia, she said it did not hurt her to see them treat Virginia this way. Virginia's subminimum wage, the hours taken away from my mother's own job, her own interests, her own life, also did not affect her. She did not understand why it impacts me as another disabled woman. Virginia and I are different. I try to explain that I look like her, that we deserve equal rights. She disagrees: I deserve a fair wage. Virginia does not.

Was Sally Hawkins's affinity for the monster like my relation to Virginia's body? Is that gap smaller than that between me and those around me? See how even I other her now. In suturing myself back together, I am learning still.

This is where I understand that if we are in *The Shape of Water* (which we are not and never would be), Virginia is always the one behind glass, prodded, unable to be heard. In our story, she always bears more risk. This is also where I understand that what I least liked about the movie was its undeniable truth: that even when allied against a common enemy, we are considered separate. We are left in the water.

I understand why #TimesUp initially forgot about disabled people, I do. We are not there. We are not visible on the carpet, in movies, in the workplace. Our bodies are not sexualized or understood as rapeable, and even those closest to us do not understand our pay.

When my grandmother named her Virginia, could she have known that she was damning her to a future of piety or colonization?

In naming me Carolyn, could my parents have known how often I would be cleaved north from south?

In saying *time's up, me too*, can you name disability as part of you?

My ex-husband once wrote a wish fulfillment in which he ended up on a red carpet. He wrote that he could not conceive of having me there with him, specifically the optics of me in a wheelchair with him. He wrote, incredulously, "How does that even work?"

Virginia has always had photos of movie stars on her walls. She used to say, "When you grow up, I'm gonna take you to Hollywood." For a long time I believed her. I moved to Los Angeles eventually, and I send postcards to her sometimes, where I know she is still watching movies on a small TV in her bedroom. She doesn't visit, but she always stays with me. Neither of us are in Hollywood.

This year when I run my tongue around my mouth, know I am sharpening those new bones into teeth.

Still Dreaming Wild Disability Justice Dreams at the End of the World

Leah Lakshmi Piepzna-Samarasinha

Psych Survivors Know

for the people in the ICE concentration camps

Whisper to each other in the corners
Evade capture
Run
Find a corner
There is always one
Even if it's only in your brain

You are still human no matter how much they treat you
    otherwise
Maybe you become partially other than human
because of what you endure

This does not make you less
There is also dignity
in feral
We have been here before
We inhabit these lands
We are with you

Bathrooms are your friends
Even if it's just five minutes
Even if it's no door

I wish we didn't have to keep
whispering
enduring
Play dead
be invisible
disassociate
Suck cock for a phone
Organize
in ways they never know how to see
bank on
their incompetence
their petty squabbles over jurisdiction
them distracted by porn on a screen

Find each other again
Disappear into the sky
Memory
Dream
as long as you need to
We have the tech for it

There will be an after
Survive for it.

Remember back in 2019, before you survived, when you got cancer and we were all afraid you would die either from the cancer or from the surgeon's ableist medical neglect killing you when you were on the table? Remember when it was just 2018, the first year disabled people built a network that gave out eighty thousand masks in one month during the wildfires? The first time you heard the term large-scale air emergency, *but not the last. Remember the first time you saw disability justice (DJ) listed as a section in the library, Audre Lorde's and Leroy Moore's faces next to each other on their books? Remember when guaranteed annual income went through, when subminimum wage got lifted and D/ID folks and people on SSDI could keep our income? Remember the medical abuse payouts? Remember when the Judge Rotenberg Center and the last forced treatment facilities for autistic youth closed and we had the mourning and celebration ceremony? Remember when you first were stockpiling masks, water, and gas, before you had the whole crip-of-color elder farm we live on and roll through now? Remember when we first built the memorial for everyone we lost—Carrie Ann, Steve, all of them?*

Alice Wong, the editor of this anthology, asked me to write a follow-up to my essay "Cripping the Apocalypse; Some of My Wild Disability Justice Dreams." I had a hard time writing it. It's hard to dream when you're terrified, and these are terrifying times. The nonstop repeated blunt force traumas of the last three years, the horrors that are often beyond the worst we could imagine, that just keep coming and coming—from the concentration camps to the public charge rule, from Kavanaugh's ascension to the Supreme Court to Muslim ban number three, forests on fire on all sides of the world and ice melting on both poles—have put me and so many people I know in a deer-in-headlights somatic state of freeze. The end of the world is easier to read about in a book, it turns out, than to experience and to know how to respond to when it happens in real life.

The past year, as I've been on tour with my book *Care Work: Dreaming Disability Justice*, I've often worn disabled queer Latinx maker and activist Annie Elainey Segarra's *The Future Is Accessible* T-shirt. Often I ask audiences to stop, go inward, and imagine that future. As disability justice movement people, we know that access is just the first step on the way to a liberated disabled future—it's not the whole of it, not by a long shot. But when I ask them to imagine that accessible future, let alone that disability justice future, they get stuck. The best they can imagine is maybe not dying in a concentration camp.

Yet as disabled people, we know that one of our biggest gifts is the Mad, sick, disabled, Deaf dreams we are always dreaming and have always been dreaming, way beyond what we are allowed to dream. Not in the inspiration-porn way that's the only way many abled people can imagine that disabled-people dream of "not letting disability stop us!" Wanting to walk or see or be "normal" above all costs, being a supercrip or an inspiration but never human. I'm talking about the small, huge, everyday ways we dream crip revolutions, which stretch from me looking at myself in the mirror—disheveled and hurting on day five of a major pain flare and saying, *You know what, I'm not going to hate you today*—to making disabled homes, disabled kinship, and community networks and disabled ways of loving, fighting, and organizing that not even the most talented abled could in a million years dream up.

And despite all the ways we are in hell, we are still dreaming right now—as we build disabled collectives, homes, care teams, conferences, art projects. As I go to three care network meetings a week for friends facing cancer, kidney surgery, and ongoing mental health needs. As I finally, finally take a deep breath and ask for and accept the care I need most from my friends, and I am able to do this because of the collective work done to make accepting that care safe and possible. As I begin to become the disabled middle-aged artist I used to be afraid of turning into, as I stop flying as much and learn to write and speak and share my work without traveling to Nebraska or Maine, in a community of other disabled writers and artists who are cripping the ways we produce, perform, and live excellent disabled artist lives.

We're dreaming brilliant disabled responses to the violence of climate change on disabled people that threatens our ability to live. Mask Oakland, a disabled- and trans-led grassroots organization, gave out eighty thousand free masks—with priority to houseless people—during the large-scale air emergency of the Paradise and Camp Fires of fall 2018 in California. As I write this during the Kincade Fire of 2019, #PowertoBreathe, a network of twelve disability justice organizations, unites to create a network of accessible hubs with generators and air purifiers by and for disabled people organizing to survive PG&E's life-threatening power shutoffs.

We are creating Black and brown disability justice public cultural space and creating what disability justice literature means, as Pittsburgh-based Black disability justice activist Dustin Gibson builds a disability justice library within a neighborhood public library that throws out the confines of the Dewey decimal system and seats Audre Lorde's and Leroy Moore's work next to each other, and as access-centered movement and Black disabled movement artists like Alice Sheppard, NEVE, and Jerron Herman reimagine what disabled dance can be.

There are so many vibrant, innovative, crip-made forms of organizing that are continuing to save everyone's asses in the face of Trump. Out of our fear, grief, and rage at the many deaths of our people, caused by insurance company denials of service and medical violence—to name one that still aches, UnitedHealthcare's denial of a $2,000 anti-biotic, resulting in the murder of beloved disabled queer Latinx fat femme activist/lawyer Carrie Ann Lucas in February 2019—Health Justice Commons establishes the first-ever Medical Abuse Hotline. Black disabled community lawyer Talila "TL" Lewis fights for Black disabled and Deaf people in prison who have been wrongfully convicted and lack access to ASL interpreters and videophones. Disabled sex workers, disabled migrants, disabled prisoners, and disabled people who use Medicaid and SSDI all self-organize for survival in the face of Trump. They are the reason why Medicaid and the ACA are still in existence and the reason Trump's public charge rule—which aimed to block disabled immigrants from being able to enter the United States because of the tired idea that they would be "burdens on the system"— was defeated.

New collectives, led by disability justice principles and disabled Black and brown people, are popping up everywhere, from Disability Justice Network of Ontario and Detroit Disability Power to Fat Rose and more, marking a new generation of disability justice activism. My sibling, queer Korean disabled organizer Stacey Milbern, buys and makes accessible her home in East Oakland—the Disability Justice Culture Club—with $30,000 in twenty-dollar bills sent in from disabled community across the world. And two hundred disabled and fat and elder people held signs that say IRREPLACEABLE and #NOONEISDISPOSABLE at the Crips and Fatties Close the Camps protest in front of the ICE office in San Francisco—part of a month of daily protests in August 2019 against Trump's torturous ICE concentration camps—these protesters, created by fat and disabled people drawing connections between our experiences (with being locked up in psych institutions, nursing homes, and back wards) and those of immigrants (including disabled immigrants) being locked up right now.

And we keep reaching for and finding each other, from Instagram hashtags and groups like #DisabledAndCute, @disabled_personals, and @disabledhikers to cultural gatherings led by Black and brown disabled artists, events like I wanna be with you everywhere, Sins Invalid, and the Disability & Intersectionality Summit.

I am writing this to remember and remind us. All of these are huge wins. Even and especially when we are frozen with fear, we are still collectively dreaming disability justice's future into being.

Remembering the Past to Dream the Future: We Have Always Found Each Other.

"You know the kind of disabled person who just wants to show up for other disabled people, doesn't ask for any credit, just wants to do the right thing?" my friend M. says to me on the phone. Of course I do. I don't tell him, but he's always been that kind of person to me.

Back in the day in Toronto, we were the two houses with ramps on our block. Long before gentrification mostly triumphed, our neighborhood was full of poor people and comfortably half-broken porches. Years before the modern disability justice movement, his house was a space where poor, multiracial, queer disabled people would hang out, support each other, plot, and laugh. For years he held Friday-night dinners where anyone could come over and eat some chicken. He would always talk to me about how important it was to him to center the least-popular crips—the ones who were cranky, angry, "difficult," crazy in ways that even other crazy people shied away from. He wanted the people who had the least community, because of all the ways ableism kills through isolation, to feel home.

A couple of weeks before that phone call, I'd been giving a workshop for a local QTPOC community center on care webs—how to create mutual-aid networks as disabled people to get and give the care we need. The first half of the workshop had gone well; I'd talked a lot about how much unpaid care work people do, how hard it is to ask for care as sick and disabled and racialized people because of all the ways we've been forced to do that work for free and then punished for needing it in the first place. People nodded and sighed.

It got rough when I said, "Okay, so think of a need you have, and take a minute to brainstorm what you need to get it met well."

I felt the temperature in the room drop ten degrees. People said, "I'm sorry, can you explain the prompt again?" multiple times. They looked triggered and angry.

I did the facilitator thing, where I say, "Hey, I'm noticing some tension in the room, do people want to talk about it?" And they did. They said they had no experience giving or receiving care in nonabusive ways. Some of them said they didn't believe that had ever happened. They couldn't imagine any time when disabled people had ever shown up for each other. Some people seemed to think I was promoting a fairy tale.

Standing at the front of that sad, angry circle of people, I felt a mix of things. I felt really sad. I felt like a bad facilitator— when I was planning the workshop, how had I somehow forgotten that so many disabled people have zero experiences of care without being treated like shit? And a part of me was also incredulous. I was like, *C'mon. No one's ever given you a cigarette when you were in line at the food stamps office? No one's ever brought you some takeout when you were sick?*

But I also got it. I thought about how huge we have become over the past fifteen years, since the term *disability justice* was invented by a small group of intersectional, radical disabled people and yet still how invisible we are if you do not know where to find us.

I thought of the examples of crip-made care I have been so lucky and lifted to witness—the care collectives, disabled fundraisers for housing or my friend's accessible van, all flying under the abled radar, all supported, only unfunded except by us. And more than the fundraisers and collectives: the ways we have hung out without trying to "fix" each other, gone to visit friends in nursing homes and played board games, creating friendships and community hangouts that are disabled at the core, that are lifesaving.

As disabled people, we are often both hypervisible and invisible at the same time. I think a lot about how some of our strongest power lies in how we organize, always, in ways unknowable to the abled. There is no national or North American–wide DJ organization you can pay dues to. Disability justice exists every place two disabled people meet—at a kitchen table, on heating pads in bed talking to our loves. Our power and our vulnerability are often in our revolutionary obscurity and the horizontal ways of organizing that can come from it. Anyone can be a part of disability justice if they organize from their own spoons, own bodies and minds, and own communities.

And: Foundations are starting to figure out that disability justice is the hot new thing they want to fund, and while we could use money, we certainly know what that usually does to movements. The nonprofit industrial/foundation complex has a long and storied history of investing in and then destabilizing and defanging movements and pitting groups against each other, often giving money to the whitest, the lightest, the ones with the most degrees and 501(c)(3)s. I firmly believe, as I have since I was a young radical studying guerrilla warfare, that our power is the strongest when we build on our own strengths and strike where the enemy is weak. We do best when we don't compromise or water our cripness down. Make something disabled and wonderful out of the disabled knowledge our bodies and minds know—with or without anyone else's money or understanding.

When I fear the loss of everything, I remember that before we had a word for ourselves, we still found each other. In my friend's house, on our ramped, half-busted front porches, and in nursing homes, in jails, in psych wards, and, yes, in camps. I know that no matter how dire the circumstances, we will always keep finding each other. Because this is what we have always done.

Wilder, Like Wildfires

I keep talking about wild disabled dreaming, so here are some wild-ass disabled dreams for some of what might be next:

As our networks, people, collectives, and cultural groups grow, do we want to imagine a loosely organized network of communication? Do we want to come up with principles of how to act in solidarity with each other when foundations or systems of power try to make us compete? For when harm and power struggles inevitably happen?

Disabled radical people—particularly BIPOC (Black, Indigenous people of color), queer and trans, and other folks—are going to keep writing, creating, and making art. What structures do we want to create to reach out to and build with each other?

Social media has been a huge tool we've used to connect and break isolation over the past decade plus, but Facebook, Instagram, and most social media sites increasingly choke-hold and shadow-ban so many of us, preventing us from being able to post or rendering us unfindable if we do post. What if we made our own social media network?

I'm never eager for any disabled person to die, but I gotta say, if the old racist parts of white disability studies and disability rights die out—and they will—we will have an opportunity. Right now, the old Disability Rights guard is angry at disability justice people because we've actually succeeded in getting more people to buy into being disabled, because we aren't racist and we're not just focused on policy work. We're focused on building homes, building a million weird little groups and actions and projects and Instagram hashtags and media networks and stories and rampshares and MCS (Multiple Chemical Sensitivity) toolkit lending libraries and housing projects and sex parties. So what happens if we can take over the Centers for Independent Living, the disability studies programs—or make something entirely new and different? An interdependence and independence center, not a center for independent living?

We've got twenty-five years until BIPOC are in the majority in the United States, and one of the wins of DJ is that more and more younger BIPOC are less afraid of disability—claiming it or integrating it into their activism. What do we do with this potential?

As we're pushed out of coastal cities due to hypergentrification and as the sea levels rise, what new disabled homes and communities will we build in the exurbs and wastelands? What crip homespaces will we build on the islands that were Florida, in the rust belt and on the rez?

What happens if we crip the Green New Deal? What if all those promised green infrastructures and jobs centered disability justice from the beginning?

As we both push to maintain Medicaid but know that existing structures of paid care attendants are underpaid, abusive, and difficult for many of us to access; and as we grow collective care structures but know that for many of us they are not accessible due to our isolation, our desire to have someone other than our friends wipe our asses, a lack of friends or social capital, or our knowledge that even if we have those things, people get exhausted: What are our dreams of a collective mutual-aid network, of a society where free, just, non-gatekept crip-led care is a human right for all? What if we could make a society-

wide mutual-aid system for care based on disability justice principles?
I'm thinking of something like the society in Ursula K. Le Guin's *The
Dispossessed*, where the anarcho-syndicalist moon-world had housing,
work, and storehouses of clothes and needed items available for all.
What if everyone had access to care like that? What if the right to care
and access was in a foundational document of any new government?
What if there was a Care Act—maybe in an existing federal govern-
ment, maybe in local Indigenous, city, state, or bioregional areas?

When she wrote the text for her housing fundraiser, my beloved
comrade Stacey Milbern said, "Disability justice dreams are what got
me here, and I'm going to keep banking on them." Sure, maybe we all
will be dead in five years because of all the climate change–fueled wildfire smoke circling the planet. However, I know we have continued
through total adversity before. And I know this:

> We have what we always have had, and more.
> We know how to mourn
> to pray
> to persist
> to find resistance in the smallest of spaces
> to find each other and make homes, alone and together
> to lay down in the middle of the road and keen with grief and
>   rage and block traffic
> to crip innovate
> to do some shit that no one says is possible
> to do something wild and unexpected under the radar
> to keep going.

Love Means Never Having to Say . . . Anything

Jamison Hill

After dating Shannon for several months, I needed to say something to her, but I couldn't. It's not that I was nervous or unsure of the phrasing. It's that I couldn't speak. My lungs and larynx couldn't create the air pressure and vibrations needed to say the words floating around my mind.

This is our reality. I can't talk to Shannon about anything—not the weather or her day or how beautiful she is. Worst of all, I can't tell her I love her.

This was never a problem in my previous relationships with women I thought I loved or perhaps didn't love at all. These women knew my voice; they heard it every day. But they never knew what I was actually thinking.

They never knew how miserable my body felt because, back then, I was able to function at a relatively normal level and hide my illness well enough to seem healthy. I could go on dates, talk on the phone, and even drive to my girlfriend's house to spend the night.

But over time my condition worsened. Lyme disease had exacerbated my existing case of myalgic encephalomyelitis, an inflammatory multisystem disease that can leave patients unable to speak or eat for years at a time.

I'm now twenty-nine and have been sick for eight years, the last three of which I have spent bedridden, mostly speechless, and unable to eat solid food. I used to be a body builder who worked out for hours every day, and I was blindsided by the rapid deterioration of my health. I couldn't care for myself. I had to delay love and many other things while I waited for my health to stabilize.

That's when Shannon came into my life.

She lives in Ottawa, about two thousand miles from my house in California. We met online, which is common, but otherwise our relationship has no precedent or guide. We are two people very much in love but also very sick.

Shannon has the same condition I do. She has been sick longer, since adolescence, but thankfully has never lost her ability to speak. Instead, she struggles with unrelenting nausea and has trouble digesting food. She is often malnourished and her weight drops below a hundred pounds—too thin for someone five feet, five inches tall.

We both have low blood volume, which makes it difficult for her to walk without fainting and impossible for me to sit up in bed without intense pain and weakness.

Since I am bedridden, the only way we can be together is for her to travel across the continent to see me. But even with her willingness to jeopardize her health by traveling so far, we are often away from each other for months at a time.

When we are together, we spend weeks in bed, mostly holding each other, our bodies aligned like two pieces of a broken plate glued back together. Because I can't speak, we often resort to communicating by text messages while cuddling in bed.

It's like a monthlong sleepover and feels surreal, being stuck in a situation so miserable that it could make your skin crawl but finding comfort knowing that your soul mate is next to you, going through something similar.

But our experiences differ. Shannon can briefly get up to use the toilet, bathe, and, on a good day, make herself a meal. I, on the other hand, have to do everything in bed—brush my teeth, bathe, and use the "bathroom"—a plastic bag for bowel movements and, for urinating, a dubious-looking plastic container attached to a tube feeding into a bucket on the floor. These are not sexy things but are part of life—my life and ours together.

I was embarrassed at first to ask Shannon to avert her eyes and try not to think of me urinating inches from where we had been kissing just seconds earlier. But I have since come to realize that it's all part of sharing our lives. It may be far from the bedroom romps we each had experienced before getting sick, but knowing that nothing about my bedridden life makes Shannon uncomfortable endears her to me.

In contrast, I have had relationships with women who became upset at the first sign of anything inconvenient—one girlfriend who threatened to break up with me because she thought my beard trimmings were clogging the bathroom sink, and another who blamed our problems on my insomnia.

These failed romances remind me of the baffling incompatibilities two people can have, but also how love can transcend even the most insurmountable obstacles when you find the right person.

Before we started our relationship, when we were just two friends with the same illness texting for hours, I asked Shannon, "Do you think two sick people can be together?"

"Yes," she replied. "I think when you're both sick it makes it easier and harder at the same time."

"I guess the downside," I said, "is there's no healthy person to take care of you."

"But when you're alone, there's no healthy person to take care of you, either," she said.

I had never thought about it like that—the possibility of two sick people being in a successful relationship together. I have always assumed that one person in the couple would need to be healthy. Two sick people can't take care of each other.

But Shannon and I take care of each other in ways I never thought possible. I may not be able to make a meal for her, but I can have takeout delivered. And she may not be able to be my caregiver, but she can post an ad looking for one. We have done these things and many others for each other, from opposite ends of North America.

We share an empathy that only two people with the same condition can feel. We know what the other person is going through on bad days; we know how exasperating it is to explain invisible symptoms to doctors only to face skepticism. And we know all too well what it's like to be immobile in an ever-moving world.

Even so, we don't know everything about each other. We don't know what we were like as healthy people. We don't know what differences lie between our current selves and the people we were before getting sick—what maturation and emotional hardening have occurred during that transformation. Most fundamentally, we don't know what it's like to have a vocal conversation with each other.

Shannon has never heard my voice. She has never heard me berate a telemarketer or mumble to myself after making a typo. She has never heard me mess up a dinner toast or tell a corny joke. She has never heard me whisper into her ear or come up with a witty reply. She has never heard me ask a question or speak my mind, to anyone.

And she may never get to hear me do any of these things, but that's okay. Here is this lovely woman, devoid of judgment, who loves me for the words I type to her on my phone.

I never loved any of my previous girlfriends the way I love Shannon. I wanted to tell her how much her companionship means to me. I had tried before, many times, without success.

Still, I felt I had to try again. Somehow I had to convey, without typing, what I was feeling. My text messages were inadequate, and I thought about using hand signals, but the heart-shaped hand gesture felt far too clichéd.

So I tried to use my voice. To my surprise, for the first time in months, I heard actual sounds coming from my mouth. With my jaw locked, I whispered through clenched teeth, "I . . . love . . . you."

"What?" she said, startled.

I took a deep breath and fought back the nearly unbearable pain in my throat and jaw. Tears began to well up in my eyes. I whispered again, this time using all the strength I had: "I . . . love . . . you."

"Oh, sweetheart," she said. "I'm so sorry. I don't know what you're saying."

I wasn't sure what was worse: the emotional torment of not being able to speak or the physical pain of trying. After everything I had been through—the months of struggling to stay alive in my sickbed—and finally finding the love of my life, I couldn't tell Shannon that I loved her.

Lucky for me, I didn't have to. As if straight from a heart-wrenching scene in *Love Story*, Shannon took my hand, gave me a soft kiss, and said, "You don't have to say anything. I love you!"

Now, months later, it still holds true: For us, love means never having to say anything.

On the Ancestral Plane
Crip Hand-Me-Downs and the Legacy of Our Movements

Stacey Milbern

My favorite boots are socks. Crip socks. Because they are made out of brown leather to look like shoes, wearing them out in public as a wheelchair user is still socially acceptable. I loved these boot socks unabashedly and wore them every day until two years ago, when I slipped in the bathroom at work. I fell because socks, unlike actual shoes, do not have gripping soles (or soles in general). A nondisabled coworker had to check on me on the bathroom floor. No incident report filed, but it was disabled childhood humiliation relived all over again. I put the boots away, dismayed and furious at how much I let myself love shoes that could cause physical injury.

I don't have these kinds of strong feelings about all articles of clothing. These boot socks are special. These boots were worn by two of my personal heroes, crip elders who became crip ancestors when they passed: Harriet McBryde Johnson and Laura Hershey.

Harriet McBryde Johnson, an American writer and disability

rights attorney, went head-to-head against ableist assholes Peter Singer and Jerry Lewis and wore them in South Carolina. Her sister sewed these boots for her. Harriet's writing meant so much to me that Harriet is the secret name I've tucked away should I ever have the honor to name someone one day. When Harriet died, or maybe before, the shoes were gifted to her friend Laura Hershey in Colorado.

Laura, a queer disabled poet and brilliant feminist thinker, was/is equally remarkable. Her poetry describes experiences the majority of people can't fathom and still resonates with people from all kinds of backgrounds. She is one of my favorite poets, just as Harriet is one of my favorite authors. When Laura died, her partner, Robin Stephens, whom I did not know at the time, asked for my address. The boot socks arrived here in California two weeks later. I don't understand why I was the lucky recipient, but I am honored to be in this lineage. Wearing them made me feel powerful and good in my body. That's why I was so let down when I fell; it felt like my ancestors let me down. Like my ancestors didn't know better, and it had an impact on me. It's not fair or reasonable to them, but it's how I felt.

I think about crip ancestorship often. It is tied to crip eldership for me, a related but different topic. So many disabled people live short lives, largely because of social determinants of health like lack of healthcare, inadequate housing, or unmet basic needs such as clean air and water. Other times the short lives are merely one truth of our bodyminds, like the neuromuscular conditions of Harriet, Laura, and myself. I do not know a lot about spirituality or what happens when we die, but my crip queer Korean life makes me believe that our earthly bodymind is but a fraction, and not considering our ancestors is electing to see only a glimpse of who we are. People sometimes assume ancestorship is reserved for those who are biologically related, but a queered or cripped understanding of ancestorship holds that our deepest relationships are with people we choose to be connected to and honor day after day.

Ancestorship, like love, is expansive and breaks man-made boundaries cast upon it, like the nuclear family model or artificial nation-state borders. My ancestors are disabled people who lived looking out of institution windows, wanting so much more for themselves. It's because of them that I know that when I reflect on the meaning of a "good life," an opportunity to contribute is as important as receiving the support one needs. My ancestors are people torn apart from loves by war and displacement. It's because of them I know the power of building home with whatever you have, wherever you are, whomever you are with. My ancestors are queers who lived in the American South. It's because of them I understand the importance of relationships and place and living life big, even if it is dangerous. All of my ancestors know longing. Longing is often our connecting place.

I believe that our ancestors laugh, cry, hurt, rage, celebrate with us. Most important, I believe they learn as we are learning, just as we learn from them. We grow knowledge and movements with them. We crip futurism with them. We demand and entice the world to change the way things have always been done, with them. We change ourselves with them. They learn through us. When we become ancestors, we will also continue to learn.

I speculate that Grace Lee Boggs is loving the conversations happening right now about disability in the context of what it means to be human and, as Grace's friends the Fialka-Feldmans said to me last week, would consider that the reason to add disability justice to social justice is not just because it's another element of diversity or representation, but rather because disability justice (and disability itself) has the potential to fundamentally transform everything we think about quality of life, purpose, work, relationships, belonging. As a new colleague Ria DasGupta said in a meeting about cripping the college campus this week, "We can no longer afford add-and-stir politics."

I speculate that a lot of the radical women of color thought leaders behind third-wave feminism are watching us give ourselves permission to be who we are in our bodies and minds. Trans liberation is changing the way some of them talk about their genders. They conceptualize the work being done at the fat-disability intersection to be an experiment in both communities talking through the things both most want to avoid. The questions we are asking about the "ethics of pace," as scholar Moya Bailey coined, tickle their brains. There are so many threads of conversation, but at the end of the day, the ancestors would be the first to say that a lot of our contemporary politics are practical ones in nature—wanting loved ones to live life well, to have needs met, to experience joy, to love, to do what needs to be done, to feel freedom. We all want things to be better for future generations, and ourselves and our ancestors, too.

I speculate that soon, our recently departed Carrie Ann Lucas will settle into her ancestorship. She will remind people to be fierce and unapologetic in all things. She'll trail-blaze wherever she is, just as she did here. She will continue to transform how we think about the world and how to be in it, especially around the importance of showing up, loving hard, remembering ritual, giving 200 percent, believing in yourself and one another when others are foolish not to, creating the community/outfit/experience/vocation you wish for yourself. I wonder what she might learn from us, too.

I wear my boots. Not on days where I need to transfer standing on tile, but often. My ancestors and I are learning and loving. Together.

The Beauty of Spaces Created for and by Disabled People

s.e. smith

The theater is dim and just warm enough that I don't need my sweater, which I leave draped on the back of my creaky wooden seat. We are hushed, waiting for the lights to come up on the swooping ramp where the dance piece *Descent*, choreographed by Alice Sheppard in collaboration with Laurel Lawson, will be performed. This is one of my favorite parts of any theatrical production, the moment *before*, when anything might happen. Where all the barriers between us have fallen away.

Sheppard and then Lawson roll out, and they begin weaving intricate patterns with their bodies and wheelchairs while the music soars over them, with Michael Maag's lighting and projection weaving around them. The audio describer speaks in a low, rhythmic voice that broadcasts to the whole room, interplaying with the performance and the music.

There is something weighty and sacred here.

It is very rare, as a disabled person, that I have an intense sense of belonging, of being not just tolerated or included in a space but actively owning it; "This space," I whisper to myself, "is for me." Next to me, I sense my friend has the same electrified feeling. This space is for *us*.

I am spellbound. I am also overwhelmed, feeling something swell in my throat as I look out across the crowd, to the wheelchair and scooter users at the front of the raked seating, the ASL interpreter in crisp black next to the stage. Canes dangle from seat backs and a gilded prosthetic leg gleams under the safety lights. A blind woman in the row below me turns a tiny model of the stage over in her hands, tracing her fingers along with it in time to the audio description.

"I really wish I could have crammed all my disabled peeps in there," I say later.

Members of many marginalized groups have this shared experiential touchstone, this sense of unexpected and vivid belonging and an ardent desire to be able to pass this experience along. Some can remember the precise moment when they were in a space inhabited entirely by people like them for the first time. For disabled people, those spaces are often hospitals, group therapy sessions, and other clinical settings. That is often by design; we are kept isolated from one another, as though more than two disabled people in the same room will start a riot or make everyone feel awkward.

The first *social* setting where you come to the giddy understanding that this is a place for disabled people is a momentous one, and one worth lingering over. I cannot remember the first time it happened to me—perhaps a house party in San Francisco or an art show or a meeting of friends at a café. The experiences blend together, creating a sense of crip space, a communal belonging, a deep *rightness* that comes from not having to explain or justify your existence. They are resting points, even as they can be energizing and exhilarating.

Crip space is unique, a place where disability is celebrated and embraced—something radical and taboo in many parts of the world and sometimes even for people in those spaces. The idea that we need our own spaces, that we thrive in them, is particularly troubling for identities treated socially as a negative; why would you want to self-segregate with the other cripples? For those newly disabled, crip space may seem intimidating or frightening, with expectations that don't match the reality of experience—someone who has just experienced a tremendous life change is not always ready for disability pride or defiance, needing a kinder, gentler introduction.

The creation of spaces explicitly for marginalized people and not for others has been fraught with controversy. Proponents insist they're necessary for people to have intra-community conversations and they create a safe environment for talking through complex issues. They also may say that people find them empowering, especially those who have been cut off from their community.

It isn't that nondisabled people are unwelcome at this dance performance. But the space has not been tailored to their needs and designed to seamlessly accommodate them, and they stand out. The experience pushes the boundaries of their understanding and expectations.

During the Q&A, the dancers roll forward and the ASL interpreter trails them.

"Any questions or comments?" one asks, the interpreter's hands moving swiftly in sync. The audience is momentarily frozen, as all audiences are at this question every time it is asked. The disabled people are still processing. We feel slightly giddy; this is a piece that speaks our common language, silently and beautifully, that reaches the deep parts of us we normally keep buttoned up and hidden away. The nondisabled people are hesitant, nervous, unsure about what to say in response to the work in progress we'd all been invited to witness.

"I liked . . . the ramp," one of the nondisabled people says hesitantly, gesturing at the set.

It must have been an unsettling experience, to be invited into our space. To be on the other side of the access divide. To see disabled people spreading their wings and soaring. To see wheelchairs turned into powerful extensions of dancers' bodies, enabling them to do things physically impossible for bipedal people.

Those in positions of power, evidently fearing that people are talking about them behind closed doors, persistently insist on barging into such spaces. They call these spaces divisive, and their organizers are told that they aren't valuing the contributions of allies. These bursts of petty outrage at stumbling upon one of the few places in the world that is not open to them inadvertently highlight exactly why such places are needed.

This is precisely *why* they are needed: as long as claiming our own ground is treated as an act of hostility, we need our ground. We need the sense of community for disabled people created in crip space. Yet, like any ground, it comes with soft spots and pitfalls, a reminder that the landscape is not uniform, can even become treacherous.

Even as some of us find a sense of belonging within these corners of the world carved out for one another, not everyone feels welcome in them; disability is a broad sociocultural identity and experience, and not everyone thinks about disability in the same way. This can be the paradox of crip space: When do we exclude others in our zeal to embrace ourselves, with our refusal to consider the diversity of human experience? How can we cultivate spaces where everyone has that soaring sense of inclusion, where we can have difficult and meaningful conversations?

Crip space is akin to a fragile natural place. It must be protected in order to preserve the delicate things within, while remaining open to change with the seasons and the passage of time. That protection sometimes requires sacrifice or challenge, awkward questions, but that makes it no less vital. Because everyone deserves the shelter and embrace of crip space, to find their people and set down roots in a place they can call home.

After the dance, after the Q&A, after the drinks and snacks in the lobby, we must regretfully disperse back out into the chilly December night. The theater is in the Tenderloin, a community in transition, nudie cuties cheek by jowl with hipster bars, and as we fan out across the sidewalk—stained with bird shit and mysterious sticky substances that cling to wheels and canes—we must return once more into the outside world, beyond crip space. The barriers begin to reappear.

A child across the street points at the phalanx of wheelchair users and says, "Look, Mommy!" Two adults stare, surprised when an adult wheelchair user unaccompanied by an attendant, braving the world alone, transfers into his car and slings his wheelchair into the backseat, pulling away from the curb with the quiet hum of an expensive German engine.

At the BART station around the corner, the elevators are, as usual, out of order.

About the Editor

Alice Wong is a disabled activist, media maker, and research consultant based in San Francisco, California. She is the founder and director of the Disability Visibility Project, an online community dedicated to creating, sharing, and amplifying disability media and culture. Alice is also the host and co-producer of the Disability Visibility podcast and co-partner in a number of collaborations such as #CripTheVote and Access Is Love. From 2013 to 2015, Alice served as a member of the National Council on Disability, an appointment by President Barack Obama. You can follow her on Twitter: @SFdirewolf. For more: disabilityvisibilityproject.com.

About the Contributors

A. H. Reaume is a feminist activist and writer whose life was changed by a head injury in 2017. Since then, writing can be painful for her, but she continues to write in order to ensure her voice and other disabled voices are heard. Reaume is a columnist for *Open Book* and finished writing her first book *Unfinished: A Novel* in 2019. She can be found on Twitter at @a_h_reaume or on her website ahreaume.com.

Alice Sheppard creates movement that challenges conventional understandings of disabled and dancing bodies. Engaging with disability arts, culture, and history, Alice attends to the complex intersections of disability, gender, and race. Alice is the founder and artistic lead for Kinetic Light, an ensemble working at the intersections of disability, dance, design, identity, and technology. Her writing has appeared in academic journals and *The New York Times*.

Ariel Henley is a writer in Northern California. She has written about issues related to beauty, equality, human connection, and trauma for outlets like *The New York Times*, *The Washington Post*, and *The Atlantic*. She shares her story in an effort to eliminate the stigma surrounding disfigurement and to promote mainstream inclusion for individuals with physical differences. Her memoir, *A Face for Picasso*, is forthcoming from Farrar, Straus and Giroux.

Britney Wilson is a civil rights attorney and writer from Brooklyn, New York. She received her BA from Howard University and her JD from the University of Pennsylvania Law School. Her work has been featured in *Longreads* and *The Nation*, on HBO's Brave New Voices, and the radio show and podcast *This American Life*.

Diana Cejas is a pediatric neurologist in Durham, North Carolina. Her essays and opinion pieces have appeared in medical publications including *JAMA: The Journal of the American Medical Association* and *Neurology*. Works of creative nonfiction and short stories have appeared or are forthcoming in *Catapult*, *Passages North*, and *Intima: A Journal of Narrative Medicine*, among others. She is on Twitter @DianaCejasMD and blogs at dianacejasmd.com. Currently, she is working on a collection of essays that describe her life as both physician and patient.

Ellen Samuels is an associate professor at the University of Wisconsin–Madison and author of *Fantasies of Identification: Disability, Gender, Race* (NYU Press, 2014). She publishes critical and creative writing on disability and chronic illness in a variety of forums and is working on a new book called *Sick Time: Disability, Chronicity, Futurity*.

Hugo and Aurora award–winning editor **Elsa Sjunneson** is a deaf-blind hurricane in a vintage dress. Her nonfiction editorial work has appeared in *Uncanny Magazine* and *Fireside Magazine*. As an author, her work has appeared in CNN Opinion, Tor.com, *The Boston Globe*, and numerous other venues. In addition to editorial and authorial pursuits, she educates authors on writing disability respectfully. She traverses the world with her guide dog and a healthy amount of skepticism.

Eugene Grant is a writer and activist in the dwarfism and disability communities.

The first Deafblind person to graduate from Harvard Law School, **Haben Girma** advocates for equal opportunities for people with disabilities. President Obama named her a White House Champion of Change. She received the Helen Keller Achievement Award and a spot on the Forbes "30 Under 30" list. President Bill Clinton, Prime Minister Justin Trudeau, and Chancellor Angela Merkel have all honored Haben. Haben believes disability is an opportunity for innovation. She travels the world teaching the benefits of choosing inclusion, and in 2019 she published her first book, *Haben: The Deafblind Woman Who Conquered Harvard Law*.

Harriet McBryde Johnson was a disability activist, lawyer, and writer who lived most of her life in Charleston, South Carolina. Her articles for *The New York Times Magazine*, her memoir *Too Late to Die Young*, and her young adult novel *Accidents of Nature* demanded that readers look not at her, but through her eyes, as she challenged stereotypes about the disability experience and the worth of disabled lives.

The Harriet Tubman Collective is a collective of Black Deaf and Disabled organizers, community builders, activists, dreamers, and lovers striving for radical inclusion and collective liberation.

A graduate of Sonoma State University, **Jamison Hill** has written essays for *The New York Times, The Washington Post, Men's Journal,* the *Los Angeles Times, Writer's Digest, Vox,* and *Vice.* Jamison was featured in *Forgotten Plague,* a documentary about myalgic encephalomyelitis, a devastating multisystem disease, as well as a Netflix original series about mysterious diseases. In 2019, Jamison's *New York Times* essay, "Love Means Never Having to Say . . . Anything," was adapted for WBUR Boston's *Modern Love* podcast and read by Pedro Pascal (*Game of Thrones* and *Narcos*). Jamison was also featured on Dax Shepard's Armchair Expert podcast.

Jen Deerinwater, a citizen of the Cherokee Nation of Oklahoma, is a bisexual, Two-Spirit, multiply disabled journalist and organizer who covers the issues her communities face with an intersectional lens. She is a contributor at *Truthout,* founder and executive director of Crushing Colonialism, and a Freedomways Reporting Project fellow. Jen's work can be found in publications such as *Bitch*, Rewire.News, and *In These Times.* Her work is included in the anthologies *Two-Spirits Belong Here* and *Sacred and Subversive.* She has been interviewed for numerous outlets on her work, and *The Advocate* named Jen a 2019 Champion of Pride.

Jeremy Woody was born in Omaha, Nebraska, and found out that he was profoundly Deaf when he was two years old, after which he learned to use American Sign Language. He attended the Iowa School for the Deaf until eighth grade, then moved to Georgia, where he was mainstreamed. He raced in National BMX races for more than seventeen years, from the time he was ten years old; he was the only Deaf competitor in the United States. He can be found on Twitter @2017JWoody and on Instagram @bmxcrazed67.

Jessica Slice is a writer living in Durham, North Carolina, with her husband, David, her son, Khalil, and their sleepy dog, Batman. She graduated from Davidson College and Columbia University, where she earned a master's degree in social work. She is an advocate for quality mental health care for people with disabilities and for accessibility in higher education. She is at work on a memoir about acquired disability, pain, transracial adoption, and motherhood.

Jillian Weise is a poet, performance artist, and disability rights activist. She is the author of three poetry collections—*The Amputee's Guide to Sex*, *The Book of Goodbyes*, *Cyborg Detective*—and a novel, *The Colony*, which features Charles Darwin and Peter Singer as characters. Weise invented the word *tryborg* to name nondisabled people who theorize about cyborgs without any ontological experience. She performs Tipsy Tullivan across social media. Her essays have appeared in *A Public Space*, *Granta*, *Narrative Inquiry in Bioethics*, *The New York Times*, and *Tin House*.

June Eric-Udorie is a twenty-year-old British writer and feminist activist. She is a cofounder of Youth for Change, an initiative that works to combat female genital mutilation and forced marriage around the world, and her advocacy has taken her to classrooms, the Southbank Centre's Women of the World Festival, and the United Nations. Her writing has appeared in *The Guardian*, *The Independent*, *ESPN the Magazine*, and *Fusion*, among others, and *Elle* UK named her Female Activist of the Year in 2017. She currently studies at Duke University, where she is a recipient of the University Scholars merit scholarship, established by Melinda French Gates.

Karolyn Gehrig is a queer disabled artist, writer, and performer. She lives in Los Angeles.

Keah Brown is a journalist and writer whose work can be found in *Glamour*, *Marie Claire* UK, *Harper's Bazaar*, and *Teen Vogue*, among others. Her debut essay collection, *The Pretty One*, published in 2019, talks about her experiences as a young African American woman with cerebral palsy. You can learn more about her at keahbrown.com.

Keshia Scott is pursuing an MS degree in cultural foundations of education with a CAS in Disability Studies from Syracuse University. She is dedicated to unmasking various channels of oppression and exploring how different modalities of oppression interact. Her interests focus on different takes on intersectionality of modes of oppression, particularly sexism, racism, and ableism. She is an intersectional feminist, an eater of all pastas and breads, and a great lover of spoken word.

Lateef McLeod is a writer and a scholar. He earned a BA in English from the University of California, Berkeley, and a MFA in creative writing from Mills College. He published his first book of poetry, *A Declaration of a Body of Love*, in 2010, chronicling his life as a black man with a disability. He currently is writing a novel tentatively entitled *The Third Eye Is Crying* and is also completing another poetry book entitled *Whispers of Krip Love, Shouts of Krip Revolution*. More of his writing is available on his website, lateefhmcleod.com, and his HuffPost blog, huffpost.com/author/lateef-mcleod. You can also hear his perspective as a cohost of the podcast *Black Disabled Men Talk*, which can be heard on a variety of podcast platforms or via the website blackdisabledmentalk.com.

Leah Lakshmi Piepzna-Samarasinha is a queer disabled nonbinary femme writer and disability justice movement worker of Burgher/Tamil Sri Lankan and Irish/Roma ascent. They are the Lambda

Award–winning author of *Tonguebreaker*, *Bridge of Flowers*, *Care Work: Dreaming Disability Justice*, *Dirty River*, *Bodymap*, *Love Cake*, and *Consensual Genocide*, and coeditor of *Beyond Survival: Strategies and Stories from the Transformative Justice Movement* and *The Revolution Starts at Home*. Since 2009, they have been a lead artist with the disability justice performance collective Sins Invalid. They are also a rust beltpoet, a Sri Lankan with a white mom, a femme over forty, a grassroots intellectual, a survivor who is hard to kill.

Liz Moore is a chronically ill and neurodivergent disability rights activist and writer. They live on their couch on stolen Piscataway-Conoy land in the D.C. metro area. You can find them on Twitter, or read more of their work at liminalnest.wordpress.com. Liz also writes disability-centered romance under the pen name Ada Lowell.

Mari Ramsawakh is a disabled and nonbinary writer, workshop facilitator, and podcaster. They have written for *Xtra*, Leafly, *Nuance*, and other publications. Their fiction has been published in the *Hart House Review* and *Toronto 2033*. Mari is also cohost and producer of the podcast *Sick Sad World*. They facilitate workshops related to disability, queerness, sexual health, and art, and they have spoken at 20:20: A Summit for the Students, by the Students; the Playground Conference; and the Make Change Conference. Mari's work is focused on increasing representation for racialized, queer, and disabled people in modeling, in all forms of media.

Maysoon Zayid is an actress, comedian, writer, and disability advocate. She is the cofounder/co–executive producer of the New York Arab-American Comedy Festival and has toured extensively at home and abroad. Maysoon is a commentator on CNN, authored "Find

Another Dream" for Audible, and appears on *General Hospital*. Her talk, "I got 99 problems . . . palsy is just one," was the most viewed TED Talk of 2014.

Patty Berne is the cofounder and the executive and artistic director of Sins Invalid, a disability-justice-based performance project centralizing disabled artists of color and queer and gender nonconforming artists with disabilities. Berne's training in clinical psychology focused on trauma and healing for survivors of interpersonal and state violence. Her professional background includes offering mental health support to survivors of violence and advocating for LGBTQI and disability perspectives within the field of reproductive genetic technologies. Berne's experiences as a Japanese Haitian queer disabled woman provides grounding for her work creating "liberated zones" for marginalized voices.

Rebecca Cokley is the director of the Disability Justice Initiative at the Center for American Progress. She joined CAP after leading the National Council on Disability for four years. From 2009 to 2013 she worked in the Obama administration at the Departments of Education and Health and Human Services, and at the White House. Rebecca began her career at the Institute for Educational Leadership. She is on the boards of Common Cause, the Community Justice Reform Coalition, and the ACLU of DC and was featured on CNN, Netflix's *Explained*, and *Last Week Tonight with John Oliver*. Rebecca has a BA in politics from the University of California, Santa Cruz.

Reyma McCoy McDeid is the executive director of Central Iowa Center for Independent Living (winner of the 2018 Organization of the Year award from the Des Moines Civil and Human Rights Commission) and serves as treasurer for both the National Council on Independent Living and the Autistic Self Advocacy Network. She is the recipient of a 2019 AT&T Humanity of Connection award, and her 2018 run for office was endorsed by the Working Families Party, the Asian & Latino Coalition, and Iowa Women for Progressive Change. She is also a single mom. Her work has been featured in VICE, Pantsuit Nation, *TIME*, the *Des Moines Register*, *The Gazette* (Cedar Rapids, Iowa), and Progressive Voices of Iowa. Her vocation is mobilizing marginalized persons—the working class, people of color, folks with disabilities, religious minorities, and others—to engage with the political process at every available opportunity.

Ricardo T. Thornton Sr. is a strong self-advocate in the District of Columbia and a former resident of the District's institution for people with disabilities, Forest Haven. He is copresident of Project ACTION!, an advocacy coalition of adults with disabilities, is an ambassador with the Special Olympics, and served on the President's Committee for People with Intellectual Disabilities. He has worked for more than forty years at the Martin Luther King Jr. Memorial Library. He is married to Donna, also a former resident of Forest Haven; they have one son and three grandchildren. The film *Profoundly Normal* chronicles their life as one of the first couples in the United States with developmental disabilities to marry.

Sandy Ho is a disability community organizer, activist, and disability policy researcher. She is the founder of the Disability & Intersectionality Summit, a biennial national conference organized by disabled activists that centers the experiences and knowledge of multiply marginalized disabled people. Sandy is a third of the team behind Access Is Love, a campaign copartnered with Alice Wong and Mia Mingus. Her areas of work include disability justice, racial justice, intersectionality, and disability studies. She is a disabled queer Asian American woman whose writing has been published by Bitch Media online.

s.e. smith is a Northern California–based journalist and writer who has appeared in publications like *Esquire*, *Rolling Stone*, *In These Times*, *Bitch*, *The Nation*, *The Guardian*, and *Catapult*. Believing that liberation for some is justice for none, smith's work is rooted in provocative conversations and cultivating emerging writers.

Shoshana Kessock is CEO of Phoenix Outlaw Productions and a narrative lead at the immersive art installation Meow Wolf. She is a producer of live-action role-playing games, a contributor to dozens of tabletop role-playing games, the author of games like Dangers Untold and SERVICE, and a creator of multiple immersive events enjoyed worldwide. When she isn't producing live-action games, she writes fiction, comics, and screenplays. She hails from Brooklyn, New York, and is now living in Santa Fe, New Mexico, with her nineteen-year-old cat, Lilo. She can be found online at shoshanakessock.com or on Twitter @ShoshanaKessock.

Sky Cubacub is a nonbinary queer and disabled Filipinx artist from Chicago, Illinois. They are the creator of Rebirth Garments, a line of wearables that challenges mainstream beauty standards through centering queer and disabled people of all sizes, ethnicities, and ages. They are the editor of the Radical Visibility Zine, a magazine for queer and disabled people of all ages based on their manifesto. As a multidisciplinary artist, they are interested in fulfilling the needs for disabled queer life, with an emphasis on joy. Sky Cubacub was named 2018 Chicagoan of the Year by the *Chicago Tribune*.

Stacey Milbern is an Oakland, California/Chochenyo Ohlone–based Disability Justice community organizer and writer. Her work is informed by her life experience as a mixed race (Korean and white) person, queer person, and disabled person with a nonnormative body. She believes our liberation requires us to be with one another and the earth interdependently. For her day job, she works for a bank in corporate HR.

Talila A. Lewis is an attorney, educator, and organizer who helps people understand the inextricable links between racism, classism, ableism, and structural inequity. Lewis created the only national database of deaf/blind imprisoned people in the United States and works to correct and prevent wrongful convictions of deaf/disabled people as the volunteer director of HEARD (behearddc.org). Lewis co-created the Harriet Tubman Collective and has taught at Rochester Institute of Technology and Northeastern University School of Law. Named a Top 30 Thinker Under 30 by *Pacific Standard* magazine, Lewis has received numerous awards, including the 2015 White House Champion of Change Award.

Wanda Díaz-Merced is an astronomer who evidenced that sound increases the sensitivity of people to detect important features in astronomy data. She is currently based at the University of Colorado Boulder.

Zipporah Arielle is a writer from a small town in Maine in the United States. She writes about everything, but her social justice work focuses primarily on issues revolving around disability, Queerness, and Jewishness. She currently resides in Nashville, Tennessee, with her service dog in training, where she spends her days writing and ordering take-out. She plans to publish a book (or two) and spend as much of her life as possible traveling before retiring to the Italian countryside (or something like that).

In a time of destruction, create something.

—Maxine Hong Kingston

We urgently need to bring to our communities the limitless capacity to love, serve, and create for and with each other.

—Grace Lee Boggs

Further Reading

Nonfiction

Andrews, A. *A Quick & Easy Guide to Sex & Disability*. Portland: Limerence Press, 2020.

Bascom, Julia. *Loud Hands: Autistic People, Speaking*. Washington, D.C.: Autistic Self Advocacy Network, 2012.

Berne, Patty, and Sins Invalid. *Skin, Tooth, and Bone: The Basis of Movement Is Our People, A Disability Justice Primer*. Second edition. Sins Invalid, October 2019. https://www.sinsinvalid.org /disability-justice-primer.

Brown, Keah. *The Pretty One: On Life, Pop Culture, Disability, and Other Reasons to Fall in Love with Me*. New York: Atria Books, 2019.

Clare, Eli. *Brilliant Imperfection: Grappling with Cure*. Durham: Duke University Press Books, 2017.

Findlay, Carly. *Say Hello*. Sydney: HarperCollins Australia, 2019.

Fries, Kenny. *In the Province of the Gods*. Madison: University of Wisconsin Press, 2017.

G, Nina. *Stutterer Interrupted: The Comedian Who Almost Didn't Happen*. Berkeley: She Writes Press, 2019.

Galloway, Terry. *Mean Little deaf Queer: A Memoir*. Boston: Beacon Press, 2010.

Girma, Haben. *Haben: The Deafblind Woman Who Conquered Harvard Law*. New York: Twelve, 2019.

Heumann, Judith, and Kristen Joiner. *Being Heumann: An Unrepentant Memoir of a Disability Rights Activist*. Boston: Beacon Press, 2020.

Huber, Sonya. *Pain Woman Takes Your Keys, and Other Essays from a Nervous System*. Lincoln: University of Nebraska Press, 2017.

Ikpi, Bassey. *I'm Telling the Truth, but I'm Lying*. New York: Harper Collins, 2019.

Johnson, Harriet McBryde. *Too Late to Die Young: Nearly True Tales from a Life*. New York: Picador, 2006.

Kafer, Alison. *Feminist, Queer, Crip*. Bloomington: Indiana University Press, 2013.

Khakpour, Porochista. *Sick: A Memoir*. New York: Harper Perennial, 2018.

Kurchak, Sarah. *I Overcame My Autism and All I Got Was This Lousy Anxiety Disorder*. Vancouver: Douglas & McIntyre, 2020.

LaSpina, Nadina. *Such a Pretty Girl: A Story of Struggle, Empowerment, and Disability Pride*. New York: New Village Press, 2019.

Leduc, Amanda. *Disfigured: On Fairy Tales, Disability, and Making Space*. Toronto: Coach House Books, 2020.

Longmore, Paul. *Why I Burned My Book and Other Essays on Disability*. Philadelphia, PA: Temple University Press, 2003.

Mairs, Nancy. *Waist-High in the World: A Life Among the Nondisabled*. Boston, MA: Beacon Press, 1997.

Montgomery, Sarah Fawn. *Quite Mad: An American Pharma Memoir*. Columbus: Ohio State University Press, 2018.

Moore Jr., Leroy F. *Black Disabled Art History 101*. San Francisco: Xochitl Justice Press, 2017.

Ortiz, Naomi. *Sustaining Spirit: Self-Care for Social Justice.* Berkeley: Reclamation Press, 2018.

O'Toole, Corbett Joan. *Fading Scars: My Queer Disability History*, 2nd ed. Berkeley: Reclamation Press, 2019.

Palmer, Dorothy Ellen. *Falling for Myself.* Hamilton: Wolsak & Wynn Publishers Ltd., 2019.

Piepzna-Samarasinha, Leah Lakshmi. *Care Work: Dreaming Disability Justice.* Vancouver: Arsenal Pulp Press, 2018.

Pottle, Adam. *Voice: On Writing with Deafness.* Regina: University of Regina Press, 2019.

Rousso, Harilyn. *Don't Call Me Inspirational: A Disabled Feminist Talks Back.* Philadelphia: Temple University Press, 2013.

Ryan, Frances. *Crippled: Austerity and the Demonization of Disabled People.* New York: Verso Books, 2019.

Sherer Jacobson, Denise. *The Question of David: A Mother's Journey Through Adoption, Family and Life.* CreateSpace Independent Publishing Platform, 1999.

Vargas, Dior. *The Color of My Mind: Mental Health Narratives from People of Color.* Self-published, 2018. http://diorvargas.com/color-of-my-mind.

Virdi, Jaipreet. *Hearing Happiness: Deafness Cures in History.* Chicago: University of Chicago Press, 2020.

Wang, Esmé Weijun. *The Collected Schizophrenias: Essays.* Minneapolis: Graywolf Press, 2019.

Fiction

Al-Mohamed, Day. *The Labyrinth's Archivist: A Broken Cities Novella.* Charlotte: Falstaff Books, 2019.

Alshammari, Shahd. *Notes on the Flesh*. Rabat, Malta: Faraxa Publishing, 2017.

Bardugo, Leigh. *Six of Crows*. New York, NY: Henry Holt & Co., 2015.

Finger, Anne. *A Woman, in Bed*. El Paso: Cinco Puntos Press, 2018.

Franklin, Tee, Jenn St-Onge, Joy San, and Genevive FT. *Bingo Love Volume 1*. Portland: Image Comics, 2018.

Griffith, Nicola. *So Lucky: A Novel*. New York: Farrar, Straus and Giroux, 2018.

Nijkamp, Marieke. *Before I Let Go*. Naperville: Sourcebooks Fire, 2018.

———, and Manuel Preitano. *The Oracle Code*. Burbank: DC Comics, 2020.

Nussbaum, Susan. *Good Kings Bad Kings: A Novel*. New York: Algonquin Books, 2013.

Shang, Melissa, and Eva Shang. *Mia Lee is Wheeling Through Middle School*. San Francisco, CA: Woodgate Publishing, 2016.

Anthologies

Brown, Lydia X.Z., E. Ashkenazy, and Morénike Giwa Onaiwu. *All the Weight of Our Dreams: On Living Racialized Autism*. Lincoln: DragonBee Press, 2017.

Catapano, Peter, and Rosemarie Garland-Thompson, eds. *About Us: Essays from the Disability Series of the* New York Times. New York: Liveright, 2019.

Cipriani, Belo Miguel, ed. *Firsts: Coming of Age Stories by People with Disabilities*. Minneapolis: Oleb Books, 2018.

Clark, John Lee, ed. *Deaf Lit Extravaganza*. Minneapolis: Handtype Press, 2013.

Findlay, Carly, ed. *Growing Up Disabled in Australia*. Melbourne: Black Inc. Books, 2020.

Gordon, Cait, and Talia C. Johnson. *Nothing Without Us*. Gatineau: Renaissance Press, 2019.

Jensen, Kelly, ed. *(Don't) Call Me Crazy. 33 Voices Start the Conversation about Mental Health*. Chapel Hill: Algonquin Young Readers, 2018.

Luczak, Raymond, ed. *QDA: A Queer Disability Anthology*. Minneapolis: Squares & Rebels, 2015.

Nijkamp, Marieke, ed. *Unbroken: 13 Stories Starring Disabled Teens*. New York: Farrar, Straus and Giroux, 2018.

smith, sb., ed. *Disabled Voices Anthology*. Nanoose Bay: Rebel Mountain Press, 2020.

Wong, Alice. *Resistance and Hope: Essays by Disabled People*. Disability Visibility Project, 2018. https://www.smashwords.com/books/view/899911.

Poetry

Alland, Sandra. "My Arrival at Crip: Poetic Histories of Disability, Neurodivergence, and Illness in Tkaronto/Taranto/Toronto, 1995–2007." *Hamilton Arts & Letters* 12 (2019–20). https://samizdatpress.typepad.com/hal_magazine_issue_twelve/my-arrival-at-crip-by-sandra-alland-1.html.

———, Khairani Barokka, and Daniel Sluman, eds. *Stairs and Whispers: D/deaf and Disabled Poets Write Back*. Rugby, Warwickshire: Nine Arches Press, 2017.

Barrett, Kay Ulanday. *More Than Organs*. Little Rock, AR: Sibling Rivalry Press, 2020.

———. *When the Chant Comes*. New York: Topside Heliotrope, 2016.

Day, Meg, and Niki Herd, eds. *Laura Hershey: On the Life and Work of an American Master*. Warrensburg, MO: Pleiades Press, 2019.

Erlichman, Shira. *Odes to Lithium*. Farmington, ME: Alice James Books, 2019.

Johnson, Cyrée Jarelle. *Slingshot*. New York: Nightboat Books, 2019.

Kaminsky, Ilya. *Deaf Republic*. Minneapolis: Graywolf Press, 2019.

Piepzna-Samarasinha, Leah Lakshmi. *Tonguebreaker*. Vancouver: Arsenal Pulp Press, 2019.

Weise, Jillian. *Cyborg Detective*. Rochester: BOA Editions Ltd., 2019.

Online Publications and Websites

Deaf Poets Society https://www.deafpoetssociety.com/

Disability column by *The New York Times* https://www.nytimes.com/column/disability

Disability Acts: Disability Essays, Screeds, and Manifestos by Disabled People for All People https://medium.com/disability-acts

Disability Visibility Project https://disabilityvisibilityproject.com/

Everybody: An Artifact History of Disability in America, National Museum of American History https://everybody.si.edu/

"In Sickness," Bitch Media, 2018 https://www.bitchmedia.org/topic/sickness

Patient No More: People with Disabilities Securing Civil Rights, Paul K. Longmore Institute on Disability https://longmoreinstitute.sfsu.edu/patient-no-more

Reclamation Press https://www.reclapress.com/

Rooted in Rights https://rootedinrights.org/

Skin Stories, Medium.com https://medium.com/skin-stories

Uncanny Magazine 30: *Disabled People Destroy Fantasy!*, September/October 2019 https://uncannymagazine.com/issues/uncanny-magazine-issue-thirty/

Uncanny Magazine 24: Disabled People Destroy Science Fiction!, September/October 2018 https://uncannymagazine.com/issues /uncanny-magazine-issue-twenty-four/

Wordgathering: A Journal of Disability Poetry and Literature http:// www.wordgathering.com/

Podcasts, Radio Programs, and Audiobooks

*Contra** https://www.mapping-access.com/podcast

Disability Visibility https://disabilityvisibilityproject.com/podcast-2/

Pigeonhole http://whoamitostopit.com/podcast-2/

Power Not Pity http://www.powernotpity.com/

Reid My Mind http://reidmymind.com/

The Accessible Stall https://www.theaccessiblestall.com/

Tips and Tricks on How to Be Sick http://sicktipsandtricks.com/

"We've Got This: Parenting with a Disability," *Life Matters*, Australian Broadcasting Corporation, 2018 https://www.abc.net.au/radio national/programs/lifematters/features/weve-got-this-parenting -with-a-disability/

Zayid, Maysoon. *Find Another Dream*. Audible, 2019 https://www .audible.com/pd/Find-Another-Dream-Audiobook/B07YVLM9NZ

Articles, Blog Posts, Essays, and Videos

Aquino-Irving, Kyla. "Celebrating the Legacy of Ki'Tay D. Davidson." Yo! Disabled & Proud, June 25, 2019. https://yodisabledproud .org/blog/celebrating-the-legacy-of-kitay-d-davidson/

Baggs, Mel. "When Orange Speaks Louder Than Words." Per-

sonal website, April 29, 2016. https://ballastexistenz.wordpress
.com/2016/04/29/when-orange-speaks-louder-than-words/.

Barbarin, Imani. "Ableism Is the Go-To Disguise for White Supremacy. Too Many People Are Falling for It." *Rewire.News*, November
19, 2018. https://rewire.news/article/2018/11/19/ableism-is-the-go
-to-disguise-for-white-supremacy-too-many-people-are-falling
-for-it/.

Bastién, Angelica Jade. "What *Crazy Ex-Girlfriend*'s Depiction of
Mental Illness Has Meant to Me This Season." *Vulture*, December 13, 2017. https://www.vulture.com/2017/12/crazy-ex-girlfriend
-mental-illness-what-it-has-meant-to-me-this-season.html.

Clark, John Lee. "Distantism." Personal Tumblr blog. August 3, 2017.
https://johnleeclark.tumblr.com/post/163762970913/distantism.

Cohen-Rottenberg, Rachel. "Seeking Great-Aunt Sarah: Learning
from the Abuse of My Disabled Ancestor." *The Body Is Not an
Apology Magazine*, July 27, 2019. https://thebodyisnotanapology
.com/magazine/reclaiming-memory-searching-for-great-aunt
-sarah/.

Cone, Kitty. "Short History of the 504 Sit-In." Disability Rights
Education & Defense Fund. https://dredf.org/504-sit-in-20th
-anniversary/short-history-of-the-504-sit-in/.

Cubacub, Sky. "A Queercrip Dress Reform Movement Manifesto."
Edited by Daviel Shy, April 22, 2015. http://rebirthgarments.com
/radical-visibility-zine.

Finch, Sam Dylan. "Why I'm Done Being a 'Good' Mentally Ill Person." The Establishment, March 27, 2017. https://medium.com
/the-establishment/why-im-done-being-a-good-mentally-ill
-person-aa1124fa4215.

Fortson, Ashanti. "I'm Not a Robot." The Nib, May 10, 2017. https://
thenib.com/not-a-robot.

Gotkin, Kevin. "Stair Worship: Heatherwick's *Vessel*." *The Avery Review* 33, 2018. https://averyreview.com/issues/33/stair-worship.

Griffith, Nicola, "Neither Dying Nor Being Cured." Personal website, October 9, 2019. https://nicolagriffith.com/2019/10/09/neither-dying-nor-being-cured/.

Joyner, Jazmine. "Why Living with Chronic Illness in a Capitalist Society Is Dehumanizing." *Wear Your Voice Magazine*, January 29, 2018. https://wearyourvoicemag.com/identities/ableism/chronic-illness-capitalist-society.

Lau, Travis Chi Wing. "William Hay; Or, An Obsession." The Rambling. February 14, 2019. https://the-rambling.com/2019/02/14/valentines-lau/.

Leduc, Amanda. "Monster or Marvel? A Disabled Life in a Superhero Universe." Literary Hub, April 26, 2019. https://lithub.com/monster-or-marvel-a-disabled-life-in-a-superhero-universe/.

Luterman, Sara. "Toxic parenting myths make life harder for people with autism. That must change." *The Washington Post*, February 26, 2019. https://www.washingtonpost.com/outlook/toxic-parenting-myths-make-life-harder-for-people-with-autism-that-must-change/2019/02/25/24bd60f6-2f1b-11e9-813a-0ab2f17e305b_story.html.

Mingus, Mia. "'Disability Justice' Is Simply Another Term for Love." Personal website, November 3, 2018. https://leavingevidence.wordpress.com/2018/11/03/disability-justice-is-simply-another-term-for-love/.

Montgomery, Cal. "Critic of the Dawn." *Ragged Edge Online* 2, 2001. http://www.raggededgemagazine.com/0501/0501cov.htm.

Ndopu, Edward. "A Photo-Essay: Decolonizing My Body, My Being." The Feminist Wire, December 12, 2012. https://thefeministwire.com/2012/12/a-photo-essay-decolonizing-my-body-my-being/.

Osunde, Eloghosa. "Don't Let It Bury You." *Catapult*, April 25, 2017. https://catapult.co/stories/dont-let-it-bury-you.

Parisien, Dominik. "Growing Up in Wonderland." *Uncanny Magazine* 12, September/October 2016. https://uncannymagazine.com /article/growing-up-in-wonderland/.

Philip, Aaron. "I'm a Black, Trans, Disabled Model—And I Just Got Signed to a Major Agency." *Them*, September 4, 2018. https:// www.them.us/story/aaron-philip-signed-to-modeling-agency.

Pryal, Katie Rose. "My Son and I Don't Do Well with Chaos—and That's Okay." *Catapult*, February 12, 2019. https://catapult.co /stories/column-we-dont-do-well-with-chaos-and-thats-okay -katie-rose-pryal.

Queen, Khadijah, and Jillian Weise. "Make No Apologies for Yourself." *The New York Times*, May 19, 2019. https://www.nytimes .com/2019/05/19/opinion/disability-poems.html.

———. "We Will Not Be Exorcised." *The New York Times*, June 15, 2019. https://www.nytimes.com/2019/06/15/opinion/disabled-poets -new-work.html.

Schulman, Howard. "As My Face Disappeared So Did My Mother and Father." *Narratively*, August 12, 2015. https://narratively.com /as-my-face-disappeared-so-did-my-mother-and-father/.

Shew, Ashley. "Stop Depicting Technology As Redeeming Disabled People." Nursing Clio, April 23, 2019. https://nursingclio.org /2019/04/23/stop-depicting-technology-as-redeeming-disabled -people/.

Soyer, Hannah. "Displacement." *mojo literary journal* 15, November 29, 2018. http://mikrokosmosjournal.com/2018/11/hannah-soyer -displacement/.

smith, s.e. "The Ugly Beautiful and Other Failings of Disability Representation." *Catapult*, October 24, 2019. https://catapult

.co/stories/the-ugly-beautiful-and-other-failings-of-disability
-representation-an-unquiet-mind-s-e-smith.

Solomon, Rivers. "Black Girl Going Mad." *Guernica*, December 4,
2017. https://www.guernicamag.com/mad-black-girl/.

Thériault, Anne. "Geel, Belgium has a radical approach to mental illness." Broadview, September 5, 2019. https://broadview.org/geel
-belgium-mental-health/.

Thompson, Vilissa. "The Overlooked History of Black Disabled People." *Rewire.News*, March 16, 2018. https://rewire.news/article
/2018/03/16/overlooked-history-black-disabled-people/.

Tischer, Ingrid. "I Remember This: What Getting My First Milwau-
kee Backbrace Was Like." Tales from the Crip, February 17, 2019.
https://talesfromthecrip.org/2019/02/17/i-remember-this-what
-getting-my-first-milwaukee-backbrace-was-like/.

Wolf, Asher. "Kindness and Other Rot." Medium.com, May 15, 2019.
https://medium.com/@Asher_Wolf/kindness-and-other-rot
-d6704331220f.

Wong, Alice. "The Last Straw." Eater, July 19, 2018. https://www.eater
.com/2018/7/19/17586742/plastic-straw-ban-disabilities.

———. "My Medicaid, My Life." *The New York Times,* May 3, 2017.
https://www.nytimes.com/2017/05/03/opinion/my-medicaid-my
-life.html.

———. "Diversifying Radio with Disabled Voices." Transom, 2016.
https://transom.org/2016/alice-wong/.

Young, Stella. "I'm Not Your Inspiration, Thank You Very Much."
TEDxSydney, April 2014. https://www.ted.com/talks/stella_young
_i_m_not_your_inspiration_thank_you_very_much/.

Permission Acknowledgments

"Selma Blair Became a Disabled Icon Overnight. Here's Why We Need More Stories Like Hers" by Zipporah Arielle first appeared on *Bustle* on March 6, 2019. Copyrighted 2019. Bustle Digital Group. 2134966:1219AT.

"To Survive Climate Catastrophe, Look to Queer and Disabled Folks" by Patty Berne first appeared in *Yes!* magazine on July 30, 2019. Reprinted with permission of the author.

"Taking Charge of My Story as a Cancer Patient at the Hospital Where I Work" by Diana Cejas first appeared in *Catapult* on May 21, 2019. Reprinted with permission of the author.

"The Anti-Abortion Bill You Aren't Hearing About" by Rebecca Cokley first appeared on *Rewire.News* on May 20, 2019. Reprinted with permission of the author.

"The Erasure of Indigenous People in Chronic Illness" by Jen Deerinwater first appeared on Bitch Media on June 8, 2018. Reprinted with permission of Bitch Media.

"How a Blind Astronomer Found a Way to Hear the Stars" by Wanda Díaz-Merced first appeared as a TED Talk in February 2016. To watch the full talk, visit TED.com.

"When You Are Waiting to Be Healed" by June Eric-Udorie first appeared on *Catapult* on September 22, 2016. Reprinted with permission of the author.

"Time's Up for Me, Too" by Karolyn Gehrig first appeared on *Guernica* on February 22, 2018. Reprinted with permission of the author.

"Guide dogs don't lead blind people. We wander as one." by Haben Girma first appeared in *The Washington Post* on August 7, 2019. Including excerpts from *Haben: The Deafblind Woman Who Conquered Harvard Law* by Haben Girma, copyright © 2019 by Haben Girma, originally published by Twelve Books, an imprint of Hachette Book Group, Inc., New York, in 2019. Reprinted by permission of Haben Girma and Twelve Books, an imprint of Hachette Book Group, Inc.

"The Fearless Benjamin Lay—Activist, Abolitionist, Dwarf Person" by Eugene Grant first appeared on *The Beacon Broadside* on April 26, 2018. Reprinted with permission of the author.

"Disability Solidarity: Completing the 'Vision for Black Lives'" by the Harriet Tubman Collective first appeared on HarrietTubman Collective.tumblr.com on September 7, 2016. Reprinted with permission of the author.

"There's a Mathematical Equation That Proves I'm Ugly—Or So I Learned in My Seventh Grade Art Class" by Ariel Henley first appeared on *Narratively* on July 18, 2016. Reprinted with permission of the author.

"Love Means Never Having to Say . . . Anything" by Jamison Hill first appeared in *The New York Times* on May 25, 2018. From *The New York Times.* © 2018 The New York Times Company. All rights reserved. Used under license.

"Canfei to Canji: The Freedom to Be Loud" by Sandy Ho first appeared on Bitch Media on August 1, 2018. Reprinted with permission of Bitch Media.

"Unspeakable Conversations" by Harriet McBryde Johnson first appeared in *The New York Times* on February 16, 2003. From *The New York Times.* © 2003 The New York Times Company. All rights reserved. Used under license.

"Falling/Burning: Hannah Gadsby, *Nanette*, and Being a Bipolar Creator" by Shoshana Kessock first appeared on ShoshanaKessock.com on July 12, 2018. Reprinted with permission of the author.

"Ki'tay D. Davidson: A Eulogy" by Talila A. Lewis first appeared on TalilaALewis.com on December 10, 2016. Reprinted with permission of the author.

"Gaining Power through Communication Access" by Lateef McLeod first appeared on "Assistive Technology," *Disability Visibility* podcast, Episode 3, on October 1, 2017. Reprinted with permission of the author.

"On the Ancestral Plane: Crip Hand-Me-Downs and the Legacy of Our Movements" by Stacey Park Milbern first appeared on the Disability Visibility Project, March 10, 2019. Reprinted with permission of the author.

"I'm Tired of Chasing a Cure" by Liz Moore first appeared on Liminalnest .wordpress.com on December 27, 2018. Reprinted with permission of the author.

"Incontinence Is a Public Health Issue—and We Need to Talk About It" by Mari Ramsawakh first appeared on *Them* on January 4, 2019. Reprinted with permission of the author.

"Why My Novel Is Dedicated to My Disabled Friend Maddy" by A. H. Reaume first appeared on *Open Book* on June 6, 2019. Reprinted with permission of the author.

"Six Ways of Looking at Crip Time" by Ellen Samuels first appeared in *Disability Studies Quarterly* 27, no. 3 (Summer 2017). Reprinted with permission of the author.

"Last But Not Least—Embracing Asexuality" by Keshia Scott first appeared on *Disability Acts* on February 19, 2019. Reprinted with permission of author.

"The Beauty of Spaces Created for and by Disabled People" by s.e. smith first appeared on *Catapult* on October 22, 2018. Reprinted with permission of author.

"How to Make a Paper Crane from Rage" by Elsa Sjunneson first appeared in *Uncanny Magazine* 26, January/February 2019. Reprinted with permission of the author.

"Imposter Syndrome and Parenting with a Disability" by Jessica Slice first appeared in *The Washington Post* on September 4, 2019, as "Parenting with a Disability Makes Me Feel Like an 'Impostor' as a Mother." Reprinted with permission of the author.

"We Can't Go Back" by Ricardo T. Thornton Sr. first appeared as "Statement of Ricardo Thornton Sr. Before the U.S. Senate, Committee on Health, Education, Labor and Pensions Regarding Olmstead Enforcement Update: Using the ADA to Promote Community Integration," on June 21, 2012. Reprinted by permission of the author.

"Common Cyborg" by Jillian Weise first appeared in slightly different form in *Granta* on September 24, 2018. Reprinted with permission of the author.

"On NYC's Paratransit, Fighting for Safety, Respect, and Human Dignity" by Britney Wilson first appeared on *Longreads* in September 2017. Reprinted by permission of the author. A version of this essay was also featured on episode 629 of the radio show and podcast *This American Life*, "Expect Delays," in October 2017. The segment was entitled "The Longest Distance Between Two Points."

"The Isolation of Being Deaf in Prison" by Jeremy Woody, as told to Christie Thompson, first appeared on the Marshall Project on October 18, 2018. Reprinted by permission of the author.

"If You Can't Fast, Give" by Maysoon Zayid first appeared on Maysoon.com on June 20, 2015. Reprinted by permission of the author.

ALSO AVAILABLE FROM

VINTAGE BOOKS & ANCHOR BOOKS

MY BELOVED WORLD
by Sonia Sotomayor

The first Hispanic and third woman appointed to the United States Supreme Court, Sonia Sotomayor has become an instant American icon. Now, with a candor and intimacy never undertaken by a sitting Justice, she recounts her life from a Bronx housing project to the federal bench, a journey that offers an inspiring testament to her own extraordinary determination and the power of believing in oneself. Along the way we see how she was shaped by her invaluable mentors, a failed marriage, and the modern version of extended family she has created from cherished friends and their children. Through her still-astonished eyes, America's infinite possibilities are envisioned anew in this warm and honest book.

Memoir

THE BREAKTHROUGH
Politics and Race in the Age of Obama
by Gwen Ifill

In *The Breakthrough*, veteran journalist Gwen Ifill surveys the American political landscape, shedding new light on the impact of Barack Obama's stunning presidential victory and introducing the emerging young African American politicians forging a bold new path to political power. Drawing on exclusive interviews with power brokers such as President Obama, Colin Powell, Vernon Jordan, the Reverend Jesse Jackson, and many others, as well as her own razor-sharp observations and analysis of such issues as generational conflict, the race/gender clash, and the "black enough" conundrum, Ifill shows why this is a pivotal moment in American history.

Current Affairs/Politics

WINNERS TAKE ALL
The Elite Charade of Changing the World
by Anand Giridharadas

Anand Giridharadas takes us into the inner sanctums of a new gilded age, where the rich and powerful fight for equality and justice any way they can—except ways that threaten the social order and their position atop it. Giridharadas's groundbreaking investigation has already forced a great, sorely needed reckoning among the world's wealthiest and those they hover above, and it points toward an answer: Rather than rely on scraps from the winners, we must take on the grueling democratic work of building more robust, egalitarian institutions and truly changing the world—a call to action for elites and everyday citizens alike.

Social Science

I LOVE A BROAD MARGIN TO MY LIFE
by Maxine Hong Kingston

Maxine Hong Kingston gives us a poignant and beautiful memoir-in-verse that captures the wisdom that comes with age. She circles from present to past and back, from lunch with a writer friend to the funeral of a Vietnam veteran, from her long marriage to her arrest at a peace march in Washington. On her journeys as writer, peace activist, teacher, and mother, she revisits her most beloved characters and presents us with a beautiful meditation on China then and now. The result is a marvelous account of an American life of great purpose and joy, and the tonic wisdom of a writer we have come to cherish.

Biography

VINTAGE BOOKS & ANCHOR BOOKS
Available wherever books are sold.
www.vintagebooks.com
www.anchorbooks.com